U.S. BUSINESS
AND TODAY'S GERMANY

U.S. BUSINESS AND TODAY'S GERMANY

A GUIDE FOR CORPORATE EXECUTIVES AND ATTORNEYS

James A. Hart
Dieter Schultze-Zeu

Q
QUORUM BOOKS
Westport, Connecticut • London

Library of Congress Cataloging-in-Publication Data

Hart, James A.
    U.S. business and today's Germany : a guide for corporate
executives and attorneys / James A. Hart, Dieter Schultze-Zeu.
       p.   cm.
    Includes bibliographical references and index.
    ISBN 0–89930–839–2 (alk. paper)
    1. United States—Foreign economic relations—Germany—Handbooks,
manuals, etc. 2. Germany—Foreign economic relations—United
States—Handbooks, manuals, etc. 3. Germany—Economic
conditions—1990—Handbooks, manuals, etc. I. Schultze-Zeu,
Dieter. II. Title. III. Title: US business and today's Germany.
HF1456.5.G3H37   1995
658.8'48'0943–dc20   94–46179

British Library Cataloguing in Publication Data is available.

Library of Congress Catalog Card Number: 94–46179
ISBN: 0–89930–839–2

First published in 1995

Quorum Books, 88 Post Road West, Westport, CT 06881
An imprint of Greenwood Publishing Group, Inc.

Printed in the United States of America

The paper used in this book complies with the
Permanent Paper Standard issued by the National
Information Standards Organization (Z39.48—1984).

10 9 8 7 6 5 4 3 2 1

To our wives
Marie Hart
and
Evelyn Schultze-Zeu

Contents

Preface

Fifty years ago, the world's attention was riveted on Berlin as it fought to repel the masses of Soviet troops, which tightened a murderous noose around the neck of Hitler's headquarters. Some two million Berliners (about half the 1939 population) struggled to survive in rubble created by the tireless daytime bombing of the U.S. Air Force and night attacks of the British.

Public transportation had been so gutted by the aerial pounding that most workers in the few operational factories could not reach their workstations. As Cornelius Ryan reported in his superb chronicle, *The Last Battle*, all production came to a halt except for eleven of the city's sixteen breweries. By government decree, these facilities were designated as "essential" production and ordered to continue making beer. Somehow, enough exhausted Berliners made the trip to work and miraculously maintained their output every day of 1945, including May 2, the date of Berlin's surrender.

Of course there were no U.S. firms left in Berlin or elsewhere in Germany in May 1945. They had been seized following Hitler's declaration of war on America on December 11, 1941. Today, more than fifty years later, Germany has welcomed back Ford, General Motors, Exxon, Woolworth, Gillette, Citibank, and some 200 other American firms ousted in 1941. They have been joined by about 1,400 additional U.S. enterprises (such as McDonald's, Merrill Lynch, and Arthur Anderson, to name only three), which have made their debut in the post–World War II period.

Germany in 1995 has weathered the Nazis, World War II, Allied Occupation, separation by its infamous Berlin Wall, the unprecedented economic and political shocks inherent in reunification, and the worst recession since the end of the war. It offers unique business opportunities to U.S. and other foreign enterprises. It is hoped that this book will contribute in a substantial manner to the understanding of Germany as a business partner.

Acknowledgments

So many people have contributed their expertise in one way or another to the authors of this book that we cannot possibly name them all at this point. Particular acknowledgment, however, is due to the following persons: Louis F. Dempsey, Senior Advisor, Brown Brothers Harriman & Co.; Professor Volker R. Berghahn (History), Brown University; Professor Richard J. Bannon (Accounting), University of Nevada—Las Vegas; Dr. James F. Hart, Member of Chicago Board of Options; Dr. Elizabeth A. Hart, Chief Foreign Economist, Northern Trust Company; Patrick J. Hart, Esq., Libertyville, Illinois; Instructor Margaret M. Hart (English), California State University—Los Angeles; and Assistant Professor Daniel E. Hart (Accounting), Southwestern Oklahoma State University.

Kathryn S. Barker, Secretary, Coronado, California, earned our special thanks for her superb preparation of the manuscript.

1

American Business with Germany: Far Better than Reported

Americans are really quite ignorant about the prosperous business relations prevailing between the United States and Germany. An unfortunate combination of reasons has given rise to this situation. First, the U.S. government, regardless of which party happens to be in power, prefers to complain about the discriminatory practices directed by Japan against American trade (sometimes justified but frequently questionable) than to exult over the open-market policies of Germany and the resultant successes of U.S. business in that nation. As will be explained shortly, the U.S. Department of Commerce insists on understating American merchandise exports to Germany by a very substantial margin—by 21 percent in 1993. This understatement of exports leads inevitably to an overstatement of America's deficit in its balance of merchandise trade with Germany—146 percent in 1993.

Second, the accomplishments of U.S. firms in Germany receive little attention in the American press, even though they are well reported in German newspapers. Finally, the American multinationals themselves seem reluctant to advertise or brag about their spectacular performances in Germany.

About 1,600 U.S. firms are now active on German soil with $140 billion in assets and employing over 600,000 workers.[1] At the same time, approximately 1,100 German companies are operating in America, with about $120 billion in assets and 500,000 employees.

Some 12,000 U.S. exporters are selling their merchandise to Germany, $24 billion in 1993 amounting to 5 percent of all of America's exports. In the same year, an unknown number of service firms were supplying Germans with a wide assortment of services, amounting to $11.2 billion (6.6 percent of all U.S. service exports).

These numbers embrace a wealth of solid accomplishments by American companies doing business with Germany. The most spectacular performance, which occurs year after year, is that achieved by U.S. multinationals through their highly efficient German subsidiaries. In 1993, fourteen of these subsidiaries did so well on the intensely competitive market of Germany that they placed in the prestigious *Top 100 German Industrial Corporations* based on sales, Germany's equivalent of the Fortune 500.[2] The same fourteen star performers also made this coveted list in 1991 and 1992.

Through its well-known subsidiary, Adam Opel, General Motors (GM) ranked seventeenth in 1993, with sales of 23 billion marks (Daimler-Benz was first with 97 billion marks). Ford, through Ford-Werke, was close behind GM, with 21 billion marks, placing it in the eighteenth position.

Philip Morris had two of its subsidiaries on the list—Philip Morris GmbH and Kraft Jacobs Suchard. The following American parents had a single subsidiary in the top 100: IBM, Exxon, Coca-Cola, Procter & Gamble, Mobil, International Standard Electrical, R. J. Reynolds, Du Pont, Hewlett-Packard, and Dow Chemical (the lowest, with sales of 2.5 billion marks).

This performance of these fourteen U.S. firms unquestionably represents the most successful penetration of a major economy by foreign multinationals ever recorded. By way of comparison, Holland had three in the *Top 100 German Industrial Corporations* in 1993, followed by one each for the United Kingdom, France, Sweden, and Switzerland. Japan did not place a single company.

U.S. newspapers have completely ignored this splendid showing by these fourteen American companies. As far as is known, they have never mentioned the appearance of U.S. firms on this list during the thirty-six years of publication.

The total sales of these fourteen companies reached a staggering $75 billion in 1993, three times as much as total U.S. merchandise exports to Germany. Five of the fourteen subsidiaries manufactured and sold more than the total global exports of their American parents. For example, exports of Ford from the United States in 1993 were $9.4 billion, while Ford-Werke sales amounted to $12.2 billion.[3]

Nine of the fourteen made a profit in Germany in 1993, a tremendous accomplishment in the year when German gross domestic product (GDP) suffered a decline of 1.1 percent. It was the largest drop in the history of the Federal Republic of Germany (FRG).

Other U.S. firms with substantial sales in Germany in 1993 were as follows in billions of marks:

Woolworth	2.5
McDonald's	2.2

Continental Grain	2.1
Du Pont (Conoco)	2.0
Gillette (Braun)	2.0
Deere	1.9
Digital Equipment	1.8
Motorola	1.7
Kodak	1.6
CPC	1.6
GM (Kabelwerke Rheinshagen)	1.5
3M	1.4
General Electric	1.2
Xerox	1.1
Toys R Us	0.8
McKinsey	0.3

Probably the best way to appreciate the magnitude of U.S. business with Germany is to measure the percentage of revenues that major American multinationals derive from German subsidiaries. For example, GM had $138.2 billion in global revenues in 1993. That broke down into $99.6 billion from the U.S. market and $38.6 billion (or 28 percent) from overseas.[4] An astounding $13.3 billion came from Adam Opel AG, its giant German subsidiary. That was about one-third of its total foreign revenue and one-tenth of its worldwide revenues. Ford tells much the same story. Ford-Werke AG had revenues of $12.2 billion in 1993, which amounted to 36.5 percent of its foreign revenues and 11.3 percent of its global revenues.

Let us summarize the situation for America's five largest multinationals on the basis of foreign revenues. The firms have held these positions between 1986 and 1993, inclusive, eight years in a row. Their foreign revenues in 1993 were as follows: Exxon, $75.6 billion; GM, $38.6 billion; Mobil, $38.5 billion; IBM, $37.0 billion; and Ford, $32.8 billion.[5] These figures are not particularly surprising.

Most readers will be surprised to know that in 1993, one-fifth of these revenues ($41.9 billion) came from five German subsidiaries of the corporate giants mentioned previously. The five subsidiaries with 1993 revenues in billions of dollars were as follows:[6]

Adam Opel AG (GM)	$13.3
Ford-Werke AG	12.2
IBM Deutschland GmbH	7.2
Esso (Exxon)	6.4
Mobil Oil AG	2.7

Even these figures do not tell the full story of Germany's importance as a source of revenues for the U.S. parents. There are smaller German subsidiaries of these five multinationals, for which revenues are not available, and we do not have the exports of these five giants to Germany.

By 1903, there were enough American firms in Imperial Germany to warrant the founding in Berlin of what is today the American Chamber of Commerce in Germany. At the outset, there were about 100 members, approximately 60 percent American citizens and 40 percent German. The preparatory committee, which was charged with promoting good trade relations between Germany and America, included New York Life Insurance Co., Associated Press, American Machinery, California Fruit, Tennessee Coal and Iron, Columbia Phonograph, and the Bradstreet Co. In 1994, the chamber boasted 2,300 members, 60 percent German and 40 percent American. There are approximately 400 U.S. companies, 650 German firms, and approximately 1,250 individual members. It is truly a very effective organization.

Today, headquarters are located in Frankfurt at Rossmarkt 12, D-60311 Frankfurt [telephone (069) 28 34 01, FAX (069) 28 56 32]. There are also representative offices in Berlin, Hamburg, Cologne, Munich, Stuttgart, and Washington, D.C.

In 1990, the fifty largest U.S. firms on the basis of sales were studied by the American Chamber of Commerce in Germany. These companies ranged in revenues from GM at the top, with 23 billion marks, down to Avon Cosmetics, with 324 million marks. Their combined sales amounted to $104 billion, or four times the total U.S. exports to Germany in 1990.[7]

American firms have competed successfully in Germany over a broad economic spectrum: autos, tractors, elevators and construction machinery, computers, petroleum and tobacco products, food, toys, commercial and investment banking, hotels, management consulting, retailing, soft drinks, chemicals, electronics, restaurants, razors, and a large variety of household products.

It is encouraging to know that U.S. firms have top market shares in Germany in eleven major segments of the economy. IBM is first in computers, with Hewlett-Packard third and Digital Equipment fourth. Exxon, Mobil, and Conoco (a subsidiary of Du Pont) are first, second, and third, respectively, in petroleum products. Coca-Cola in soft drinks, Toys R Us in toys, McDonald's in restaurants, Xerox in copiers, Otis in elevators, Continental in grain trading, and Gillette in razors are all first in their fields. Philip Morris and Reynolds are first and third in cigarettes. McKinsey leads in management consulting, and Boston Group is third.

GM and Ford are also quite impressive as fourth and fifth in auto production, the only foreign manufacturers to penetrate the highly competitive German market. GM's new modern plant in Eisenach in eastern Germany is generally regarded as the most advanced in Europe.

It is obvious that U.S. firms are far more solidly established in the industrial structure of Germany than their German counterparts in America. Only two German companies, both chemical giants, placed in the largest 100 industrial firms in the United States in 1993. Hoechst AG (Hoechst Celanese) ranked eightieth on the Fortune 500, with sales of $6.8 billion, and Bayer AG (Miles) placed eighty-fourth, with sales of $6.5 billion. The fourteen U.S. companies in Germany piled up total sales of $75 billion in 1993, while the two German firms in the United States reported $13 billion in sales.[8]

Since colonial times, America has enjoyed good commercial relations with Germany. The first export statistics were published by the United States for 1790. In that year, Americans exported a total of $20 million, $7 million of it to the United Kingdom. The only two other customers listed were France with $1 million and Germany with "less than $500,000."[9] The United States imported $23 million in 1790 and thus ran a deficit of $3 million. We have no figures on imports from Germany until 1821, when they were valued at $1 million.[10]

American trade with Germany expanded enormously in the following years, reaching exports of $322 million and imports of $189 million in 1913, the last full year of peace before the outbreak of World War I. Only the United Kingdom and Canada did more trading with the United States than Germany.

Trade with Germany came back slowly after the conflict; and in 1919, the first full year of peace, the United States exported $93 million and imported $11 million. By comparison, exports to the United Kingdom were $2.2 billion; Canada, $734 million; and Japan, $366 million.

By the eve of World War II (1938), U.S. exports to Germany had only increased to $107 million, and imports to $118 million. Continued global depression and Hitler's drive to reduce German dependence on imports in preparation for war crippled trade between the two nations.

When World War II ended in 1945, defeated Germany was divided into two states. American trade with East Germany was severely restricted; and by 1989, the United States exported only $94 million in goods and imported $139 million.[11]

In 1946, a severely battered West Germany struggled to restore trade with the United States. America exported only $83 million and imported $3 million in that year. Slowly this expanded, and eventually exports began to rocket, as did imports. For 1993, the U.S. Department of Commerce reported American exports to Germany of $18.9 billion and imports of $28.5 billion, a deficit of $9.6 billion.[12]

Regrettably, the data on exports are severely flawed. The figures issued for the same year by the Federal Statistical Office (FSO) of Germany showed U.S. exports of $24.2 billion and imports of $28.3 billion.[13] The two sets of U.S. import statistics are reasonably close to each other, a mere $200-million difference.

The gap in U.S. exports to Germany is stunning. The German statisticians say American exports for 1993 were $5.3 billion more than reported by the U.S. experts, an incredible 28 percent higher.

Year after year 12,000 American exporters are selling more goods to Germany than reported by their government, and the amount of unreported exports has grown from $2.4 billion in 1987 to $5.3 billion in 1993. This huge disparity arises because the U.S. Department of Commerce employs a faulty method of measuring U.S. exports to Germany. It counts only those goods shipped directly by American exporters to German importers. Items sent first to third-country ports like Amsterdam and then transshipped to Germany are not tabulated as exports to Germany but as exports to Holland. The German statisticians realistically count such goods as exports to Germany.

Washington could very simply end this farce by accepting statistics prepared by Germany's FSO. This would not only provide more reliable and more encouraging information to American business but would also save money.

The suggestion that the U.S. Department of Commerce accept the German statistics on our exports to that market is not as radical as it first sounds. We have such an arrangement with Canada, and it works well. Who is going to say that the Germans are less trustworthy than the Canadians as statisticians?

Since the U.S. Department of Commerce understates our exports to Germany by a substantial margin every year, it unavoidably goes on to overstate our bilateral trade deficit with that country by a huge margin. For 1993, the statisticians from Washington, D.C., reported a deficit with Germany of $9.6 billion. This is an astounding $5.7 billion (146 percent) greater than the $3.9-billion figure published by the Germans. This unnecessarily frightening deficit issued by Washington year after year was particularly unfortunate for 1991, when the German figures showed a small surplus for the United States amounting to $300 million, while the U.S. Department of Commerce insisted that we had a deficit of $4.8 billion.

It is worth noting that *The Economist,* the prestigious London periodical; *Commerce Germany,* published by the Frankfurt-based American Chamber of Commerce in Germany; and other international publications employ the data prepared by the Germans rather than those issued by Washington, D.C.

Not surprisingly, the recurrent understatement of U.S. exports to Germany slops over into a ridiculous overstatement of American exports to Holland. In 1992 (the last year for which official Dutch figures are available), the U.S. Department of Commerce reported $13.4 billion in merchandise exports to that country, while the Netherlands said such exports were only $10.4 billion. As in the case of Germany, the statistics published on U.S. imports from Holland were reasonably close (the U.S. Department of Commerce reported $5.3 billion, and the Dutch statisticians $4.7 billion).[14]

Germany usually is the fifth-largest buyer of U.S. goods after Canada, Japan, Mexico, and the United Kingdom. It is also usually the fifth-largest supplier of products to the United States after Canada, Japan, Mexico, and China.[15]

Manufactured goods dominate U.S. exports to Germany, and the same prevails in the opposite direction. In 1993, America sold $17.1 billion in manufactures to Germany and bought $27.7 billion.[16] The principal manufactures exported by the United States were as follows (in billions of dollars):[17]

1. Automatic data-processing machines	1.6
2. Aircraft and spacecraft and parts	1.1
3. Parts for office and automatic data-processing machines	1.0
4. Motor vehicles	0.9
5. Measuring instruments	0.7
6. Parts for motor vehicles	0.6

The leading manufactures imported from Germany were as follows (in billions of dollars):[18]

1. Motor vehicles	5.4
2. Internal-combustion piston engines	0.9
3. Textile and leather machinery	0.9
4. Parts for motor vehicles	0.6
5. Measuring instruments	0.6
6. Electrodiagnostic apparatus	0.5

America exported $1 billion in agricultural products to Germany, chiefly oil seeds ($252 million), fruits and nuts ($205 million), and tobacco ($162 million).[19] In the same year, German farm products imported only amounted to $500 million, mostly food and live animals ($324 million).[20]

The United States is normally the fifth-best customer of Germany, after France, Italy, the United Kingdom, and Holland. It usually rates fourth as a source of imports after France, Holland, and Italy.

The U.S. Department of Commerce published an excellent forty-seven-page brochure in 1991 entitled *Marketing in the Federal Republic of Germany.* Among other things, the document has a wealth of data on exports and imports of both the United States and Germany. Ironically, the study uses six pages of statistics issued by the FSO of Germany. On page 43, one of these German tables shows U.S. exports to Germany in 1989 as $20.3 billion. However, on page 4, the text cites such exports for 1989 as $16.6 billion (as reported by the U.S. Department of Commerce statisticians). At no place in the brochure is any explanation offered for this huge discrepancy.[21]

American firms selling services to Germany turn in far more favorable results than the nation's exporters of merchandise. In 1993, the United States exported $11.2 billion in services to Germany and imported $7.3 billion, creating a surplus of $3.9 billion. This favorable balance had grown from only $88 million in 1986.[22]

The United States is far better equipped to compete in services than Germany. It had 72 percent of its GDP in the service sector in 1992, while Germany had 57 percent.[23] In 1993, America was first in global sales of services, with $172 billion, and sported a $59-billion surplus. Germany ranked fourth, with $67 billion, and had a deficit of $37 billion.

The 1993 favorable balance in services with Germany was principally based on surpluses in the following categories: royalties and license fees, $1.6 billion; travel, $1.3 billion; passenger fares, $0.6 billion; legal services, $73 million; management consulting and public relations, $37 million.[24]

Combining a $3.9-billion surplus in services with a $3.9-billion deficit in merchandise trade (German version) for 1993 resulted in an overall balance with Germany in that year. Using this same formula, America's deficit worldwide in 1993 was only $75 billion, far less disturbing than the much-cited $132-billion shortage in merchandise alone.[25] Germany, on this same basis, had only a surplus of $7 billion in 1993 instead of its vaunted $44-billion surplus in merchandise trade.[26]

Foreign direct investment in Germany by U.S. firms is presented by the U.S. Department of Commerce on a historical-cost or book-value basis. Thus, no attempt is made to calculate the much higher current-cost value and market value of American corporate facilities in Germany.

Substantial American foreign direct investment did not begin until after World War II. Even in 1929, the global total on the historical-cost basis was only $7 billion. In 1950, it was $19 billion; but two decades later, it had shot up to $75 billion. By 1993, it had soared to $548 billion.[27]

West Germany had $4.3 billion of American direct investment in 1970, well behind Canada (with $21 billion) and the United Kingdom (with $8 billion).[28] By 1980, West Germany had climbed to $15 billion. There was never any foreign direct investment in East Germany because that Marxist state prohibited all such operations. After reunification in 1990, approximately 220 U.S. firms invested about $3.6 billion in the East, involving some 40,000 jobs.[29]

By 1993, there was $37 billion of U.S. direct foreign investment in Germany on the historical-cost basis. However, the United Kingdom had more U.S. capital, with $96 billion, followed by Canada with $70 billion. Switzerland had $32 billion, and Japan $31 billion.[30] It should be remembered that common language, legal systems, and business cultures are strong attractions in the United Kingdom and Canada. Furthermore, America fought as a military ally with these nations against Germany in World Wars I and II.

In manufacturing alone in 1993, the United States had $22.2 billion in foreign direct investment in Germany, compared with $22.8 billion in the United Kingdom and $34 billion in Canada.[31]

Germany has attracted 7.2 percent of all the world's foreign direct investment. Only the United States, with 28.6 percent, and Britain, with 9.9 percent, have drawn more. Japan, by contrast, has only 0.7 percent; France has 4.2 percent; and Italy has 3.6 percent of the global total.[32]

We can only make a broad guess on foreign direct investment by U.S. firms in Germany on a current-cost basis and a market-value basis. The U.S. Department of Commerce reported $548 billion as the total foreign direct investment position for the whole world at the end of 1993 on a historical-cost (book-value) basis. It went on to estimate current-cost value at $716 billion and market value at $993 billion. Unfortunately, the "source data needed to make these adjustments by country and industry are not available."[33] While the U.S. Department of Commerce hesitates to publish a market-value estimate for Germany, it would probably amount to about twice the historical-cost valuation, or $74 billion.

Breaking down the $37-billion figure for historical-cost in 1993, we find that $22 billion is invested in manufacturing, distributed as follows (in billions of dollars):[34]

Machinery	6.2
Transportation equipment	5.9
Chemicals	3.8
Food	2.0

Nonmanufacturing investment in Germany (in billions of dollars) includes the following:

Finance (except banking, insurance, and real estate)	5.1
Wholesale trade	2.9
Petroleum	2.4
Banking	2.2
Services	0.8

Another approach to studying foreign direct investments of the United States is to count the assets of foreign nonbank affiliates. In 1991, total assets amounted to $1.69 trillion worldwide, almost four times the $467 billion attributed to foreign direct investment on a historical-cost basis. American firms had $356 million of such assets in the United Kingdom, $203 billion in Canada, $175 billion in Japan, and $140 billion in Germany.[35]

Looking only at assets of U.S. manufacturing affiliates overseas in 1991, the German affiliates did far better. They had $76 billion in total assets, compared with $77 billion in the United Kingdom, $75 billion in Japan, and $72 billion in Canada.[36]

A study of the gross product of nonbank majority-owned foreign affiliates of U.S. firms also deserves our attention. In 1991, such American affiliates produced a total of $356 billion, compared with $421 billion in merchandise exports in that year. Affiliates in the United Kingdom led with $59 billion, followed by Germany, $49 billion; Canada, $47 billion; and Italy, $20 billion.[37]

Looking only at the gross product of majority-owned U.S. manufacturing affiliates overseas in 1991, Germany led all nations with $34 billion. The United Kingdom was second with $28 billion, followed by Canada with $23 billion and Japan with $7 billion.[38]

In 1993, U.S. firms invested more new capital in these manufacturing affiliates in Germany ($4.1 billion) than in any other nation. Affiliates in the United Kingdom drew $3.5 billion, while those in Canada attracted $3.1 billion and the Japanese attracted $1.3 billion.[39] Remember once more that Germany suffered its worst decline in GDP during 1993 in the history of the FRG.

A survey by the U.S. Department of Commerce conducted in 1993 questioned the U.S. parents of these foreign manufacturing affiliates as to their plans for new capital expenditures during 1994. German affiliates led all others with $4.2 billion, followed by the United Kingdom with $4.1 billion, Canada with $3.7 billion, and Mexico with $2.2 billion.[40]

According to the German government, in 1992 U.S. firms had by far the highest direct investment in that country, with 53 billion marks. Holland was second with 29 billion, followed by Switzerland, 25 billion; the United Kingdom, 13 billion; Japan, 14 billion; and France, 12.6 billion.[41]

In the interest of objectivity, it is imperative that we examine the obstacles that tend to hinder U.S. direct investment in Germany:

1. *Rising dollar value of German mark.* Since its creation in 1948, the mark has increased from 30 cents to 64 cents at the end of 1994—a climb of 113 percent. From 1948 to 1973, the mark was under International Monetary Fund (IMF) control and only rose by 4 cents to 34 cents.

With the end of controls in 1973, the mark's price became subject to the market forces of supply and demand. During the next twenty-one years, it climbed 30 cents to 64 cents.

Understandably, U.S. multinationals found direct investments more attractive in the 1948–1973 era than they have since then. Conversely, German companies have become decidedly more interested in the United States.

2. *Highest hourly labor costs (wages and benefits combined) in manufacturing in the world.* In 1970, American hourly labor costs were the world's highest (15.8 marks), and West Germany ranked fifth (9.4 marks). Twenty-three years later, in 1993, German labor costs at 42.7 marks were at the peak, while the U.S. costs were 25.57

marks.[42] This change was primarily a result of the rapid rise in the German wages.

3. *Shortest workweek in the world.* The shortest workweek makes the Germans the envy of workers throughout the world, but it disturbs U.S. firms considering a move into that country. In 1991, it was 37.6 hours, compared with 40 hours in the United States and 41.5 hours in Japan.[43]

4. *Most vacation days in the world.* The German manufacturing worker received forty-two days of vacation in 1991, compared with twenty-five for the Japanese and twenty-three for the Americans. Including holidays, the German worker was on the job 1,499 hours for all of 1991; the Americans, 1,847 hours; and the Japanese, 2,319 hours.

5. *More frequent sick leave.* In 1992, the average German worker took 146 hours sick leave, compared with 55 hours in the United States and 36 hours in Japan. The Swedes held the world record with 208 hours.[44]

6. *Inflexibility of labor unions.* German unions are much stronger than their American counterparts, thanks to more supportive labor laws, much higher union membership, and a more cooperative spirit between employers and unions. This bothers many U.S. multinationals.

7. *High taxes.* This factor is probably the most significant impediment to American investment. A study by the Deutsche Bank showed the following percentages of 1992 GDP absorbed in taxes:[45]

Germany	43.7
United States	30.7
Japan	29.3

While very little appears in the U.S. media on the strength of business relations with Germany, negative criticism is all too constant. Complaints most frequently voiced by American firms are that wages and taxes are too high, labor unions too strong, labor legislation too restrictive on employers, and government regulation too excessive.

Certainly, there are disadvantages in direct investments in Germany; but there are also many powerful advantages, such as 63 million affluent westerners and 17 million easterners in humbler but gradually improving conditions. Also, Germany has a stable currency, excellent exporting skills, reliable government, superb educational facilities at all levels, and high-quality workers. We cannot forget that German products can move freely without duties into the other eleven members of the European Union (EU), a market of 250 million additional customers.

The simple fact is that for some 1,600 U.S. firms, the advantages outweigh the disadvantages of doing business on German soil. Many of them arrived before World War II, a few even in the nineteenth century. Each American company must decide for itself after a very painstaking feasibility study whether to take the plunge in Germany. Some businesses have pulled out in recent years, but far more have started up in this high-powered economy.

NOTES

1. *Commerce Germany,* Frankfurt, American Chamber of Commerce in Germany, 6 (1994): 34.

2. *Frankfurter Allgemeine Zeitung,* July 5, 1994.

3. *Fortune,* New York, August 22, 1994, p. 132.

4. *Forbes,* New York, July 18, 1994, p. 276.

5. Ibid.

6. *Frankfurter Allgemeine Zeitung,* July 5, 1994.

7. *Commerce Germany,* Frankfurt, American Chamber of Commerce in Germany, 7 (1991): 19.

8. *Fortune,* New York, April 18, 1994, p. 222.

9. *Historical Abstract of the United States,* Part 2 (Washington, D.C.: U.S. Department of Commerce, 1974), p. 906.

10. Ibid., p. 907.

11. *Statistical Abstract of the United States 1994* (Washington, D.C.: U.S. Department of Commerce, 1994), p. 824.

12. *U.S. Foreign Trade Highlights 1993* (Washington, D.C.: U.S. Department of Commerce, 1994), pp. 17, 21.

13. *Statistisches Jahrbuch 1994* (Wiesbaden: Federal Statistical Office, 1994), p. 318.

14. *Statistical Yearbook of the Netherlands 1994* (The Hague: publishers of Netherlands publications, 1994), p. 326.

15. *U.S. Foreign Trade Highlights 1993* (Washington, D.C.: U.S. Department of Commerce, 1994), pp. 30, 31.

16. Ibid., pp. 34, 38.

17. Ibid., p. 90.

18. Ibid., p. 91.

19. Ibid., p. 90.

20. Ibid., p. 91.

21. *Marketing in the Federal Republic of Germany* (Washington, D.C.: U.S. Department of Commerce, 1991), pp. 3, 43.

22. *Survey of Current Business,* Washington, D.C., U.S. Department of Commerce, September 1994, p. 106.

23. *The Economist,* London, February 20, 1993, p. 63.

24. *Survey of Current Business,* Washington, D.C., U.S. Department of Commerce, September 1994, pp. 110, 114, 132, 133.

25. *U.S. Foreign Trade Highlights 1993* (Washington, D.C.: U.S. Department of Commerce, 1994), p. 11.

26. *International Financial Statistics,* Washington, D.C., International Monetary Fund, December 1994, p. 250.

27. *Survey of Current Business,* Washington, D.C., U.S. Department of Commerce, August 1994, p. 137.

28. *United States Statistical Abstract 1981* (Washington, D.C.: U.S. Department of Commerce, 1981), p. 836.

29. *Commerce Germany,* Frankfurt, American Chamber of Commerce in Germany, 1 (1994): 9.

30. *Survey of Current Business,* Washington, D.C., U.S. Department of Commerce, August 1994, p. 137.

31. Ibid.

32. *New York Times,* January 5, 1992.

33. *Survey of Current Business,* Washington, D.C., U.S. Department of Commerce, August 1994, p. 128.

34. Ibid., p. 137.

35. *Survey of Current Business,* Washington, D.C., U.S. Department of Commerce, July 1993, p. 56.

36. Ibid.

37. *Survey of Current Business,* Washington, D.C., U.S. Department of Commerce, February 1994, p. 63.

38. Ibid.

39. *Survey of Current Business,* Washington, D.C., U.S. Department of Commerce, March 1994, p. 42.

40. Ibid., p. 43.

41. *German American Business Journal Midwest,* Chicago, German-American Chamber of Commerce, August 1993, p. 17.

42. *Der Spiegel,* Hamburg, 52 (1994): 20.

43. *New York Times,* May 26, 1992.

44. *Der Spiegel,* Hamburg, 52 (1994): 19.

45. *Die Zeit,* Hamburg, June 11, 1993.

2

German Business with the United States: Extremely Stable

The United States and Germany are now intimately bound in a wide variety of business relationships. Traditional exports and imports of goods and services, direct and portfolio investments, license agreements, joint ventures, franchises, leases, security underwriting, export financing, dealerships, agencies, branch offices, subsidiaries, and representative offices have grown over the years. Very rarely does one read or hear of U.S. or German firms withdrawing from such relationships. One readily recalls Volkswagen's flop with its American assembly line and several U.S. commercial banks that gave up their branches in Germany, but these were exceptions.

Business relations with Germany have prospered in part because of the large waves of German immigration flowing into America since colonial times. William Penn, founder of the colony of Pennsylvania and a strong Quaker, offered religious freedom to prospective settlers (Maryland and Rhode Island were equally tolerant). He also developed a strong sales organization for selling his land in Germany, which proved quite effective. In 1683, a ship anchored at Philadelphia with the first German colonists—thirteen families from Krefeld. The colony had 100,000 German settlers at the time of the American Revolution, about one-third of Pennsylvania's population. One-fourth of the members of the colonial legislature were German. The English majority felt so threatened that one governor required Germans to take a loyalty oath to the British crown. In the colonies as a whole in 1776, every sixth settler was German.

Benjamin Franklin, Philadelphia's most famous citizen, saw an opportunity to make some money from these immigrants and started a German-language newspaper in 1732, the *Philadelphische Zeitung*. However, Franklin's German was poor and the paper folded after the second issue.[1]

One amusing two-century-old legend, which Germans love to bring up to Americans, revolves around the alleged vote in Congress to replace English with German as the official language of the infant United States. Supposedly the hatred of Britain was still so intense that the proposal only lost by one vote, the vote of a German-born Congressman who had to go to the toilet just before the roll was called.

Since American businesspersons are bound to be surprised by this hoary tale in Germany, this book has the obligation to provide them with the answer. The truth is that in 1775 Congress cast a procedural vote to keep alive (and thus not kill) a bill requiring all Federal laws to be translated and published in German. This move failed to carry by 1 vote, 40 to 41.

The U.S. Census has reported that between 1820 and 1990 some 58 million people immigrated into the United States, and Germany led with 7 million. Italy was second with 5.4 million, followed by the United Kingdom (5.1 million), Mexico (4.8 million), and Ireland (4.7 million).

In the 1980 census, for the first time, Americans were asked about their ancestry. The published report surprised most citizens when it showed 49.5 million English, 49.2 million Germans, 40.1 million Irish, 12.8 million French, and 12.1 million Italians. For the 1990 census, the question was changed; but it showed the Germans far out in front with 57.9 million, or 23.3 percent. The Irish were second with 38.7 million (15.6 percent), followed by 32.6 million English (13.1 percent) and 14.7 million Italians (5.9 percent).[2]

There have been many attempts to explain these statistics, but they are not very satisfactory. Perhaps the main reason is that with the passage of time since World Wars I and II, people of German ancestry are more inclined to acknowledge their origins. By way of illustration, a German couple started a very good restaurant in San Diego after World War II and timidly called it the "Swiss House." Only after many years did they have the courage to change the name to "Rhine Lander."

Another illustration concerns the Hotel Bismarck in Chicago's loop, built before World War I. During that conflict, public hostility toward Germany after U.S. entry in 1917 forced the owners to change the name to Hotel Randolph (after the street name). After the war, the hostelry became Hotel Bismarck again. During World War II, it continued as the Bismarck. Chicago street philosophers maintain that the citizenry was so infuriated with the Japanese after Pearl Harbor that it did not have enough energy to hate the Germans with the intensity registered in World War I.

Germany began its foreign direct investments after Bismarck founded the Empire in 1871. It was far behind the older colonial powers like Britain,

France, Holland, and Belgium. However, it moved quickly and by 1914 had substantial investments in many countries.

When America declared war against Germany in 1917, German investments in this country were seized by the U.S. government under the provisions of the Trading with the Enemy Act of 1917. These assets were not returned after the fighting ended. The same scenario was played out again during World War II. As a result, Germany was very hesitant about making direct investments in the United States after 1945. Even the thought of investing in America seemed unreal as long as the available capital was needed for urgent reconstruction of the war-damaged domestic economy.

Many well-known German companies watched Washington seize their American assets during World Wars I and II. Bayer AG undoubtedly took all honors in persistent fighting to recover its confiscated property.

Bayer had invented "Bayer Aspirin" in 1897, the world's first analgesic pain killer. It was probably the most widely used and most profitable drug ever discovered. The tradename and trademark (the famous "Bayer Cross"), along with all other assets of the firm, were seized by the United States in 1917. In 1918, these valuable rights were sold at public auction to Sterling Winthrop for $5 million.

Sterling Winthrop had a fabulous success with its "Bayer Aspirin" but had to fight frequent lawsuits brought by Bayer. U.S. legal protection for the trade rights ran out in 1921, but that did not stop Sterling from promoting Bayer as the quality pain killer. In 1970, Sterling sold Bayer the rights outside the United States and Canada for $2.8 billion. In 1986, Bayer paid $25 million to use the Bayer name in the United States on its chemical products.

In 1994, Kodak—which now owned Sterling Winthrop—sold the Bayer tradename and trademark for the United States and Canada (along with some other assets of Sterling) to Smith Kline Beecham for $2.9 billion. Bayer had bid against Smith Kline for this packet but had failed in its effort.

Bayer lost little time in approaching Smith Kline and within a month signed a contract to reacquire its tradename and trademark, together with other assets, for $1 billion. This brought to an end a prolonged struggle for Bayer.[3]

Schering AG, a leading pharmaceutical firm in Berlin, had the dubious distinction of losing its American assets in World Wars I and II. Ernst Schering started the business as a Berlin drugstore in 1851, developed a medication for gout, and later developed one for diphtheria. In 1876, an American subsidiary, Schering & Glatz, was established. It was seized by the U.S. government during World War I and dissolved.

By 1929, Schering was back and Schering Corporation was created in New York City. It specialized in hormone research and synthesized steroid drugs. This subsidiary was seized in World War II and then sold by the U.S. government in 1951. In 1971, it merged with the Plough firm in Memphis, which owned St. Joseph children's aspirin.

Schering-Plough developed an antibiotic called Garamycin, then a more potent one called Netromycin. It bought Dr. Scholl's Foot Care and developed the Maybelline line of cosmetics. The company has been tremendously profitable, reporting $4.3 billion in sales in 1993 (ranked 117 on the Fortune 500) and $730 million in net income, a profit margin of 16.8 percent.

Back in war-torn Berlin, the former parent, Schering AG, watched its plant in the eastern part of the city get pounded into rubble by American and British air power as well as Soviet artillery. The property was then seized by Marxist Germany. Undaunted, Schering built a new plant in West Berlin, just a few blocks from the Wall (but it kept business records in West Germany).

In 1993, Schering AG ranked fifty-third in sales among German industrial firms with DM 5.6 billion. Net profit was DM 255 million, and it was the largest Berlin employer—with 24,000 workers.

Lice powder, penicillin, and hormonal contraceptives have been leading products in recent years. In 1976, Schering started its third wave of investment in U.S. subsidiaries: Schering Berlin and Scherex Chemical in Dublin, Ohio; Berlex Laboratories in Wayne, New Jersey; Chemcut in State College, Pennsylvania; and Nor-Am Chemical in Wilmington, Delaware.[4]

Starting in the 1970s, West Germany began to directly invest more outside the country than foreign business invested in Germany. The gap increased constantly over two decades, exploding in the 1985–1990 period. In those five years, 90 billion marks more left West Germany than came in from abroad. In 1990 alone, the Germans invested 36 billion marks in foreign countries, while only 3 billion marks were invested in Germany.[5]

The prestigious Institute for the German Economy (DIW) commented that this outflow would not be disturbing as long as the chief motive was market expansion and protection. DIW found that one-third of all foreign direct investment was made because of unfavorable production conditions facing German firms at home.[6]

President Hans Peter Stihl of the influential German Industry and Commerce Association (DIHT) has discussed hourly labor costs in the firm, which he directs. The company has plants in Waiblingen (Germany), Wil (Switzerland), and Virginia Beach (United States). In 1984, the hourly labor cost was DM 25.15 in Germany, DM 23.30 in America, and DM 20.51 in Switzerland. By 1991, the German cost had soared 51 percent to DM 38.02. The Swiss cost was up 23 percent to DM 25.18. The American cost actually fell 4 percent to DM 22.34.[7]

In 1993, total foreign direct investment in the United States came to $445 billion, and $34 billion was of German origin. Germany ranked fifth in such investments after Japan with $96 billion, the United Kingdom ($95 billion), Holland ($68 billion), and Canada ($39 billion).[8]

The German government reported that at the start of 1992, German firms had 258.8 billion marks of direct investment in foreign countries. The largest amount by far was in the United States, a total of 59.4 billion marks. The country-by-country allocation (in billions of marks) is as follows:[9]

United States	59.4
France	22.8
United Kingdom	19.2
Belgium	19.1
Holland	16.2
Japan	5.2

According to the German Ministry of Economics, there were more than 1,100 German firms operating in the United States in 1993 with some 500,000 workers.[10]

Forbes publishes an annual list of the 100 largest foreign investments in the United States based on sales. In 1993, fourteen German companies placed on this list.[11] Tengelmann, a huge food retailer (which owns 53 percent of A&P), ranked seventh out of 100 and led all German firms with total revenues of $10.3 billion. Hoechst, Bayer, and BASF—the Big Three chemical firms—accounted for $6.8 billion, $6.4 billion, and $5.2 billion, respectively, in revenues. Siemens, second only to Daimler-Benz in Germany, turned in revenues of $5.5 billion in the United States; Daimler reported $3.06 billion. Franz Haniel in foods had $6 billion in revenues; Allianz, $4.3 billion in insurance; Henkel, $4.2 billion in household products; RWE, $2.9 billion in principally coal mining; Bertelsmann, $2.3 billion in publishing; and Michael Otto, $2 billion through catalog retailing. Thyssen, the German steel firm, had $1.5 billion, and Robert Bosch, $1.4 billion in revenues from auto parts production in America.

Eight of the fourteen German firms reported a profit in 1993, two lost money, and four made no disclosure. BASF recorded the highest profit in 1993 ($410 million), while Siemens recorded the largest loss ($168 million). The other two of the Big Three chemicals also made solid profits in 1993: Hoechst, $101 million, and Bayer, $131 million. Daimler-Benz did not disclose.

BMW announced in June 1992 that it would build an assembly plant in Spartanburg County, South Carolina, investing $400 million and employing 2,000 people. South Carolina, with probably the best industrial recruiting organization in America, was in competition with many other locations, including Mexico. The final choice was narrowed down to Nebraska or South Carolina; but the latter's offer of about $150 million in tax breaks, access highways, water and sewer improvements, and other inducements won the investment.

One very interesting tax break is a fixed dollar (undisclosed amount) deduction for each worker on the payroll for the next twenty years. The basic

South Carolina tax rate on corporation income is 5 to 6 percent, the lowest of all the southeastern states.

BMW opened the plant in November 1994, with only 570 workers turning out thirty cars a day. By 1997, daily production should reach 3,000 units. Half of the vehicles will be exported to 100 different countries. Each worker at the new Spartanburg plant costs BMW $40,000 per year, half the cost in Germany and about one-third less than the unionized workers hired by GM and Ford in the United States. BMW forecasts that total production costs in South Carolina will be 30 percent below Germany's.[12]

Spartanburg County now has eighty foreign factories, thirty-four of them German. Hoechst AG is one of the oldest, dating back to the 1960s. Robert Bosch AG (1985), Bertelsmann AG (1986), and Adidas AG (1988) came more recently. BMW is also expected to bring in nineteen parts manufacturers, employing about 2,000 people.

The population of Spartanburg County is now 225,000, with 8,000 of them German nationals. Twenty-five years ago, it was a textile center with 86 percent of its workers in this declining industry. The former governor of South Carolina and a local Chamber of Commerce executive saw the problem and set out to bring in foreign textile and textile machinery manufacturers. All kinds of other manufacturers joined in moving to Spartanburg County. Today, textiles provide only 41 percent of the jobs.[13]

In September 1993, Mercedes-Benz AG—the auto-manufacturing subsidiary of Daimler-Benz AG—announced that it would follow BMW to the southeastern United States to Vance, Alabama (not far from Tuscaloosa). After five months of competition, Alabama outbid South Carolina and North Carolina—the other finalists in a field, which, at the outset, included thirty-five states. The prize is a $300-million assembly plant, where 1,500 workers will turn out a luxury sport-utility car (about 65,000 cars per year). It is expected that supplier firms may hire as many as another 8,000 workers.

To win this plant, Alabama is paying out about $250 million in extras, including tax breaks, job training, and other incentives. Low labor costs, weak unions, transportation facilities, favorable business climate, and education levels were about equal in all three finalist states; but Alabama's total package was a bit richer, possibly as much as $10 million. A unique incentive is the "Saturday School" to be run by the University of Alabama to keep German students up to back-home standards in math and science. As one resident of Vance said, "We probably gave away half the state, but it is probably worth it."[14]

The U.S. Department of Commerce reported that 512 foreign firms completed investment contracts to operate in the United States in 1992. Japan led with 195 transactions, Germany placed second with 58, and the United Kingdom was third with 52. Many of the investors did not publicize the value of their transactions. However, of those with value disclosed, five French investments piled up $3.6 billion to lead, but twenty German firms placed second with $2.9 billion, and eighty-nine Japanese companies reported $2.7 billion.[15]

NOTES

1. Adolph Schalk, *The Germans* (Englewood Cliffs, N.J.: Prentice-Hall, 1971), p. 427.

2. *Statistical Abstract of the U.S. 1992* (Washington, D.C.: U.S. Department of Commerce, 1993), p. 43.

3. *Wall Street Journal,* New York, September 13, 1994.

4. Thomas Derdak (ed.), *International Directory of Company Histories,* Vol. 1 (Chicago: St. James Press, 1991), p. 683.

5. *Frankfurter Allgemeine Zeitung,* February 24, 1992.

6. Ibid.

7. *Frankfurter Allgemeine Zeitung,* January 29, 1992.

8. *Survey of Current Business,* Washington, D.C., U.S. Department of Commerce, August 1994, p. 126.

9. *German American Business Journal Midwest,* Chicago, German-American Chamber of Commerce, August 1993, p. 17.

10. *Frankfurter Allgemeine Zeitung,* October 5, 1993.

11. *Forbes,* New York, July 18, 1994, p. 266.

12. *The Economist,* London, November 19, 1994, p. 73.

13. *Los Angeles Times,* August 25, 1992.

14. *The Economist,* London, January 8, 1994, p. 32.

15. *Foreign Direct Investment in the U.S., 1992, Transactions* (Washington, D.C.: U.S. Department of Commerce, August 1993), p. 5.

3

The Three Economic Superpowers: Germany, Japan, and the United States

Practically all analysts today agree that the United States, Germany, and Japan are the world's economic superpowers. All three have certain strengths that set them apart from other nations. A careful examination of these assets is helpful at this time.

POPULATION

The United States, with 255 million people in 1992, was more than twice the Japanese population of 124 million. Germany, with 80 million people, was about one-third the population of America. Russia today has only 149 million people, quite in contrast with the awesome 276 million once boasted by the Soviet Union.

LAND AREA

The United States has 3.5 million square miles of territory. Japan, with 145,000 square miles, is equal only to the state of Montana. Germany, with 137,000 square miles, is slightly smaller than Montana. Russia (76% in area of the Soviet Union) still controls 6.5 million square miles, almost twice the size of America.

GROSS DOMESTIC PRODUCT (GDP)

In 1992, the United States led Japan in GDP by a wide margin of 58 percent and Germany by 237 percent. The figures for the leading nations of the world were as follows:

United States	$5.4 trillion
Japan	$3.4 trillion
Germany	$1.6 trillion
France	$1.2 trillion
Italy	$1.1 trillion
United Kingdom	$0.9 trillion
Russia	$0.4 trillion

On a per capita basis, in 1992 the three superpowers ranked as follows (with no adjustment for purchasing power):

Japan	$27,400
United States	$21,400
Germany	$20,000

Russia, by contrast, had only $2,700.

When one corrects these figures to reflect purchasing power, the three countries in 1992 stood as follows:[1]

United States	$22,700
Germany	$19,900
Japan	$19,400

Of course there is no guarantee that these three will still be at the summit of economic power in the years ahead. In 1870, Britain was the world's only superpower, supreme in military strength and by far the richest nation in the world. The British per capita GDP was 25 percent higher in purchasing power than the United States, twice that of Germany, and five times that of Japan (then about the same as Mexico).[2]

ECONOMIC GROWTH

One measures economic growth by the annual rate of increase or decrease of real GDP. All three nations have enjoyed solid growth since 1980. However, the United States suffered a decline of 0.7 percent in 1991 and then resumed growth with 2.6 percent in 1992, 2.8 percent in 1993, and an estimated 4 percent in 1994. Germany continued to grow after absorbing East Germany in 1990, recording increases of 1.7 percent in 1991 and 1.9 percent in 1992. It stumbled in 1993 by 1.1 percent and then recovered by an estimated 2.8 percent in 1994. Japan shrank to a growth rate of only 0.1 percent in 1993 but recovered to an estimated 0.5 percent in 1994.[3]

INDUSTRIAL PRODUCTION

Between 1985 and 1993, all three of the economic superpowers experienced growth in industrial production. The United States increased 18.8 percent in this eight-year period, Japan 13.6 percent, and West Germany 10.8 percent.[4] America dropped 1.8 percent in 1991 but then started to climb again in 1992. In October 1994, it was 6.2 percent above the previous year. Japan declined 5.3 percent in 1992 and 4.5 percent in 1993. This fall continued into 1994, but an upturn came; and by October, it was 4.6 percent above October 1993.

Western Germany lost 1.2 percent in 1992 and then 6.0 percent in 1993. Recovery did not set in until February 1994, and by October, industrial production was 5.2 percent above the previous October. Eastern Germany probably fell 42 percent between the second half of 1990 and its lowest point in January 1993. By the end of 1994, the East had recovered to about the second half of 1990.[5]

PRODUCTIVITY

Reliable productivity studies of eastern Germany are still very difficult to complete, and thus all figures here deal only with the West. The European Commission in its study of comparative productivity put the United States in first place in 1993 with a rating of 138.7. West Germany was well behind the United States with 119.8, closely followed by Japan with 118.7.[6]

Another study covering productivity in 1990 showed the American worker producing an average of $49,600 in goods and services to lead the world. By comparison, the average West German produced $44,600 and the Japanese $39,600.[7]

MERCHANDISE EXPORTS

With few exceptions, the United States, Germany, and Japan regularly rank first, second, and third in exports of goods. In 1993, the United States reported $465 billion (12.6% of the world total). Germany had $366 billion (9.9%), and Japan $361 billion (9.8%).

Of course, on a per capita basis, the Germans overwhelm both the United States and Japan by a huge margin. In 1993, there were $4,500 exports for each German, 2.5 times the American figure ($1,800) and well in excess of the Japanese ($2,900).[8]

Even in total exports, the 80 million Germans have been neck and neck with 256 million Americans in recent years. West Germany took world leadership away from the United States for the first time in 1986, a spot enjoyed by the latter for more than seventy years. Bonn held this lead in 1987 and 1988. America recaptured first place in 1989. In 1990, a reunited Germany grabbed the top position again; but the United States bounced back to lead in 1991, 1992, and 1993.

Germany is far more dependent on exports than the United States and Japan. In 1991, the Germans exported 24 percent of their GDP, as compared with 11.5 percent in the United States and 9.4 percent for Japan. This American percentage is expected to grow even further in the years ahead.

Belgium/Luxembourg is the most dependent of nations on foreign trade (57%), followed by Holland (47%), Switzerland (27%), and Austria (25%). Percentages for some other countries with dependencies less than Germany were Britain and France with 18 percent each, Italy (15%), and Spain (11%).

While Germany and Japan consistently pile up surpluses in their balances of merchandise trade, the United States regularly reports a deficit. In 1993, Japan exported $152 billion more than it imported. Germany had a surplus of $33 billion, and America's deficit was $115 billion.

West Germany's trade surplus reached its peak in 1988 when it amounted to $79 billion. This fell substantially in 1990 to $71 billion and then precipitously to $23 billion in 1991. This reflected the problems of reunification, which pulled much of the West's production out of international trade and into what had formerly been East Germany. In 1992, the trade surplus grew again to $39 billion; and in 1993, it was $33 billion.

STRONG CURRENCY

A nation must have a strong currency to become an economic superpower and also to maintain that status. Both Germany's mark and Japan's yen have proved particularly robust.

One important reason for the strength of the mark and the yen has been the large monetary reserves held by their central banks. As of the end of 1992, the Bundesbank led the world with $91 billion in various foreign currencies available to defend the mark on the foreign exchange markets of the world. Japan had $71.6 billion, and the United States had $60 billion.[9]

Germany gave birth to the mark on June 21, 1948, within the IMF, which maintained a system of controls until 1973. Since then, the mark has been free to float under the forces prevailing in the global foreign exchange market. During the forty-six years of its life, the mark has gone from 30 cents to 64 cents at the end of 1994, an increase of 113 percent.

Japan's yen was fixed at 0.27 cent in 1949 by American occupational authorities under the auspices of the IMF, a rate that prevailed until 1973. By the end of 1994, the floating yen had moved upward to 1 cent, a climb of 233 percent.

Germans and Japanese find that their currencies have far greater purchasing power in the United States than at home. For Americans, the reverse is true.

Germans vacationing in the United States are particularly attracted to Florida, Southern California, and other warm regions. Some German tourists combine family clothing purchases with annual vacations in America, thereby saving enough to substantially reduce their travel costs.

SAVINGS

Germany and Japan greatly surpass the United States in personal savings. In 1990, household savings in these and some other countries as a percentage of disposable income were as follows:[10]

Germany	13.9%
Japan	13.6%
France	12.2%
Canada	10.4%
United Kingdom	9.0%
United States	5.2%

WORKING HOURS

The Germans work only 1,590 hours per year and thus have by far more leisure time than citizens of other countries. Longer vacations, more holidays, and shorter workweeks all contribute to this statistic. By comparison, Americans work 1,950 hours, and the Japanese 2,120.[11]

TAX BURDEN

The German people carry a much heavier tax load than the Americans and the Japanese. In 1992, combined German taxes and social security payments took 43.7 percent of GDP. By contrast, the same percentage was 30.7 percent in the United States and 29.3 percent in Japan.[12]

CREDIT RATINGS

Credit rating agencies consistently place Germany, Japan, and the United States in their highest ratings. In July 1993, *Standard & Poor's* rated them and some other nations as follows:[13]

Country	Rating
United States	AAA
Germany	AAA
France	AAA
Britain	AAA
Japan	AAA
Netherlands	AAA
Norway	AAA
Austria	AAA
Switzerland	AAA
Belgium	AA+
Denmark	AA+
Canada	AA+
Sweden	AA+
Singapore	AA+
Taiwan	AA+
Australia	AA
Italy	AA
Spain	AA
Finland	AA-
Ireland	AA-
New Zealand	AA-
Portugal	AA-
South Korea	A+
Hong Kong	A
Iceland	A
Malaysia	A
Thailand	A-
Chile	BBB
China	BBB
Israel	BBB
Greenland	BBB-
Indonesia	BBB-
Turkey	BBB-
India	D+
Mexico	D+
Uruguay	D+
Venezuela	D

CONSUMER RANKING
OF SUPERPOWER GOODS

Japanese, German, and American products are far more highly regarded by worldwide consumers than those of Britain, France, Canada, and Italy. A Gallup poll published in 1994 showed that 38.5 percent of the 20,000 consumers in twenty countries rated Japanese goods "excellent" or "very good." Germany ranked at this level of quality with 36 percent of the consumers, and the United States with 34.3 percent. Britain was a poor fourth with 20 percent, followed by France, Canada, Italy, Spain, China, Taiwan, Mexico, and Russia.[14]

Japanese customers showed the greatest consumer patriotism; 76 percent of them rated their products excellent or very good. Germans were second with 49 percent. In America, 41 percent of the customers rated U.S. products in the top two categories; 36 percent picked the Japanese; and German goods were third. In Europe, German products led with a score of 44 percent, Japanese products drew 35 percent, and American products 27 percent.

INFLATION

During the 1985–1993 period, the United States suffered far more inflation than Japan and West Germany. America's consumer price index (CPI) climbed 34 percent in these eight years, compared with 19 percent in West Germany and 15 percent for Japan.[15]

West Germany was able to hold its inflation under that of Japan between 1985 and 1991 (10.7% to 11.8%). The strains of reunification began in 1992. Eastern Germany had inflation of 11.1 percent in 1992 (largely because of ending rent control) and 8 percent in 1993. However, eastern inflation subsided in 1994 and was only 3.2 percent in June, compared with 3.0 percent in the West.[16]

REAL WAGES

In the 1983–1993 period, American workers were hit by a 9-percent decline in real wages. During the same period, the Germans enjoyed a 20-percent increase and the Japanese 12 percent.[17]

UNEMPLOYMENT

During the 1983–1993 period, unemployment in the United States dropped from 10 percent to 6 percent, while Japan remained fairly stable at about 3 percent. The German situation was far more complicated. East Germany officially had no unemployment before the Berlin Wall fell in November 1989. Then it suffered a massive loss of jobs, reaching a peak rate of 17.1 percent in February 1994, or 1,300,000 jobless. Western Germany also hit a high in the same month, 8.9 percent or 2,740,000 out of work. Both parts of Germany slowly improved after that. The eastern rate was 14.8 percent (1,120,000) in June 1994, while the westerners had a rate of 8.0 percent (2,480,000).[18]

CORRUPTION

There is, unfortunately, some corruption to be found in all three economic superpowers. It would appear on the basis of one study that Japan has a greater problem than the United States and Germany. A study cited in *The Economist* divides nations into three levels of corruption: high, middle, and low. Germany and the United States were in the low category along with others such as Taiwan and Singapore. Japan was classified in the middle corruption group, including China, Brazil, and Malaysia. The high category of corruption embraces such countries as Russia, Venezuela, and the Philippines.[19]

NOTES

1. *New York Times*, July 4, 1993.
2. *The Economist*, London, June 20, 1992, p. 107.
3. *Economic Report of the President*, Washington, D.C., 1994, p. 395; *Financial Times*, London, March 28, 1994.
4. *Financial Times*, London, December 28, 1994.
5. Ibid.
6. *Wall Street Journal Europe*, Brussels, June 29, 1993.
7. *New York Times*, February 27, 1994.
8. *The Economist,* London, April 16, 1994, p. 115.
9. *Frankfurter Allgemeine Zeitung*, May 4, 1993.
10. *New York Times*, January 17, 1993.
11. *New York Times*, October 2, 1992.
12. *Die Zeit*, Hamburg, June 11, 1993.
13. *Frankfurter Allgemeine Zeitung*, July 23, 1993.
14. *Financial Times*, London, February 11, 1994; *Frankfurter Allgemeine Zeitung*, March 12, 1994.
15. *Financial Times*, London, July 19, 1994.
16. *Frankfurter Allgemeine Zeitung*, July 12, 1994.
17. *New York Times*, March 14, 1994.
18. *Frankfurter Allgemeine Zeitung*, July 7, 1994.
19. *The Economist*, London, March 19, 1994, p. 86.

4

Merging Two German States

COMPARISON OF EAST AND WEST

German reunification is a continuing and complex process that is gradually integrating East and West Germany. It is going to take much longer than anyone expected on that euphoric midnight in October 1990, when Chancellor Kohl proclaimed to a crowd of 100,000 standing outside the Reichstag Building in Berlin that the two German states were once again united.

The stark contrasts between East and West Germany could not be fully understood, even by the very able scholars who had specialized in studying the German Democratic Republic (GDR). In the West, these researchers had to rely at least in large part on the data supplied by the East German government, which had fabricated its statistics so effectively that very few of its own top officials really knew what was going on in Marxist Germany.

Once the Berlin Wall fell on November 9, 1989, the enormity of the eastern propaganda effort slowly began to surface. Dr. Breuel, President of Treuhand, was quoted as saying: "The former East German government claimed that it was the eighth largest industrial power in the world. And we believed it. That speaks for an unlimited naiveté on our part."[1]

The basic economic differences between the two German states in 1989 were dramatic. In population, the West had 62 million, the East 16 million. Gross national product (GNP) amounted to $1.2 trillion in the West ($19,300 per capita) and $75 billion in the East ($4,500 per capita). Employment statistics in 1988 showed 27.3 million western workers and 8.6 million easterners. Exports in 1988 amounted to 15 percent of GNP in the West and 14 percent in the East. In that same year, there were 620 telephones per 1,000 West Germans, as opposed to 240 in the East. Similar ratios of auto ownership were 450 and 220, respectively.[2]

The most glaring contrast was in per capita GNP, $19,300 in the West and $4,500 in the East. This was a tremendous gap of more than 4 to 1. On July 1, 1990, the Monetary Union gave the easterners a big boost to about $7,800.[3]

In 1991, disposable income per capita in the East was only 47.1 percent of that in the West. By 1992, it was up to 58.1 percent; and in 1993, it reached 62.1 percent. Gross wages per employee in the East were 47.6 percent of the West's level in 1991, 62.1 percent in 1992, and 68.5 percent in 1993.[4]

The superior western standard of living was vividly illustrated by automobiles, not only in the comparative affordability but also in the quality and in the average waiting period. In West Germany, 97 percent of the households had a car, while only 52 percent had one in East Germany. The western cars were predominantly Volkswagens, Opels, Fords, or Japanese or French imports; while the great mass of East Germans drove Wartburgs or Trabants—flimsy domestic cars that sounded like lawn mowers and left a polluting blue flag emission as they moved through traffic. The westerner could buy his car at once, while the easterner had to wait about ten years.

MONETARY UNION
(JULY 1, 1990)

This historic event established the social market economy of West Germany for all of Germany. The East German Ostmark gave way to the West German mark as legal tender. The Bundesbank became the central bank of all Germany, and the fate of the East German population became the responsibility of Bonn.

At 10,000 banks and booths around their country, East Germans between the ages of fourteen and sixty had a week to change up to 4,000 Ostmarks for marks at a rate of 1 to 1. Those over sixty could exchange an additional 2,000 at that parity rate, and those under fourteen only 2,000. All cash and deposits in excess of these limits could be converted at a rate of 2 to 1.

Wages and salaries were converted at a rate of 1 to 1 under labor contracts, provided they were in force on or before May 1, 1990. The same rate applied to alimony, rentals, stipends, and other forms of recurring payments. Not included were payments to and from life insurance companies covering life policies and private pension contracts. These were converted at a rate of 2 to 1. Government pensions were fixed at a rate of 1 to 1. All other claims and liabilities denominated in eastern marks were converted at a rate of 2 to 1, except for claimants residing outside East Germany or claims arising after December 31, 1989 (to be settled at a rate of 3 to 1).

The mechanics of monetary union were effectuated by the Bundesbank. Despite many problems, the transformation from the limping East German mark to the western mark went off with comparative smoothness. One of the coauthors was in an East Berlin hotel as midnight approached on June 30. The bar had already switched all its prices to marks but continued to accept the East German currency until the magic stroke of 12. Patrons holding Ostmarks were speeding up their drinking markedly as midnight approached.

The next morning was a beautiful Sunday, and as usual the stores were closed. Shop windows in East Berlin were full of new merchandise, all priced in marks. Window-shoppers were out on the sidewalks in force, puzzling like foreign tourists over strange products in a new currency. One small group was very excited as they discussed a store window featuring Kellogg's Corn Flakes, previously unavailable in eastern stores.

Nobody realized on that delightful day how costly and frustrating the integration process would be for both East and West Germans. The universal optimism generally prevailing among West Germans at the time of monetary union was traceable, in part, to their widespread faith in the mark. It would, they believed, affect the eastern Germans much as it had the westerners in 1948. Even the sober and conservative Deutsche Bank was carried away by this dogma.

There are strong indications that the East German economy will show the same positive trends over the medium term which the Federal Republic experienced following the Currency Reform of 1948. At that time, the real GNP grew in the double digits for the first two years. Between 1950 and 1960, real economic growth in West Germany averaged close to 8 percent. The setting for a strong economic upswing in East Germany is similarly excellent. Once the expected influx of significant amounts of private capital into East Germany and the massive public financial support from West Germany is fused with the release of productive forces in the East, then currently low levels of East German productivity and capacity utilization will be a memory of a bygone past.[5]

POLITICAL UNION
(OCTOBER 3, 1990)

The unification ceremony took place in Berlin at midnight of October 2 as thousands of thoughtful (very few jubilant or intoxicated) citizens gathered around the Reichstag Building to watch the impressive liturgy enacted on the western steps of this historic structure. After the ceremony, Chancellor Kohl and his party sat in the lobby of the Hotel Kempinski. Kohl was still glowing with understandable pride. He had disproved his many critics, who have tended to underestimate this prodigious politician, by consummating a German union comparable to that of Bismarck but without the military action of his predecessor. Kohl's response to his many well-wishers was strikingly modest, far from Bismarckian.

The Bundestag was increased in size to 662 members, and the first all-German elections were held on December 1, 1990. Chancellor Kohl's coalition won a comfortable majority of 398.

TREUHAND ANSTALT

This incredible and highly controversial agency of the German government has played a central role in merging the German states. Treuhand Anstalt (Trust Agency) was created by the East German government in March 1990, seven months before unification. After unity, Treuhand was housed as a unit of the Ministry of Finance in Bonn; but its main office remained in East Berlin. Originally, Treuhand took over ownership of some 8,000 East German enterprises. Under the enabling statutes, Treuhand was required to do the following:

1. Convert them into corporations under West German law.
2. Reorganize those firms capable of surviving in a capitalistic society.
3. Sell the reorganized companies to private corporations.
4. Enter joint ventures or other cooperative contracts on behalf of its companies.
5. Liquidate those companies unable to compete in a market economy.
6. Return nationalized businesses to original private owners.
7. Return properties once owned by local and state governments, which had been nationalized by the East German government.

In firms with over 500 workers, Treuhand was further charged with appointing supervisory boards (comparable to U.S. boards of directors). West German business leaders and bankers, many retired, were recruited for the vast majority of seats on these boards.

To make its holdings more salable, Treuhand was authorized to break up the larger units and repackage them. This increased the total to 13,781. Clearly, Treuhand has been conducting the largest and most controversial going-out-of-business sale in world history. Prime Minister Thatcher's much advertised privatization program in the 1980s only involved about forty British companies.

Treuhand's main office in Berlin was a sprawling building on Leipziger Strasse, which once served Hermann Goering's Air Ministry. Incredible chaos reigned at the outset, but fortunately, the situation improved. Fifteen regional offices were located throughout eastern Germany, and foreign offices opened in New York and Tokyo.

Some enterprises have been easier to move than others. Treuhand has had great trouble selling textile factories; shipyards; steel mills; machine tool

makers; and manufacturers of chemicals, autos, electronics, and heavy machinery. It has done well with construction companies, hotels, restaurants,
food processors, and breweries. West German brewers rushed to buy the eastern facilities and convert them to western quality. Germany's largest brewer,
Brau and Brunnen AG (maker of Dortmunder Union and Schultheiss among
others), bought six eastern breweries and watched its sales climb 15 percent
in 1991 over the previous year.[6]

Western German corporations did not exactly reenact the Oklahoma Land
Rush to buy up properties. Chancellor Kohl repeatedly lectured them pub-
licly and privately for their hesitancy. The government gradually increased
tax and other inducements (most of them also available to foreign investors).
Furthermore, Treuhand itself began to offer more attractive terms to both
German and non-German prospects.

By October 1993, Treuhand had sold 732 of its firms to foreign corporations. Swiss firms (about 114) lcd in total buyers, followed by the United
Kingdom (102), Austria (100), France (71), and the United States (70). Most
surprising was the fact that only three Japanese companies had acquired
Treuhand firms.[7] Japan's multinationals have long shown a reluctance to make
direct investments in any part of Germany, preferring to use Britain as their
springboard within the European Community.

Some critics have portrayed U.S. business executives as unduly timid in
this area. Such criticism is unjustified for two reasons. First, there were very
serious difficulties for both Germans and Americans in Treuhand acquisitions.
Second, there were usually more effective strategies available to U.S. companies for reaching the eastern German market. As of May 1993, some 200
U.S. corporations had invested DM 6 billion in the East according to a statement by the U.S. Ambassador, Robert Kimmitt. These were both acquisitions
of Treuhand firms and investments outside of Treuhand, which have maintained or created some 42,000 jobs.[8]

By the end of 1994, when Treuhand was terminated, only 65 firms of its
original 13,781 were still for sale. These firms became the responsibility of a
newly created agency, Beteiligungs-Management-Gesellschaft (Managing
Holding Company), housed in the Ministry of Finance.[9]

Thus, in four and one-half years of its existence, Treuhand had disposed
of 13,716 firms. Some 3,701 were liquidated or in the process of being liquidated. About 3,000 were returned to state and local governments, from which
the Marxist central government had seized them between 1949 and 1990. The
remaining 9,649 were privatized by sale or return to the individual owners
from which they had been confiscated.[10]

What will happen to the 65 firms still belonging to Treuhand? Many are
big companies in basic industries. They are going to be difficult to sell and
even more difficult to close. Many of them will probably remain in federal or state
ownership because it is so politically unpopular to shut down major employers.

Speedy return was essential for the local governments, which could not borrow funds to improve these properties until title questions were clarified.

The federal and eastern state governments have designed a wide variety of financial assistance programs to encourage private firms, both German and foreign, to invest in the East. These benefits are applicable to investments in Treuhand firms and outside Treuhand as well. The West German authorities long had experience with such programs used to stimulate investment in West Berlin and areas on their side of the Iron Curtain, whose benefits are now being removed.

CLAIMS FOR NATIONALIZED PROPERTY

Claims for property confiscated in what was once East Germany are divided into three classes: 1933–1946 (Nazi period), 1946–1949 (Soviet Occupation), and 1946–1990 (East Germany). They have presented a highly emotional and very expensive set of problems for the German government. Over the past five years, these difficulties have unleashed a fury of debate in the legislature and a battle royal in the courts, both of which are sure to continue for at least another decade.

The Property Act of 1990 (*Vermögensgesetz*) was the first statutory effort in this field, providing that, in general, property seized in 1933 to 1946 and 1949 to 1990 should be returned to its original owners; otherwise, monetary compensation should be paid. However, claims originating in 1945 to 1949 under Soviet rule were excluded from this legislation. This exclusion applied to 14,000 landowners (mostly of large holdings) and many business firms.

Amendments were made seven times to the Property Act of 1990 in an effort to improve its provisions, but nothing was done to extend its benefits to Soviet victims. Finally, the Reparation Act of 1994 (*Entschädigungs-und Ausgleichsleistungs—Gesetz*) provided some relief to the class of claimants. They cannot recover their property, but former landowners can obtain limited compensation.

There is a very good chance that this part of the law will be declared unconstitutional. The legal argument against it is that treating those damaged by Soviet nationalization less favorably than the other two groups of claimants violates the principle of equality set forth in Article 3 of the German Constitution.

A deadline of December 31, 1992, was fixed in the Property Act of 1990 for filing claims under that statute. By that date, some 1.2 million claims had been registered, covering 2.6 million titles. About 150,000 claims were filed against property in eastern Berlin, half of which were settled by the end of 1994.

On December 2, 1949, a list was published called "Liste 3," covering the Soviet confiscation of land belonging to about 1,600 aristocratic landlords and business firms—mostly large but some middle-size—with a total estimated value of $26 billion. Two of the firms on the list—Wertheim Department Store in Leipziger Strasse and a book printer in Bernauer Strasse, both in East Berlin—filed individual lawsuits asking for return of their property. They argued that their claims be treated as claims against East Germany rather than the Soviet Union because the confiscation procedure begun in the Soviet period was not finally carried out until December 2, 1949, with the publication of the list by East Germany, which was founded on October 7, 1949. Both actions were denied by the Federal Administrative Court in February 1995.[11] The court held that the confiscation was effectuated by laws enacted during the Soviet Occupation and mere publication in the East German period was of no legal significance.

Some German lawyers have filed suits using legal theories which do not rely on the aforementioned statutes. One group of cases consists of appeals to the European Court of Human Rights in Strassburg, which argue that Germany has violated the rights of the claimants under the Human Rights Convention of 1950 and the Geneva Convention of 1949.

Another theory employed has been to sue the German Foreign Minister and the former State Secretary of this same Ministry for fraud and perjury, inasmuch as they gave false testimony before the Federal Constitutional Court to the damage of the claimants. They testified that the Soviet Union had insisted on the exclusion of 1945–1949 claims as a price for its approval of German reunification in 1990. One can expect additional statutes and court decisions which will lead to still further modification of German law in this field.

Accordingly, we must urgently advise any person who things he or she has a valid claim to consult a competent lawyer as soon as possible. The statutes are voluminous, highly technical, and frequently illogical. There are different deadlines varying with the nature of the claim, and the claims themselves are processed in the order that they are filed.

One West Berliner filed a claim for the return of a parcel of land in downtown Berlin on which the twenty-six-story International Trade Center and the eleven-story Hotel Metropol had been built by the East German government. A Swiss citizen claimed title to one of the lots on which the soaring East Berlin television tower was constructed. Assuming that these claims are upheld, the owners will be entitled only to compensation for their commercial land and not for the improvements.

Communist officials routinely seized houses of people who migrated to the West or were hostile to the regime. The new occupants placed in such houses paid only nominal rents, often only a few dollars, to the state.

Because the preferred property for investors in the big cities is so often involved in legal battles over title, many entrepreneurs have moved to the virgin farmland on the edge of the cities where no such problem exists. Office parks and shopping malls have been rising on plowed-up farms. So many have been built around Leipzig that city officials worry about their ability to survive.

An interesting case involving a nationalized business was reported in February 1991.[12] Heinz Janetski started a private firm in 1945 after World War II that made medical centrifuges near Leipzig. He originally had eleven workers, but by 1958, Janetski had eighty-five on his payroll. He needed to expand and applied for a government loan. The East German government supplied the investment in return for an 80-percent interest in the firm. The state took 80 percent of the profit and taxed his 20-percent share at a 92-percent rate (a typical arrangement).

Nevertheless, Janetski made a success of the business. By 1972, he had 330 workers and was selling in forty-five foreign countries. Sales were 28 million east marks (worth about $5 million at the time). In 1972, East Germany nationalized the business as part of a nationwide program, and Janetski was out on the street.

In the summer of 1990, Janetski applied for and recovered the business, which had been neglected and allowed to fall into serious deterioration. It was so bad, he said, that he "wept and wept." There were 480 underworked employees, a number he quickly trimmed to 180. The state had not brought out a new model of the centrifuge since it nationalized the business in 1972. Janetski has already incorporated Western and Japanese technology and now has a full line of eighteen different models, ranging in price from DM 1,000 to DM 45,000.

U.S. CLAIMS

American claims for property nationalized in East Germany had been assembled by the U.S. Department of State before reunification. The Foreign Claims Settlement Commission, a government agency, had processed all American requests and had recognized 1,899 as valid, including those of Woolworth, GM, ITT, and Singer.

Total recognized claims amounted to $78 million. With compound interest at 6 percent until 1990, the United States was asking for $370 million.[13] By a treaty between Germany and the United States dated May 13, 1992, the total was fixed at $190 million. American claimants now have the option of pursuing such claims under the terms of this treaty (confiscated property passes to Germany) or under the terms of the Property Act of 1990 as amended (described earlier).

COSTS

The federal government, together with the western states and communities, has now been pouring funds into the East for over four years. Such transfer payments amounted to DM 121 billion in 1991. They shot up to DM 142 billion in 1992 and DM 150 billion in 1993.[14] Anticipated transfer payments for subsequent years were as follows in billions of DM:[15]

1994	154
1995	194

NOTES

1. *Frankfurter Allgemeine Zeitung*, March 27, 1992.

2. *The Economist*, London, October 6, 1990, p. 143.

3. "German Survey," *The Economist*, London, May 23, 1992, p. 4.

4. *Financial Times*, London, May 4, 1994.

5. *German Economy and Monetary Union* (Frankfurt: Deutsche Bank, 1990), p. 53.

6. *Frankfurter Allgemeine Zeitung*, March 23, 1992.

7. *Financial Times*, London, June 14, 1993.

8. *German-American Business Journal Midwest*, Chicago, German-American Chamber of Commerce, August 1993, p. 28.

9. *Frankfurter Allgemeine Zeitung*, December 31, 1994.

10. *Wall Street Journal*, New York, December 9, 1994.

11. *Frankfurter Allgemeine Zeitung*, February 9, 1995.

12. *New York Times*, February 14, 1991.

13. *Frankfurter Allgemeine Zeitung*, June 26, 1990.

14. *Financial Times*, London, May 4, 1994.

15. *Der Spiegel*, Hamburg, 44 (1994): 116.

5

Principal Methods of Selling to Germany

U.S. firms have developed an impressive variety of approaches to the German market. Some of these methods are relatively inexpensive, while others involve substantial investment. Each firm must decide which method or combination of methods will best promote the sale of its products or services on the German market.

Exports of merchandise have traditionally received the most attention; but it has long been clear that U.S. firms, through their German subsidiaries, manufacture and sell in Germany far more than American business exports to that country. In 1993, total merchandise exports to Germany came to $24.2 billion, but the German subsidiaries of GM with $13.2 billion and Ford with $12.2 billion ($25.5 billion combined) produced and sold more than total U.S. exports to Germany.

The methods most frequently used to sell to the Germans are described in this chapter.

EXPORTS DIRECTLY TO GERMANY

Exporting from the point of production in the United States to the German customer is a simple and comparatively inexpensive method of reaching the German market. Most firms use this as their first approach; and if they receive a satisfactory response, they adopt one or more additional strategies.

Torel Inc. of Yoakum, Texas, is a good illustration of this strategy. Founded in 1961, Torel manufactures western-style belts, wallets, and other leather products. The first German orders arrived in 1978 from visitors at U.S. trade fairs. In 1981, Torel took its products to the Nürnberg trade show and rented its own exhibit. The response from German retailers was most gratifying, and Torel continues to exhibit every year at the Nürnberg Fair. In 1985, Torel went a step further by retaining a dealer in leather products located in Heidelberg.[1]

Torel does not publish annual sales figures, but they are estimated at $10 million. It now exports 10 percent of its production, 4 percent going to about 1,000 German retailers. Torel found early that German customers prefer products "Made in Texas" rather than "Made in USA." They also like the gaudier "John Wayne" type of leather goods.

EXPORTS THROUGH TRADE INTERMEDIARIES

There are about 2,500 trade intermediaries in the United States, accounting for some 10 percent of all U.S. exports. They pay about 15 percent below the best discount price of small manufacturers and then sell the products overseas. These trade intermediaries are sometimes called export management companies. They save their customers, typically small manufacturers, the considerable expense of setting up their own export department.[2]

SALES ORGANIZATION IN GERMANY

One of the best sales organizations in Germany is that of IBM. It has long dominated the computer market of western Germany, where it has substantial manufacturing facilities. After German reunification in 1990, IBM moved quickly to achieve the same position in the East. It has no plans to manufacture there, but a strong sales organization has been established as one phase of its operations. Its total expenditures on its eastern market came to DM 154 million in 1990 and DM 253 million in 1991.[3]

GERMAN AGENTS

An agent under the law enters sales contracts on behalf of his or her principal (the seller) and is paid a commission for his or her services. This method is popular because of its low cost to the American principal. It has also been attractive to firms that did not want to manufacture in eastern Germany after political union in 1990. Dow Chemical, with about $20 million in sales to East Germany in 1988, led all U.S. firms; and 3M was second with $10 million. Both of these companies, with probably the broadest experience in this region, decided not to buy a Treuhand firm or build a new plant in the East. Instead, they are using agents and supplying customers for the present from long-established manufacturing facilities in western Germany and other countries.

GERMAN DISTRIBUTORS

A distributor or dealer differs from the agent in that he or she enters contracts in his or her own name. The distributor normally buys and takes title to the goods, which are then sold to the customer. Caterpillar has long had a distributor in western Germany and decided to use the same firm for this purpose in the East rather than set up its own sales organization in the new states. GM, Ford, and Chrysler all use distributors throughout Germany.

REPRESENTATIVE OFFICES

Banks and financial institutions, as well as law firms and accounting firms, often use this strategy. The First Union National Bank of North Carolina (Charlotte) has a representative office in Dusseldorf, which cannot accept deposits or make loans. It can only solicit deposits and loans on behalf of its home office. Citibank AG originally opened a representative office in Dresden in 1990 and then later changed it to a full branch.

BRANCHES

A branch office is simply an extension of the home office and has no separate legal identity. Bank of America has a branch in Frankfurt, which conducts business much the same as a branch in California. Both bind the parent company in San Francisco.

ACQUISITION OF
EXISTING GERMAN CORPORATIONS

Many U.S. firms have used this method to get inside the German market. The best-known example is Adam Opel AG, which was a going concern when purchased by GM in 1929 as its German subsidiary.

ESTABLISHMENT OF
NEW GERMAN CORPORATIONS

Most U.S. firms have used this method. Ford wanted a German subsidiary and decided to create Ford-Werke AG, a brand new corporation to manufacture and sell its cars in Germany.

JOINT VENTURES

In May 1990, GM signed a joint venture with Automobilwerke Eisenach GmbH, the former manufacturer of the Wartburg, the larger of the two much-derided automobiles once made by East Germany. GM negotiated this contract with Treuhand Anstalt, which still owns Automobilwerke, thus avoiding an acquisition. It has invested $16 million to take 80 percent of the stock in the joint venture known as Opel-AWE GmbH, which assembles Vectras. By October 1990, Vectras were rolling off the Eisenach line at the rate of 10,000 per year. Otis Elevator, Honeywell, IBM, and Hewlett-Packard have also entered joint ventures with Treuhand companies.

In September 1992, Maytag entered a joint venture agreement with Bosch-Siemens Hausgeräte GmbH of Munich for the cooperative sales worldwide of their respective household appliances. Bosch-Siemens had sales of $4 billion in 1991, and Maytag $3 billion. Bosch-Siemens (second only to the Swedish firm Electrolux in European production) makes products under the name of Bosch, Siemens, Constructa, and Neff. Maytag produces under the following brand names: Maytag, Hoover, Magic Chef, Admiral, and Norge.[4]

A very interesting joint venture was announced in October 1993 by United Air Lines (the second largest in the United States after American Airlines) and Lufthansa AG, a government-owned German carrier. This agreement followed, by ten days, an air-traffic treaty between the United States and Germany, which froze for two years the number of flights by U.S. airlines to Germany and from Germany to third countries. This gave Lufthansa a respite from mounting competition from American companies. The joint venture agreement enables United Air Lines to book its passengers via Lufthansa to smaller German cities after landing in Frankfurt, Berlin, and other major hub airports. Lufthansa can do the same on United flights in the United States. Both airlines honor each other's frequent-flyer programs and share ground crews, checking in customers, and catering.[5]

Before reunification, only Pan Am (among U.S. carriers) was allowed to fly into Germany; but Pan Am has been liquidated, and United, American, and Delta are now battling for this business. The joint venture should enable United and Lufthansa to reciprocally generate more revenue miles. Both suffered losses in 1991, 1992, and 1993. United had revenues of $14.5 billion in 1993 and a loss of $50 million. Meanwhile, Lufthansa was reporting $10.3 billion in sales and a loss of $66 million. There were 83,000 workers on the United payroll (of whom 8,000 are pilots), while Lufthansa had 63,000.[6]

LICENSE AGREEMENTS

The owner of a patent may grant commercial use of the patent to another party under terms of a license agreement, which requires the licensee to pay a fee to the licensor. The owner of unpatented know-how may also enter into such a license agreement, which is equally binding on the licensee. However, unprotected know-how is less salable to the prospective licensee, who views a patent as an indication of novel technology protected from copying and thereby justifying the payment of a higher license fee. Nor does the know-how have to be secret in order to be the subject of a license agreement.

The licensor may grant an exclusive license to both manufacture and distribute the subject matter. This exclusion clause may go so far as to exclude even the licensor. On the other hand, the agreement may permit manufacturing but not the distribution or vice versa.

The licensor may restrict the licensee to one or more uses of the patent, retaining to itself all other rights. There may be restrictions as to territory, time, and distribution. The patent holder may retain under the terms of the license agreement the right to sell and transfer the patent.

During the Marxist era in East Germany (1949–1990), most of the methods of selling discussed in this chapter were prohibited by law. Only exports, joint ventures, license agreements, and representative offices were available to U.S. (and other foreign) firms if they wanted to reach East German consumers. The trade officials responsible for such matters were particularly sympathetic to license agreements because this arrangement gave them maximum control over the foreign product being manufactured and distributed in their nation. Also, they could pay license fees with bartered goods, thereby conserving their limited hard currencies.

Two highly publicized license agreements of this time involving U.S. firms were made by IBM and Pepsico. IBM for many years licensed the building of and sale of some of its computers by Robotron, the huge state-owned combine responsible for such machines. Pepsico entered a license agreement with East Germany in 1974, under which it manufactured and sold Pepsi near Rostock for several years.

RETAIL OUTLETS

Woolworth organized its German subsidiary in 1926, which a year later opened its first store, a "Twenty-Five and Fifty Pfennig" general merchandise unit in Bremen. It prospered, and Woolworth gradually covered the country with outlets. Germany's defeat in 1945 brought the loss of thirty stores for Woolworth (sixteen in the German territory allocated to Poland by the Allies and fourteen in what became East Germany).[7]

The East German stores were nationalized by the Marxist government without compensation and converted into state-owned retail outlets. Woolworth stated in June 1990 that the firm had filed claims for damages with the proper German authorities but would not wait to begin building new stores in the East.[8]

In 1991, Woolworth filed a claim with Poland to recover one of its nationalized stores. The government has contested the case with several legalistic tricks; but the real reason is fear of a precedent, thus triggering a huge wave of German claims. To date, the claimant has completely failed.[9]

Woolworth reported that immediately after the fall of the Berlin Wall in November 1989, East Germans flocked to some thirty West German stores lying close to the border, where sales quickly doubled their previous volume.[10]

Most of this sudden increase took place in West Berlin, where Woolworth had twenty-three stores.[11] In 1990, nine of its ten most profitable stores worldwide were in Germany.

The first store in the East opened in East Berlin in April 1990, only five months after the Berlin Wall fell and six months before reunification on October 3, 1990. During 1991, six outlets were started in the East and sixteen in the West.[12] It should be noted that Woolworth stores in Germany handle a wider variety of goods than those in the United States, particularly in the higher-priced categories.

German sales for 1989 were DM 1.9 billion, and profits were DM 43.5 million, giving a profit margin of 2.2 percent on sales. Business shot up after the Berlin Wall fell on November 9, 1989; and for 1990, sales were up a sensational 47 percent to DM 2.8 billion. Profits were even more sensational, up 73 percent to DM 75.3 million.[13] Profit margin rose to 2.6 percent.

In 1991, sales of Woolworth climbed an additional 4 percent to DM 2.9 billion; and profits were also up 4 percent to DM 78.3 million, making a profit margin of 2.9 percent.[14]

Woolworth's spectacular rise of 47 percent in German sales in 1990 over 1989 was far ahead of other American corporations. Actually, the others did not benefit substantially from the fall of the Berlin Wall and reunification until 1991. In that year, Coca-Cola led all other U.S. firms with a brilliant sales increase of 66 percent, far ahead of second-place Procter & Gamble with 24 percent. As previously noted, the East Germans for the most part came west to established stores to boost Woolworth sales in 1990. On the other hand, Coca-Cola had to establish production and marketing facilities in the East to achieve its big jump in 1991.

German operations have been regularly the most profitable in the global performance of Woolworth. In 1991, the German stores constituted only 5 percent of the total; but they accounted for 16 percent of worldwide sales and 23 percent of net profits.

Sales in 1992 were off a mere 0.7 percent to DM 2.92 billion, but profits fell 72 percent to DM 21 million. Management stated this was to be expected after the extraordinary run-ups in 1990 and 1991.[15]

Woolworth's organization in Germany is rather unique and deserves some attention. An American subsidiary corporation, Retail Company of Germany, based in Frankfurt, handles all German operations. It owns F. W. Woolworth Co. GmbH, the old subsidiary dating back to 1926, which in 1993 operated about 330 traditional general merchandise stores in Germany. In addition, Retail Company of Germany owns the following specialty chains:

Rubin GmbH (jewelry)	40 outlets
Moderna GmbH (shoes)	100 outlets
Der Schuh (shoes)	100 outlets

Lady Plus (for larger women)   18 outlets
New Yorker Süd (jeans and sportswear)   18 outlets

In 1991, general merchandise stores generated 90 percent of all German sales, compared with 10 percent for the specialty chains. This was quite in contrast to the global Woolworth mix, where general outlet stores brought in 53 percent and the specialty 47 percent.

It should be noted that the Foot Locker chain of stores in Germany is not owned by Retail Company of Germany but is directly held by the Woolworth Corporation. The mother company quietly launched the Foot Locker concept in 1972, selling many brands of shoes and apparel. Today, there are more than 2,000 outlets worldwide, most of them in North America. Sales are $1.5 billion annually and they are the largest source of profit for Woolworth. It is believed that Foot Locker accounts for one-half of all Woolworth earnings.[16]

Foot Locker opened an attractive store on the Kurfürstendamm in Berlin in early 1993. During the National Basketball Association (NBA) playoffs the store was selling large quantities of equipment carrying the insignia of the Chicago Bulls. The customers were predominantly under thirty years of age.

In 1994, Woolworth still had 589 stores in Germany. Toys R Us reported forty-four stores, Timberland reported two stores, and Walt Disney reported two stores. Canada supported 1,297 Woolworths; but Germany was second among foreign countries, followed by 485 in Australia and 46 in Mexico.[17]

Exxon, through its German subsidiary, Esso AG in Hamburg, operated 1,663 filling stations in 1992, which reported DM 19 billion in revenue and profits of DM 457 million, a 2.3-percent return on sales.[19]

FRANCHISES

Franchising has become a powerful segment of the U.S. economy. There were 3,000 franchisers in this country in 1992 with 540,000 franchises. Total sales were $758 billion (up 6 percent over 1991) or more than 35 percent of total retail sales in the nation. Restaurant franchises (103,000) were far ahead of second-place nonfood retailers (57,000).[19] Most franchisers charge an initial fee to the franchisee. McDonald's collects $22,500 while Domino's Pizza takes $6,000. Start-up costs vary greatly for all of them. Costs for Domino's Pizza range from $76,000 to $187,000.[20]

However, only one in three franchises is operating outside the United States. Another third said they plan to go international by 1997.[21]

Franchises have been very popular in Germany in recent years. Some 2,200 new franchises were granted in 1992, bringing the total to 16,000.[22]

McDonald's celebrated its twenty-fifth birthday in 1993 and boasted 13,000 restaurants in sixty-six countries, the world's largest chain. Some 9,000 of the units are franchises, again the global leader.[23] In Germany alone, there were 442 restaurants (249 franchises), to rank first in restaurants and franchises. In 1992, McDonald's had 153 franchise owners of these 249 franchises. Total sales came to DM 1.2 billion. In the first five months of 1993, McDonald's received over 1,000 inquiries from parties interested in a franchise. Under the franchise contract used in the East, McDonald's assumes building and outfitting costs of about $1 million; and the franchisee invests $540,000. Over 300 applications were filed for the first six eastern franchises.

Goodyear, through its German subsidiary, Deutsche Goodyear GmbH in Cologne, was the only other U.S. firm in the top twenty franchisers in Germany in 1992. It had 120 franchises for tire and auto service.

Franchising is beginning to thrive in the new Länder as well, with over 1,400 eastern German franchises active as independent partners of western German franchisers. Interestingly, a number of well-established western German companies, which, prior to the fall of the Berlin Wall, did not use franchising, have begun to do so with their eastern German partners.

LEASING BUSINESS FROM GERMAN OWNERS

Hilton International has used this method in Dresden and Weimar. It announced in 1992 that it had entered a long-term lease with Deutsche Interhotel AG, the largest hotel chain in the East, under the terms of which Hilton would operate as lessee of the two hotels. Hilton also bought a hotel originally built as the Dom in eastern Berlin and renamed it the Berlin Hilton. This brought the number of hotels operated by Hilton in Germany to seven.[24]

By far, the most publicized business lease by an American is that of Tom Dooley III, about thirty years old and the son of a wealthy Boston trash hauler. Tom was one of the first Americans to go to eastern Germany after reunification. He and his father drove along the Baltic coast in January 1991 in search of business opportunities.

The prize that caught his interest was the famous Seebrücke (Sea Bridge) Restaurant, hanging over the surf and supported by wooden piles in tiny Ahlbeck. It is a landmark of the lovely island of Usedom and the last survivor of several Sea Bridge restaurants built one hundred years ago and designed after those found on the south coast of England.

The Usedom beach is probably the most beautiful in Germany and was extremely popular before World War II. It extends about twenty miles, and the Sea Bridge is at the eastern end near the Polish border. Just about two miles to the west on the beach is Heringsdorf, the famous bathing resort of German royalty and upper society from all over Europe. Ahlbeck is more plebeian and attracted middle-class families, particularly from Berlin, which is only seventy miles to the south. It was called "Children's Bathtub of Berlin"; and its most famous citizen, a tailor named Egelinski, fathered his thirty-third child in 1913 by his second wife. The Kaiser honored him as "The Richest Father in the World in Children."[25]

Dooley discovered that the Sea Bridge was owned by the town of Ahlbeck, which was entertaining bids from prospective lessees. Although he had no experience as a restaurateur, or any other business, he won a unanimous city council vote over thirty-nine bidders. The town officials were impressed by his father's wealth, Tom's charm, and his promise to make the area "Berlin's Cape Cod." He retained excellent lawyers, who got him an airtight lease for an incredible twenty-five years at a ridiculously low rent of DM 5,000 per month.

Dooley fired and replaced the entire restaurant staff twenty-four hours before a banquet for Germany's President von Weizsäcker, but the affair went off without a serious hitch. Then he opened a late-night disco which kept the citizens awake. He clothed his waiters in jogging suits and served mediocre food on dirty tablecloths. Dooley did not trust locals for security guards and, at first, hired Poles and then later members of the Lebanese militia living in Berlin. Unknown persons cut his water line and broke his windows. Dooley claims that the mayor threatened him by warning that he would be beaten up in the dark streets if he did not surrender his lease. Dooley reported the threat to the U.S. Ambassador and requested his protection.

The mayor canceled the lease in November 1991, citing failure to pay a security deposit. After this was paid, the town council balked on reinstating the contract unless Dooley agreed to pay a higher rent, shut down the disco, and give up other benefits.[26]

The town of Ahlbeck filed eviction proceedings in the Local Court but failed. The restaurant, as had been the custom, closed between November 1 and May 1 when it reopened for the 1992 season. Business was stimulated by the start of daily airplane service from Berlin. Dooley has invested about DM 1 million to improve his leased property and aimed at DM 3 million in revenue in 1993.

Probably the most curious aspect of this legal brawl is a clause in the lease calling for Dooley to rebuild by the end of 1994 a pier destroyed by a winter storm in 1941. Dooley's lawyers insisted that this meant an 80-meter structure similar to the one destroyed, which would cost about DM 400,000. The mayor said the town needs a 200-meter pier that can accommodate Baltic steamboats and would cost an estimated DM 5 million. Dooley told the mayor he would stick with the 80-meter pier.[27]

Dooley has made very few friends, but the Beck Brewery (the largest German beer import into the United States) has given him financial backing. Tom's father advised him after the first season to cut his losses and sell, but he was determined to stay.

As of March 1993, with his third season starting May 1, Tom was still embroiled with the town of Ahlbeck. It had prepared an amended contract that he refused to sign. The new agreement would have doubled his rent to DM 10,000 ($6,000) per month and require him to make a compensation payment to the town of DM 400,000 ($240,000), which would be used for the construction of the pier.

However, the controversy between Dooley and Ahlbeck has apparently been settled, and he is making money. All the media attention seems to have helped his restaurant's business. He has also profited from all the favorable publicity given another Tom Dooley, born in Germany of an American father, who became a star for the U.S. soccer team in 1993.

EQUIPMENT LEASING TO GERMANS

This is a comparatively new but expanding line of business. Volume in 1992 expanded to $31 billion in the United States, up 10.5 percent over 1991. Whirlpool was the first firm to lease large household appliances to retail customers in Germany. Its subsidiary, Whirlpool Hausgeräte Vertriebs GmbH, in Nürnberg, had revenues of DM 296 million in 1992, an increase of 10 percent. Eastern German revenues were DM 30 million, a 50-percent increase. During 1993, Whirlpool began leasing to wholesale customers.[28]

NOTES

1. *Wall Street Journal*, New York, November 13, 1990.
2. *Wall Street Journal*, New York, February 2, 1993.
3. *Frankfurter Allgemeine Zeitung*, April 10, 1992.
4. *Frankfurter Allgemeine Zeitung*, September 16, 1992.
5. *The Economist*, London, October 9, 1993, p. 75.
6. *Frankfurter Allgemeine Zeitung*, October 4, 1993.
7. *Financial Times*, London, April 6, 1990.
8. *Wall Street Journal*, New York, June 20, 1990.
9. *Frankfurter Allgemeine Zeitung*, July 9, 1993.
10. *Handelsblatt*, Dusseldorf, June 23, 1990.
11. *Berliner Morgenpost*, July 11, 1990.
12. *Financial Times*, London, April 6, 1990.
13. *Frankfurter Allgemeine Zeitung*, November 9, 1992.
14. *Frankfurter Allgemeine Zeitung*, July 11, 1990; *Financial Times*, London, May 9, 1992; *Wall Street Journal*, New York, November 9, 1992.
15. *Handelsblatt*, Dusseldorf, June 30, 1993.
16. *Wall Street Journal*, New York, November 9, 1992.
17. *Financial Times*, London, April 11, 1994.
18. *Frankfurter Allgemeine Zeitung*, June 16, 1993.
19. *Wall Street Journal*, New York, October 16, 1992.
20. *New York Times*, October 4, 1992.
21. *Wall Street Journal*, New York, November 13, 1992.
22. *Frankfurter Allgemeine Zeitung*, June 28, 1993.
23. *Frankfurter Allgemeine Zeitung*, May 10, 1993.
24. *Frankfurter Allgemeine Zeitung*, February 24, 1992.
25. *Frankfurter Allgemeine Zeitung*, March 25, 1993.
26. *Wall Street Journal*, New York, April 10, 1992.
27. *Frankfurter Allgemeine Zeitung*, June 4, 1992.
28. *Frankfurter Allgemeine Zeitung*, May 17, 1993.

6

German Government

Germany has 80 million inhabitants, of whom 6.8 million (8 percent) are aliens. This figure is high for a European country. It arises out of generous policy toward asylum seekers and the need for foreign workers in the 1960s and 1970s.

The number of aliens rose 6 percent during 1993, and the leading nationalities were as follows (in millions):[1]

Turks	1.90
Yugoslavians	1.20
Italians	0.50
Greeks	0.30
Poles	0.20
Rumanians	0.16
Spanish	0.13
Portuguese	0.09
Americans	0.08

While all nations in Western Europe have been the havens for asylum seekers, in 1992 Germany had become the residence of more cases than all others combined. The totals were as follows:[2]

Germany	438,000
Sweden	83,200
France	28,900
United Kingdom	24,600
Austria	16,200
Spain	12,700
Italy	2,500

As of July 1, 1993, the Constitution was amended to restrict the number of asylum seekers. The effect of this may be less than anticipated if foreigners become illegal immigrants sneaking over the borders.

Germany geographically lies almost entirely north of the United States–Canada boundary. It has three geographic regions:

1. Northern Germany is part of the immense plain sweeping from France into Russia, a convenient highway for hostile armies over the centuries.
2. The central segment turns hilly.
3. The southern region is mountainous. Zugspitze, south of Munich on the Austrian line, is the highest German mountain, rising 9,999 feet.

Berlin lies in the flat northern plain, about parallel with Calgary, Canada, but having a mean annual climate equal to that of Chicago. However, Berlin is warmer in winter and cooler in summer than Chicago. There is also less snow, and it melts faster.

Berlin is Germany's largest city, with 3.4 million—equal to Los Angeles. Its area of 340 square miles is much smaller than the 465 square miles of Los Angeles and larger than New York's 301 square miles. Before World War II, Berlin reached a peak population of 4.3 million; only 2.3 million were still there in 1945.

Fortunately for the Germans, they borrowed more heavily from the British than the Americans in formulating their Constitution of 1949. In the first place, their president is a figurehead like the English monarch. Second, their chief executive, a chancellor comparable to England's prime minister, is elected by Parliament—not by state primaries, national conventions, and presidential elections over a ten-month period, which beats the electorate into a state of insensitivity. The members of Parliament have a solid period of working with their elected leaders before elevating them to the office of chancellor. They have no fear of being saddled with some inexperienced governor out of nowhere. If the chancellor becomes impossible, Parliament does not have to wait months or years until the four-year term expires. They can vote him out with a majority vote whenever his conduct justifies it.

As Adlai Stevenson once said, "In America every young man born here can be elected president. It is a risk we all have to take."

The Constitution of 1949 was slightly amended at the time of reunification in 1990 to take care of problems arising out of the merger. Parliament set up a commission in 1991 to study proposed amendments and to make recommendations to Parliament by 1994. The sixty-four-member commission is composed of thirty-two members of the Bundestag and thirty-two from the Bundesrat. In its first eighteeen months of pondering, the commission showed little interest in change.[3]

On October 3, 1990, not just the Constitution but the entire legal system of West Germany (with a few exceptions) became the law of what had formerly been East Germany. On certain very sensitive points of conflict, it was agreed between the two Germanies that they would retain their respective statutes until the new all-German Bundestag was elected on December 2, 1990. Then this united legislature would enact laws for the entire nation.

One area in which different East and West German laws survived reunification was the amount of alcohol legally permissible in the blood of an automobile driver. Until January 1, 1993, easterners continued to drive under their old Marxist statute, which punished even the slightest amount of alcohol in the bloodstream. Meanwhile, westerners could still drive legally as long as alcohol was not in excess of 0.8 promille. After debating for more than two years, the Bundestag finally applied the western limit of 0.8 promille to all of Germany, effective January 1, 1993.[4]

Now business lunches for those in the East who enjoy a second martini with their meals have become more relaxed. Under the old 0.0 promille limit, scientific types figured that one libation with lunch would disappear from the bloodstream by 5:00 P.M. and that they could safely drive home at the end of the day. Two drinks, however, would still produce incriminating evidence.

Another point of divergence from October 2, 1990, to January 1, 1993, was the speed limit on the autobahn. Westerners continued to drive without a limit, while easterners observed their long-standing legal restraint of 100 kilometers per hour. Here again, there was prolonged argument; but eventually the Bundestag extended the western law to the East.

When West Germany was founded in 1949, Bonn became the temporary capital. After reunification, a vote of the Bundestag in 1991 declared that Berlin was once again the German capital. Moving from Bonn is proving to be a slow process. Losing 22,000 government jobs will be a severe blow to this city of 300,000. It will cost about $2 billion to $20 billion over a ten-year period, depending mostly on how many new government buildings are eventually built in Berlin and how many ministries remain in Bonn. Moreover, many western members of Parliament have never liked Berlin and would prefer to prolong their stay in Bonn.[5]

The president of the FRG is elected for a five-year term by a convention made up of two groups: the Bundestag and the state legislatures. The president cannot serve more than two terms.

Germany has had seven presidents thus far, as follows:

1949–1959	Theodore Heuss (Free Democrat)
1959–1969	Heinrich Luebke (Christian Democrat)
1969–1974	Gustav Heinemann (Social Democrat)
1974–1979	Walter Scheel (Free Democrat)
1979–1984	Carl Carstens (Christian Democrat)
1984–1994	Richard von Weizsäcker (Christian Democrat)
1994–1999	Roman Herzog (Christian Democrat)

President von Weizsäcker's term expired on July 1, 1994. The next president, Roman Herzog, a former judge of the Federal Constitutional Court, was the first elected by a convention including the six new states.

Real power in Germany is vested in the chancellor, who is not popularly elected but selected by the lower house of Parliament, the Bundestag. Like Britain's prime minister, the chancellor can be removed by majority vote of the lower house; but there is a significant difference. The Bundestag must in the same vote name a successor, which makes it more difficult to remove the chancellor.

The Bundestag now has 662 members, half of them elected from specific districts like the House of Representatives in the United States. The other half are elected on the basis of votes cast for the parties presenting lists in the particular states. The voter thus gets two votes on the Bundestag ballot. With the first vote, one votes for an individual candidate among those listed for that particular district on the ballot. With the second vote, one votes for the party list one favors.

In order to seat even one deputy, the particular party must either poll a minimum of 5 percent of the total vote cast or win three seats in the single-member districts. This has proved a very wholesome feature in the electoral system in that it has eliminated the small splinter parties which proved so troublesome in Germany during the Weimar Republic (1920–1933) and in many other countries.

The upper house of the German Parliament is the Bundesrat, with sixty-eight members. Each of the sixteen state governments elects three, four, or six members based on its population. In December 1994, the Social Democratic Party (SPD) controlled a majority of the sixteen states and had a majority of forty-one members in the Bundesrat. Thus, the government of Chancellor Kohl (Christian Democratic Union–Christian Social Union [CDU-CSU] and Free Democratic Party [FDP] in coalition) with a slim majority in the Bundestag found itself in a minority in the upper house.[6]

The Bundesrat must approve by a majority vote all laws effecting changes in the sovreignty of the states and the distribution of tax money. All constitutional amendments require a two-thirds majority of both Bundestag and Bundesrat.

In all other cases, members of the Bundesrat cannot interfere with the legislative process of the Bundestag except when a piece of legislation goes so entirely against their grain that they choose to invoke a conference committee set up to arbitrate between the two chambers. There, a consensus proposal must be drafted; this then goes to both houses for a second reading. It can, however, still fall through in the Bundestag if it is rejected by a two-thirds majority. The Bundesrat can then overturn this decision if it manages to line up a two-thirds majority against it. In the forty years of German parliamentary history between 1949 and 1989, the conference committee of the two houses was invoked 507 times to settle a contentious issue. In all, fifty-two laws subsequently failed to clear the necessary hurdles—not many when one considers the huge number of laws passed during those four decades.

The Bundesrat members selected by the various state governments are generally high-ranking officials of these same state governments. They do not serve for a fixed term but solely at the pleasure of their respective states. The Bundestag passes all federal laws, which then must be submitted to the Bundesrat.

During its history, the FRG has had six chancellors, in the following sequence:

1949–1963	Konrad Adenauer (Christian Democrat)
1963–1966	Ludwig Erhard (Christian Democrat)
1966–1969	Georg Kiessinger (Christian Democrat)
1969–1974	Willy Brandt (Social Democrat)
1974–1982	Helmut Schmidt (Social Democrat)
1982–	Helmut Kohl (Christian Democrat)

Since the creation of the FRG in 1949, the Germans have been fortunate in the stability of their government. There have been only five changes in administration in forty-five years, all achieved with a minimum of friction. Two of these transfers of power involved a change of party leadership, the first, in 1969, from the CDU-CSU to the SPD. The second, in 1982, saw power return to the CDU-CSU.

The Constitution of 1949 was deliberately designed to overcome some of the weaknesses in the Weimar Constitution of 1920, which was torpedoed by Hitler's Nazi dictatorship in 1933. While the Weimar Republic had a short, troubled life of thirteen years, the FRG has now enjoyed forty-five years of peace and prosperity.

One factor contributing powerfully to political stability in post–World War II Germany has been the high quality of its leadership, namely, Konrad Adenauer, Willy Brandt, Helmut Schmidt, and Helmut Kohl. Chancellor Adenauer (1949–1963) was the ideal politician to bring the defeated Germans out of their miserable condition and into an era of respectability. As mayor of Cologne and a member of the Reichstag, Adenauer had vigorously opposed the Nazis; and they had forced him out of political life. Starting in 1949, Adenauer led the combined CDU-CSU to three parliamentary victories. His government provided a wholesome climate conducive to the German economic miracle.

Willy Brandt was chairman of the SPD. This organization, dating back to 1875, had been Marxist in its platform and had never won a parliamentary election. Brandt, a pragmatic Socialist, persuaded his SPD colleagues to exorcise themselves of Marxism in 1959; and ten years later, his party placed first in the 1969 Bundestag elections. During his chancellorship (1969–1974), he led a movement to reduce tensions with East Germany, the Soviet Union, and other nations in the Communist bloc.

A scandal forced Brandt to resign in 1974, but the Socialists were fortunate to have Helmut Schmidt as a replacement. As chancellor from 1974 to 1982, Schmidt proved to be one of the world's ablest politicians. A moderate in his economic policies, he won the respect of conservative German business leaders and provided conditions for further growth in his nation's prosperity. He also earned the confidence of foreign political leaders who continued to consult him after he was forced to leave office.

Gorbachev phoned Schmidt for advice in 1990 when his fortunes were collapsing in Moscow. The German statesman listened carefully and then said, "There is only one thing to do. Emigrate to Canada."[7]

Helmut Kohl, chairman of the CDU, was sworn in to follow Schmidt as chancellor in 1982 and has known the glory of reunification in 1990 as well as the resulting economic problems. But Kohl has survived efforts from inside and outside his own party to oust him. Born in the Rhineland-Palatinate in 1930, Kohl reminds many Americans of the late Mayor Richard Daley of Chicago (now called Richard I to distinguish him from his son, who is currently mayor of that city). Kohl's organizational skills in building a well-functioning political machine are superb, and his combative instincts are devastating.

Although Helmut Kohl earned a Ph.D. in political science at Heidelburg, he does not use the title like most German politicians. He has frequently been criticized for not speaking a foreign language, but he replies, "What do you want, a translator or a chancellor?" Mayor Daley of Chicago even had trouble speaking his own language, but nobody ever questioned his administrative genius "in the city that works."

German political parties have greater power and are better organized than those in America. Parties hold regular annual conventions that elect strong chairmen as chief executives. Usually, the chairman is also nominated as the party's candidate for chancellor; but occasionally, different people are selected.

German party discipline is such that ambitious members must render loyal service before being nominated for chancellor or for prime minister of one of the states or as mayor of a city. There are no primaries, as in the United

States, to nominate candidates—which permit politicians to come out of nowhere to run for high office.

In the Bundestag election in 1990, the first for reunited Germany, six parties were able to elect members as follows:

CDU-CSU	319
FDP	79
SPD	239
PDS	17
Alliance 90	8
Total	662

It will be noted that the Party of Democratic Socialism (PDS) and Alliance 90 polled under 5 percent but still won seats in the Bundestag. Parties limited to eastern Germany had little time to organize in western Germany. Accordingly, the law was amended as to these organizations solely for the 1990 election to let them take seats if they won 5 percent of the vote in the East. The PDS, with only 2.4 percent nationally, was still able to get seventeen seats in the East. Alliance 90 took 1.2 percent overall in Germany but was strong enough in the new states to elect eight members to the Bundestag.

The CDU-CSU polled the largest number of votes in the 1990 Bundestag elections. While it operates as one party in Bonn, the CSU functions in Bavaria and the CDU fields candidates in the other fifteen states. The two parties have separate structures, but they form a common caucus in the Bundestag. Chancellor Kohl is chairman of the CDU, and Minister of Finance Theo Waigel heads the CSU.

The CDU-CSU is a moderately conservative political party, generally comparable to the Republicans in the United States except for their stronger support of social security programs and labor unions. The CDU tends to be a bit more liberal on social issues than the Bavarian CSU. The word *Christian* in the names of both parties is significant in that they tend to espouse the social teachings of the German Lutheran and Catholic churches. For example, both are generally opposed to abortion.

As mentioned earlier, the SPD dates back to 1875. In 1919, the radical wing broke off to form the Communist Party, which then fought bitterly with the Socialists in the period leading up to Hitler's seizure of power.

Rudolf Sharping, prime minister of Rhineland-Palatinate, was elected chairman of the SPD in 1993 and was the party's candidate for chancellor in the October 16, 1994, Bundestag elections. Helmut Kohl had the same office before moving to the national political stage in Bonn.

The FDP is a small but influential political organization that is basically liberal in the European sense of the word. In Europe, liberal politicians believe in the maximum freedom for the individual and reject all forms of religious interference in government. By contrast, in America a liberal is one urging government intervention and reform in both political and economic policies.

Because neither the CDU-CSU nor the SPD has always been capable of winning a majority of seats in the Bundestag, the FDP has been invited to form a coalition to give the larger party a working majority. In 1990, for example, the CDU-CSU only won 319 seats (43.8%) and not 332 (needed for an absolute majority of the 662 seats); and the FDP was invited to bring its 79 seats into a CDU-CSU-FDP coalition. That gave Kohl a working majority of 398 (54.8%).

Klaus Kinkel was elected chairman of the FDP in 1993 and became Deputy Chancellor and Foreign Minister in Kohl's cabinet. Kinkel was the party's candidate for chancellor in 1994.

The PDS was organized in 1989 as the successor to the Socialist Unity Party (SED) of East Germany. As a hard-line Marxist party, the SED ruled the East Germans with an iron fist until the collapse of the Berlin Wall signaled the end of German Marxism.

The PDS renounced the most extreme tenets of the SED but took over an efficient and well-financed party organization in the East, where it has about 150,000 members. However, in the West it can only claim 1,000.[8]

In January 1993, the PDS elected Lothar Bisky as its new chairman. Bisky, aged 51, came up as a member of the Brandenburg state parliament. He was elected PDS leader in this body. By profession, he is a professor of cultural theory and served as rector of the SED's College of Film and Television in Potsdam from 1956 to 1990.[9]

The Green Party was organized in the 1970s, drawing environmentalists, opponents of nuclear power, and voters against the North Atlantic Treaty Organization (NATO). In the 1987 Bundestag election, the Greens won 8 percent of the vote and forty-four seats. In 1990, the Green vote fell to 3.8 percent; and it lost all seats in the Bundestag. However, the Greens in 1993 merged with the Alliance 90, and the resulting Alliance 90–Green organization surmounted the 5-percent hurdle in 1994. Alliance 90 is an association of small political groups that sprang up in East Germany in 1989 to protest the East German dictatorship.

The Republicans are a neo-Nazi party, which is highly nationalistic, anti-foreigner, and strongly advocates the recovery of territory lost during World War II. Fortunately, it has never cleared 5 percent at the national level.

The Constitution of 1949 provided for eleven states. With unification in 1990, the number was increased by five (Brandenburg, Mecklenburg-Vorpommern, Saxony, Saxony-Anhalt, and Thuringia). The sixteen states (*Länder*) of Germany exercise more power than the fifty state governments in the United States.

Berlin is completely surrounded by Brandenburg, and the two economies are closely integrated. There is a movement to merge these two states, and this will probably take place by 1999.

Under the German Constitution, the state legislatures (*Landtage*) have the power to enact certain statutes to apply within their boundaries. They are generally limited to matters of cultural policy, education, and the maintenance of law and order. In a conflict between a federal and a state statute, the federal enactment prevails.

An interesting example of a state statute was passed by Bavaria providing that prostitution was legal in cities having a population of 20,000 or more. The mayor of Landsberg, some forty miles west of Munich, proudly announced in 1987 that his municipality had reached 20,000. Much to his consternation and that of the citizens, prostitutes moved in; but their stay was short. In November 1988, the results of the national census were published showing that the city had a populaton of only 19,500 souls. The Landsberg police immediately drove them out of town. Since then, the population has been edging back up to 20,000; but the Bavarian state legislature came to the rescue and increased the legal limit to 30,000.[10]

Each state has its own constitution and its own one-house legislature. Political parties must win at least 5 percent of the vote to win a seat in the legislature. While the Republicans failed to seat a member of the Bundestag in 1990 and 1994, they did better in state elections.

On October 16, 1994, Germany held its second Bundestag election as a united nation. The Kohl coalition (CDU-CSU-FDP) won again, but its majority was drastically reduced from 134 to 10. The seats now held by the various parties are (with 1990 seats in parentheses):

CDU-CSU	294	(319)
FDP	47	(79)
SPD	252	(239)
Alliance 90–Green	49	(8)
PDS	30	(17)

NOTES

1. *Frankfurter Allgemeine Zeitung*, March 31, 1994.
2. *New York Times*, August 10, 1993.
3. *The Economist*, London, July 24, 1993, p. 49.
4. *Frankfurter Allgemeine Zeitung*, June 3, 1993.
5. *Wall Street Journal*, New York, June 22, 1992.
6. *Financial Times*, London, January 13, 1995.
7. *New York Times*, December 25, 1992.
8. *Focus*, Munich, 25 (1993): 50.
9. *Frankfurter Allgemeine Zeitung*, February 1, 1993.
10. *New York Times*, July 1, 1989.

7

German Legal System

COMPARISON WITH U.S. SYSTEM

The fundamental difference between the U.S. and the German legal systems arises out of the fact that America inherited the common law tradition from England, while Germany, France, and practically all countries outside the English-speaking world developed code law structures for their people. Thus, an American lawyer trained in the British common law system is understandably ill at ease when he begins to study the law of Germany.

The common law originated in England when the judges began to apply the customary law to disputes in their courts. Their decisions gradually became the accepted law of the country, which was followed by subsequent judges in controversies involving similar situations. Parliament later began to pass written statutes, which, in case of conflict, overruled the common law. Statutory law often applied to questions not yet decided by the common law judges. The basic premise then and today is that in the absence of a statute covering a dispute before the court, a judge will apply the common law.

The first colonists in America quite naturally brought this English system of law with them, and it continued after independence. Each state now has developed its own common law, which governs that particular state unless its legislature or the Congress passes statutes to the contrary.

A good example is common law marriage, which provides that a man and woman living together and holding themselves out to the world as husband and wife are to be regarded as legally married, even though they have not gone through a ceremonial marriage. This common law rule still applies in several states, but the great majority have replaced it with a statute that sets forth the requirements of a ceremonial marriage and stipulates that only such a marriage will be regarded as legally valid in that state.

At common law, one could not make a binding contract unless he or she was 21 years of age. This is still the rule in a few states, but in all others a statute passed by the state legislature has lowered the age requirement—in most cases to age 18.

With the passage of time and the increasing complexity of modern life, Congress and state legislatures have ground out an ever-increasing mass of statutes. The net result is that most of American law today is statutory rather than common.

Although there were much earlier legal codes adopted, France must be given credit for founding the modern code law family in the early years of the nineteenth century. The five codes then enacted are usually called the Napoleonic Codes, not because Napoleon Bonaparte wrote them but because he prodded French jurists into writing them. They were as follows:

Civil Code
Code of Civil Procedure
Criminal Code
Code of Criminal Procedure
Commercial Code

They were designed to cover the whole spectrum of legal relationships in French society at that time. Germany adopted a similar set of codes between 1871 and 1900, based in large part on the French models but adjusted to its own special needs. Practically all other non–English-speaking countries have embraced the code law arrangement with variations to suit their own particular requirements.

The underlying philosophy of the code system is that all basic rules should be contained in the codes and other statutory enactments, which the judges can then apply to all cases coming before them. The decision itself should have no application beyond the particular case and the litigating parties. Theoretically, this decision should not in itself have the force of law. This squares with the constitutional views of the highly respected French legal philosopher, Montesquieu, who insisted that the three branches of government—the legislative, executive, and judiciary—should be kept separate and independent.

Subsequent experience has shown that even the most efficient legislatures cannot produce laws with enough speed and wisdom to regulate everything. Thus, it has been gradually conceded that the judge must fill in the gaps of the statutory law. These decisions, particularly those of the higher courts, are frequently cited and followed by the lower courts. To this extent, they have become precedent and have practically the meaning of law; but lower courts are not bound to follow such decisions. Judges in code law countries are more influenced than American jurists by what scholars have written in textbooks, commentaries on the statutes, and articles in legal periodicals.

Between 1917 and 1991, some countries operated under a Marxist legal system designed by the Soviet Union. Until 1917, the Russian Empire was a code law country; but when Lenin (who was a lawyer) seized power, he issued a decree that the statutes of the collapsed regime should no longer apply. The courts were ordered to base their decisions on the decrees of the worker and peasant government and to decide in accordance with the "socialist consciousness of law."

East Germany operated under Marxist law from 1945 until 1990. With reunification the eastern Germans became subject to the law of the FRG. The present German legal system came into existence in 1871 with the creation of the German Empire. There were basic constitutional law changes when the empire became the Weimar Republic in 1920, as it was replaced by the Nazi dictatorship in 1933, as Allied Occupation followed in 1945, and as the FRG was established in 1949.

The FRG today has three basic sources of law, which rank as follows in order of priority:

1. Constitution (*Verfassung*)
2. Statutory Law (*Gesetz*)
   A. Federal Statutes
   B. State Statutes
3. Decrees
   A. Regulation (*Verordnung*)
   B. Administrative Order (*Verwaltungsakt*)

The German political leaders of 1949 refused to use the term *constitution* (*Verfassung*). They argued that there could be no constitution until both German states were united and that this temporary document should be called the "basic law" (*Grundgesetz*). Actually, it was and remains the German Constitution, and there have been very few changes since reunification in 1990.

It is a very elaborate instrument with a lengthy Bill of Rights consisting of nineteen articles and well-organized provisions for the executive, legislative, and judicial branches of government. It draws heavily on the British, Weimar, and U.S. constitutions but still has many original features.

Statutes passed by the Bundestag and applying throughout the entire FRG are next in importance. If in conflict with the constitution, they are unconstitutional and unenforceable. Federal statutory law can take the form of a code

(*Gesetzbuch*), such as the civil code (*Bürgerlichesgesetzbuch*), covering a large segment of the law; or it can be passed as an individual statute dealing with a specific area of the law (e.g., the Installment Sales Act [*Gesetz betreffend die Abzahlungsgeschäfte*]).

The next source of German law is the mass of decrees, which has poured forth from the competent organs of government. There are two kinds of decrees: regulation (*Verordnung*) and administrative order (*Verwaltungsakt*). A regulation supplements a statute and is of general application. An administrative order is issued pursuant to a statute but is limited in application to a specific case.

Max Rheinstein, a distinguished German legal scholar who taught for many years at the University of Chicago, estimated that 80 percent of the cases brought to court under private law (involving disputes between individuals) would have the same results in either the United States or Germany. The 20 percent with different decisions can be traced to variations in historical development and methods of legal thought.[1]

It is never very easy to compare legal systems. The frustrations involved led one student of comparative law to write:

German law prohibits everything, except that which is permitted.

French law permits everything, except that which is prohibited.

Russian law prohibits everything, including that which is permitted.

Italian law permits everything, especially that which is prohibited.

DEVELOPMENT OF GERMANIC LAW

The origins of the German legal system stretch back to pre-Christian times when the Germanic tribes began to push their way into what is now Germany. Driving out of the north and the east, they gradually displaced the Celts, who had previously inhabited this area. When the Roman legions under Julius Caesar crossed the Alps and pushed northward about 50 B.C., the Germans vigorously resisted. Eventually, the Romans were wise enough to build their outposts along the south shore of the Danube and west side of the Rhine, using these fast-flowing, powerful rivers as defense lines. When the legions of Emperor Augustus foolishly departed from this strategy in A.D. 9, they were cut to pieces by the forces under the heroic Hermann in the Battle of Teutoburg Forest. As a result, Roman law and culture had little impact on this larger part of Germany until after the collapse of the empire. The Germans had already developed tribal law (*Stammesrecht*) with variations from one tribe to another. It grew out of custom and the conviction of what the law ought to be. The law of each tribe applied to all its members and to anyone else living in tribal territory. Moreover, the tribesman was viewed as taking his own law with him when he moved into territories peopled by other tribes.

This law was extremely primitive and harsh. When a child was born, it was shown to the father, who had the right to decide whether it would be raised or exposed to die. This rule endured until after the baptism of Clovis, the chieftain of the Franks in 496, and the acceptance of Christianity by the Germanic tribes. To prove one's capacity to make a will, a man had to take his sword and shield and then mount a horse from a stone about fifteen inches high. Imagine how many will contests this would generate today if the law were still in force. A man raised his finger to signify agreement; to express the contrary, the finger was bent.

With the passage of time, these tribal rules became territorial law (*Landrecht*), and the principle of carrying one's law around with him on his travels disappeared. Starting about the year 400, the tribes began to reduce their territorial laws to writing. One of them was the Law of the Alamans, published about 720. It was organized into three parts, dealing with the Alaman relations to the church, to the duke, and to each other.

For murdering the duke, the penalty was death and permanent confiscation of the murderer's property. Lesser offenses were punishable by fine in terms of the solidus, a gold coin worth about $5.00. For example, anyone starting a fight in the duke's courtyard was to be fined 40 solidi "for his folly." If the wrongdoer was a slave, he lost his right hand or his owner could save him by paying the 40 solidi.

As to crimes against fellow Alamans, the code is quite detailed. If anyone strikes another in anger, the fine is 1 solidus. When a bone is broken, the fine goes up to 6 solidi. This is the same punishment for pulling someone off his horse. Forty solidi are payable for knocking out an eye or cutting off a hand.

The code also makes provision for payment of the judge: "Let him always receive a ninth part of the fine so long as he judges correctly." Another section deals with punishment of the judge in the event of bribery:

> If a judge adjudicates wrongly after accepting a bribe, let that man who took something unjustly from another through juridical decision restore what he obtained. Let a judge who adjudicates falsely be compelled to pay twofold to him who suffered a loss, since he attempted to pass judgement against the regulations of our law. And let him be compelled to pay forty solidi into the public treasury.

As the Roman Empire weakened and finally came to an end in 476, the stronger Germanic tribes pushed out to fill the vacuum. The Angles, Saxons, and Jutes took Britain; and the Lombards seized northern and central Italy.

The most powerful tribe was the Franks, destined to be the political organizers of both France and Germany. Under the leadership of Clovis (481–511), they pushed out from their home along the east bank of the Rhine to absorb France, Holland, and Belgium, as well as much of western and southern Germany.

More than two centuries later, Charlemagne became King of the Franks (768–814). During his forty-six-year reign, Charlemagne attacked in all directions. He battered the Moslems in Spain and the Lombards in Italy and took substantial territories from German tribes to the east (the Saxons, Bavarians, and the Austrians).

On Christmas Day in A.D. 800, Charlemagne was crowned Holy Roman Emperor in St. Peter's in Rome by Pope Leo III. The Pope realized that he could no longer count on the emperor in Constantinople. He hoped that the Catholic King of the Franks could provide him with the necessary protection.

It was a connection between the German monarchy and the Roman church that would deeply affect both institutions. In good times and bad, the Holy Roman Empire endured for a thousand years. Eventually, it divided into a bewildering variety of small and large states with lay rulers and others under control of princes of the church, a total of several thousand. They were all more or less under the rule of the emperor.

Among other problems, the Holy Roman Empire had no constitution for its first five centuries. There was no rule of succession, and picking a new emperor usually produced a battle royal, which would have made great television entertainment. Thus, the title of emperor went to the strongman of the day.

Finally, in 1355, the King of Bohemia—with his capital in Prague—was named Emperor Charles IV. He reigned with distinction until 1378; and among other accomplishments, he issued the Golden Bull in 1356, an Imperial Constitution. Under this document, seven of the more powerful rulers of the constituent states (four lay and three clerical) were appointed permanent Electors of the Emperor. They would meet in Frankfurt when a vacancy occurred and, by majority vote, pick the next emperor. Later, the number of electors was expanded to nine.

Under this system, the electors alternated in their imperial choices between the rulers of Austria, Bavaria, and Bohemia. After 1437, the Austrian Hapsburgs (with one short interruption) always wore the imperial crown until Napoleon ended the Holy Roman Empire in 1806.

For a period of about four centuries, from about 1100 to 1500, the old Roman law and the Canon law of the church were gradually infused into the German legal system. In the twelfth century, the law professors at the University of Bologna began to study Roman law, including the Code of Civil Law (*Corpus Juris Civilis*) proclaimed by Emperor Justinian between 529 and 535. German and other European law students came to Bologna and eventually took back to their home countries a knowledge and respect for the Roman law, which gradually became an integral part of the legal curriculum at other European universities.

There had long been the fiction that the emperors of the Holy Roman Empire were the successors of the old Roman emperors. Understandably, the former readily accepted the Roman law with its support of strong central power in the emperors. In 1495, an Imperial Court was created, which was to base its decisions (in the absence of statutes or custom) on the Roman law.

This infusion of the Roman law into the German legal system (generally called "the reception of Roman law") was made easier by the fact that it really filled a vacuum. The simple rules of thumb, popular customs, and crude procedures prevailing in the territorial law systems of the diverse German states were just not capable of solving the increasingly complex problems of life in the later Middle Ages. Roman law appealed to scholars as systematic, universal, and sophisticated. Men trained in the Roman law were gradually retained by the German princes to modernize their legal systems. This body of law was particularly influential in reforming constitutional law, contracts, torts, and real and personal property. Canon law was also taught in the universities, and jurists educated in this discipline were also hired in many German states. Their contribution was most evident in improving the laws of domestic relations and inheritance. They also brought to the primitive German courts the efficient procedures of the church courts, including the right of appeal to a higher tribunal and proper documentation.

The innumerable German states were reduced in number by the Treaty of Westphalia in 1648, which brought the disastrous Thirty Years' War (1618–1648) to a close. It lowered the number to something over 300. This still served the interests of the major European powers in keeping the Germans disunited and relatively powerless. France, Britain, Russia, Sweden, and Holland had already achieved some measure of national unity by this time.

In 1815, the Congress of Vienna was charged with redrawing the map of Europe after the downfall of Napoleon. Among other things, it reduced the number of German states to thirty-nine. By this time, two of these countries— Austria and Prussia—had by conquest expanded into major world powers.

These thirty-nine countries formed a loose organization called the German Confederation (*Deutscher Bund*), with its own parliament, which met at Frankfurt under the presidency of Austria. The Confederation made substantial progress in the unification of German law, adopting a Law of Negotiable Instruments in 1848 and the General German Commercial Code in 1861.

Germany was not fully unified until 1871 when the German Empire came into existence. The Constitution of 1871 was largely the personal handwork of Otto von Bismarck, who had been Prime Minister of the Kingdom of Prussia since 1862. This constitution with no bill of rights served as the basic law of the Empire until its collapse in 1918 at the end of World War I. It was presented to a Reichstag, elected by universal male suffrage, which approved it with only a few changes. It was Bismarck who said that men should not know how their laws and sausages are made.

The imperial crown was vested permanently in the Prussian royal family. Thus, King William I of Prussia became Emperor William I of Germany. The Constitution called for two legislative chambers: the Reichstag (elected nationwide) and the Bundesrat (Federal Council) composed of delegates sent by the various state governments. These states retained their own election laws, and Prussia controlled twenty-six of the fifty-one seats in the Bundesrat.

The powers of the popularly elected Reichstag were severely restricted. First, there was no ministerial responsibility; thus, the imperial chancellor (Bismarck) and his cabinet served at the pleasure of the emperor, not the Reichstag. Second, all federal legislation had to be approved by both the Reichstag and the Bundesrat. This gave Prussia a veto over all proposed laws.

This German Empire was a federation of twenty-five states, differing greatly in land area and population. The mighty Kingdom of Prussia ruled over more than half the Empire's territory (113,000 of 180,000 square miles). Prussians numbering 37 million accounted for a majority of the 62 million German citizens. The Principality of Waldeck, however, the smallest of the twenty-five, had a mere 500 square miles (about the size of Los Angeles today) and only 55,000 subjects. It was really a fascinating chessboard: four kings, six grand dukes, five dukes, seven princes, and three mayors of the city-state republics of Hamburg, Bremen, and Lubeck. Austria, of course, remained outside the German Empire.

This constitution laid the foundation for creating a unified German legal system, built on the five major codes, which were all in force by 1900. Conceptually, these codes were greatly influenced by Roman law, and they exercised a powerful unifying effect on the states.

The five codes had the same names as those first adopted in France: criminal code, code of criminal procedure, civil code, code of civil procedure, and the commercial code. Each of them was carefully drafted to cover systematically a broad area of the law.

In summary, it can be said that modern German law has historically been drawn from four sources: customs, Roman law, Canon law, and statutes. Roman law and Canon law have been enacted into statutory law. Customary law, which originally accounted for all German law, has almost disappeared in the same way by being incorporated into statutes. In fact, legal scholars are divided as to whether there is really any customary law remaining as a current source of German law. All of them agree that the present legal system is either entirely statutory or almost so as to its sources.

One superb German law wisely protects children from their parents inflicting stupid names on the defenseless offspring. Each community has a *Standesamt* (Personal Status Office), which maintains separate registries for births, marriages, and deaths.

The parents of a newborn are legally required to file the name selected with this office. The name must clearly indicate the sex of the child and must not offend against custom and good taste. If the name is rejected by the officials, the parents have the right to appeal to the court. Court decisions over the years show a primary concern that the name does not degrade or hold its bearer up to public ridicule. Recent cases have rejected the names of business firms such as Whoopy, McDonald, Agfa, and Omo. The forename Matzedaju was also rejected by the court because it was not a proper name but a title of nobility in Japan. Brika was turned down because it was created by merging and shortening Brigitte and Karl. Schroeder was disallowed because it was not a proper forename for a child, even though such a character exists in the Peanuts comic strip. Americans cursed with oddball names may well wish that their parents had been constrained by such a law.[2]

COURTS

The Constitution of 1871 did not establish a court system but granted the Reichstag the power to legislate as to the "whole domain of civil and criminal law, including judicial procedure." The Reichstag passed a series of statutes designed to secure uniformity in the administration of justice. The resulting court system survived the abolition of the empire in 1918 and served the judiciary requirements of the Weimar Republic (1919–1933). It suffered severe blows under Hitler but was still breathing at the end of World War II in 1945.

Germany still operates (with minor changes) under this judicial structure. Courts today are divided into two classes: ordinary and special. The ordinary courts have exclusive jurisdiction in all criminal matters and in civil cases involving disputes between citizens. There are five sets of special courts established to handle civil disputes arising out of administrative law. The four successive levels in the ordinary court system are as follows:

1. Local Courts (*Amtsgerichte*), which have three divisions: civil, criminal, and family.
2. State Courts (*Landesgerichte*), separated into three divisions: civil, criminal, and commercial.
3. State Courts of Appeal (*Oberlandesgerichte*). In Berlin, this tribunal is called the *Kammergericht.*
4. Federal Supreme Court (*Bundesgerichtshof*).

There are more than 600 Local Courts, which are the tribunals of original jurisdiction for minor crimes, civil claims involving DM 10,000 or less, and family law problems. A single professional judge sits in the civil, family, and minor criminal matters. In crimes punishable by two years or more, there are two lay judges (*Schöffen*) with equal voting power. This is called a mixed tribunal (*Schöffengericht*) and is considered to be a more effective instrument to protect the rights of the accused than the use of a jury, which was abolished during the Weimar Republic. As in America, the accused is presumed innocent until proven guilty.

The second level of ordinary courts includes about 100 State Courts, each having civil, criminal, and commercial divisions. The civil division has three professional judges and hears appeals from the Local Court when the claim exceeds DM 1,500 (in lesser amounts, the judgment of the lower judge is final). In the commercial division of the State Court, one professional judge sits on the bench with two lay judges, businessmen with expertise in the matter before the court.

The third judicial level comprises some twenty State Courts of Appeal. They hear appeals from the civil and commercial divisions of the State Court and from the family division of the Local Court. It has no appellate function in criminal matters, but it tries in the first instance persons accused of treason and other crimes of comparable importance and unconstitutional acts.

At the apex of the judicial system is the Federal Supreme Court, located in Karlsruhe, with no original jurisdiction but serving as the final court of appeal in both civil and criminal matters. This court has 100 judges, divided into twenty chambers of five members each.

Bavaria (alone among the states) has added another tribunal, called the Bavarian State Supreme Court (*Bayerisches Oberstes Landesgericht*). It functions as an appellate body between the State Court of Appeals and the Federal Supreme Court.

As to the special courts in Germany, the Labor Court (*Arbeitsgericht*) has original jurisdiction in all labor disputes, with one professional judge and one lay judge representing the labor unions and a second being picked by management. Appeal can then be taken to the Court of Labor Appeals (*Landesarbeitsgericht*) and finally to the Federal Labor Court (*Bundesarbeitsgericht*). There is a Court on Social Matters (*Sozialgericht*) to exercise original jurisdiction over disputes involving health insurance, unemployment benefits, and old-age pensions. Here appeals can be taken first to the Court of Appeals on Social Matters (*Landessozialgericht*) and then to the Federal Court on Social Matters (*Bundessozialgericht*), which, like the Federal Labor Court, is located in Kassel. The Tax Court (*Finanzgericht*) hears disputes over tax claims in the first instance; in order to expedite the flow of cases, there is only one appeal here to the Federal Tax Court (*Bundesfinanzhof*) in Munich. A single Federal Patents Court (*Bundespatentgericht*) to handle patent and intellectual property matters sits in Munich, with appeals to the Federal Supreme Court. All other administrative disputes go to the Administrative Court (*Verwaltungsgericht*), with appeal to the Court of Administrative Appeal (*Oberverwaltungsgericht*) and then to the Federal Administrative Court (*Bundesverwaltungsgericht*) in Berlin.

The Constitution of 1949 created one new tribunal, the Federal Constitutional Court (*Bundesverfassungsgericht*), to review the constitutionality of all decisions of other courts, as well as legislative and executive actions at the federal and state levels. Judicial review had never existed before in the German legal system, and Hitler had come to power without serious opposition in the courts. Thus, it was believed that the Federal Constitutional Court would better protect the Constitution, the law, the courts, and other democratic institutions from a future dictator.

This court is the highest and most important in Germany because of its judicial authority and its political role. Unlike the other courts, it is administratively and financially independent of the Ministry of Justice and the judges can be removed only by a motion of the court itself. There are sixteen judges appointed for twelve-year nonrenewable terms. It is divided into two divisions of eight judges each, called Senates. The First Senate hears cases involving basic constitutional rights granted by Articles 1 to 19 in the Constitution. The Second Senate is concerned with disputes between different government institutions and a variety of other matters. Any law can be reviewed as to its constitutionality by the Federal Constitutional Court. The opposition party in the Bundestag can even challenge a statute being passed by the government majority.

At the state level, State Constitutional Courts (*Landesverfassungsgerichte*) have been established to perform the same task. These tribunals hear cases challenging activities that are believed to violate the constitutions of the individual states.

Judicial proceedings under German law follow the inquisitorial principle. Under this system, the judge is a more active participant in the fact-finding process and intervenes more energetically to establish the evidence in the case to see that justice is done. Furthermore, in principle, cross-examination is not permitted under the German system. In a civil case, there will be a number of isolated meetings and written communications between the parties, their attorneys, and the judge. During the course of these meetings, evidence will be introduced, testimony given, motions and rulings on procedure made, and areas of agreement and disagreement gradually marked out. The proceedings tend to be very unconcentrated.

This has a number of consequences. First, the pleadings are very general. Issues are defined as the case proceeds; and it is possible to introduce new motions, causes of action, and issues with relative ease. Second, there is much less pressure on the German attorney to forearm himself with information and argument on every fact or claim that might possibly arise and prove relevant. If unsuspected facts do emerge or unforeseen allegations are made, the attorney will always be given an opportunity to search for and present additional proof. It is, therefore, hardly surprising that the German attorney is not equipped with the common law attorney's powers of discovery, those effective means backed by the power of the court, for tracking down and finding out the facts that may be relevant.

It is not left to the parties to drum up as many witnesses as they choose. The German judge will do his very best to minimize the number of factual issues that can only be resolved by hearing witnesses. Significant enough, witnesses can only appear pursuant to a special order made by the judge, stating which witnesses are to be examined and on what factual issues. Such an order is not subject to appeal and will be made only on controversial issues the judge believes crucial to the disposition of the case.

Last, German civil procedure has no counterpart to the highly complicated rules of the common law regarding the exclusion of various kinds of evidence. Doubtless these rules were intended to prevent the jury being misled by untrustworthy testimony. Since the evidence is evaluated by professional judges in German civil procedure, any evidence, including hearsay evidence, is admissible in principle; and the judge decides how much weight it deserves.

It should be added that experts are not, technically speaking, witnesses at all. They are usually appointed by the court, act under the court's instructions, and owe the court a duty of loyalty and impartiality. Hence, in a German court one rarely sees head-on clashes between experts, called by the parties and paid to be partial, subjected to fierce examination and cross-examination by attorneys who have just acquired a smattering of their expertise for the purpose.

LAWYERS

Becoming a licensed lawyer takes much longer in the FRG than it does in the United States. The average law student takes nine years from the start of his legal studies until admitted to practice.

To qualify for the study of law in Germany, the applicant must have the *abitur*, which is granted upon graduation from the gymnasium after thirteen years of school. The *abitur* is about the same as completing a community college two-year program in the United States and certifies that its recipient is qualified to enter a university. The student is usually nineteen or twenty when starting law school.

After a minimum of 3.5 years (seven semesters), fixed by the law of the judiciary (*Richtergesetz*), the student is eligible to sit for the first state examination. In practice, many students take additional courses. The average time in law school is now 5.3 years before presenting oneself for the first exam. This rigorous test (written and oral) is administered by the Ministers of Justice of the sixteen states.

If the candidate fails, he or she may take the test a second time. The average student passes after 5.75 years and then applies for admission for the practical training (*Referendariat*). This involves a waiting period of 1.25 years. Now an average of seven years has elapsed.

The practical training lasts 2.5 years during which the student is a temporary civil servant, receiving an allowance and the title of *Referendar*. The practical course includes a number of months in the various courts (except the Supreme Court); in the office of a public prosecutor and a practicing lawyer; and in civil service. This extends the total training period to an average of 9.5 years.

The *Referendar* can also ask for six months' additional training in a foreign country in the office of a German Chamber of Commerce or a lawyer.

Now the candidate can take the second state examination. About 90 percent of the applicants (approximately one-third of those who started law school) pass this test and now receive the title of *Assessor*.

An *Assessor* can apply for any field of activity he or she desires: judge, prosecutor, lawyer in civil service, notary, practicing attorney, or legal counsel in a business firm.

The entire legal education is designed to train students as judges, even though only about 20 percent apply and are accepted for a judicial career. Most go on the bench at this point, unlike the American custom of appointing or electing judges after some years of experience as lawyers and usually after service to a political party.

A practicing lawyer in the FRG is called a *Rechtsanwalt*. As of 1992, there were 47,300 (77 for each 100,000 citizens), as compared with 655,000 in the United States (279 per 100,000). On the other hand, Germany has 28 judges per 100,000 and the United States only 12. America's ratio of prosecuting attorneys is 10 per 100,000, and Germany's is 6 per 100,000.[3]

Germany provides for exams for lawyers specializing in tax law (*Fachanwälte für Steuerrecht*). It is also possible to qualify as a specialist in labor law (*Fachanwälte für Arbeitsrecht*). There are also exams for administrative lawyers (*Fachanwälte für Verwaltungsrecht*). Last, there are special exams for social security lawyers (*Fachanwälte für Sozialrecht*).

There is a statute that lists and defines in great detail every possible act of advice or litigation. It also provides that for every act so defined the attorney is entitled to one basic fee or to a multiple or fraction thereof. An attorney is normally entitled to three basic fees for conducting a lawsuit, one being payable when the action starts, another when the oral argument begins, and the third when evidence is taken. Under the statute, the amount of the basic fee is related to the amount involved in the action or other matter handled by the attorney. In principle, therefore, the attorney's fee is the same whether the case involves much work or a little, whether it is complex or simple, whether the client is rich or poor, whether the attorney is well known and experienced, and whether he is successful in the case. Where the lawyer gives advice or acts for the client in some other way outside court, there may be some scope for flexibility in putting a value in the matter, so the schedule of statutory fees may operate less rigidly. In litigation, the value of the matter will be evident from the sum claimed, or else it will be fixed by the court, as in the case of divorces and other nonpecuniary claims. An agreement to pay a fee higher than the statute prescribes must be in writing; to charge a lower fee is considered unethical. To work for a contingent fee is not just a breach of etiquette.

The Federal Supreme Court has held such an agreement void as contrary to public policy.

The advantage of this method of charging for legal services is that the client may make a reasonably accurate estimate of the cost of a lawsuit, since the attorney's fee is based on the value of the claim rather than on the relatively unpredictable amount of time he may have to spend on it. On the other hand, it may be argued that the attorney will be underpaid if a case of small value involves much work, while he may receive a windfall for handling a simple matter with a large price tag. This danger is probably more apparent than real. In the former case, the attorney may stipulate for a fee above the statutory tariff, or he may do only as much work as the statutory fee justifies. In the latter situation, cases involving much money and little work are fairly rare.

Court costs, unlike those in the United States, are by no means negligible. They are fixed by statute and consist of one or more basic units. The number of units payable depends on the number of stages the proceedings have run, not on how long the proceedings take or how complex they are or how much work they require of the court. In a fully contested case, three units will be payable, the amount of the unit being fixed by the statute in relation to the amount involved in the litigation. According to the code of civil procedure, the loser must reimburse the winner not only for the court costs he or she may have had to pay but also for the attorney's fees, including disbursements by counsel incident to the case and other expenses. This applies, however, only to expenses that a reasonable litigant would have incurred under the circumstances, and a loser who thinks he or she is being overcharged in the bill presented by the opponent may ask the court to review it.

As in other civil law countries, the notary (*Notar*) is an important figure on the legal scene in the Bundesrepublik. In order to be admitted as notary, one must have the qualification for judicial office. Whereas attorneys may be admitted without limit, notaries are admitted only in such numbers as are required for the proper administration of law. Notaries have an exclusive statutory right to perform certain administrative acts required by law, such as certifying a person's signature to a document (*Beglaubigung*) or attesting a declaration or agreement (*Beurkundung*). For a *Beurkundung*, the notary draws up a document containing the names of the parties and the exact text of their declarations, which they sign, and then the notary certifies in the document that he has read these statements back to the parties and that they have approved and signed them. Notarial attestation is required by law for a number of important transactions, such as agreements to buy or sell real estate, promises to make a gift, marriage contracts, and the transfer of shares in a limited-liability company (GmbH). As to wills, while a testator may make a perfectly valid will all by himself if he writes it out and signs it, many people prefer to have their will drawn up and attested by a notary. In making an attestation, the notary is required to ascertain the true intention of the parties, to advise them of the legal consequences involved, to see that inept and inexperienced parties are not disadvantaged, and to put their statements in as clear and unambiguous form as possible. The rule requiring notarial attestation clearly has something more than an evidentiary function; it also embodies the idea that in certain important transactions the public interest requires the presence of an impartial person who can give the parties legal advice and ensure that their intentions are properly carried out.

NOTES

1. Max Rheinstein, *Collected Works*, Vol. 1 (Tübingen, J. C. B. Mohr [Paul Siebeck], 1979), p. 250.
2. *Wall Street Journal*, New York, July 15, 1993.
3. Rheinstein, *Collected Works*, p. 250.

8

Legal Aspects of European Union

Since its creation in 1957, the European Union (EU) has adopted more than 1,500 rules, covering some 10,000 pages. This enormous mass of legislation has become a part of the legal systems of the twelve member countries. When an EU rule contradicts a law of Germany or any other member state, the latter must give way.

Originally, it was believed that only the Treaty of Rome (1957) founding the EU and other treaties ratified by the twelve nations as constitutional law took precedence over the law of the members. The European Court of Justice has held that not just the treaties but all EU laws prevail over national law.

STRUCTURE OF EUROPEAN UNION

Students of history are fascinated with this unprecedented international organization, which has often promised more than it can deliver to its 360 million inhabitants speaking nine different languages. It is still expanding some thirty-seven years after its founding, and U.S. firms in Germany must be aware of the areas in which the EU can affect them.

The twelve member nations vary greatly in population, shown by the following figures (from 1992) in millions:

Germany	79.8
Italy	57.8

United Kingdom	57.4
France	57.1
Spain	39.5
Holland	15.1
Greece	10.1
Belgium	10.0
Portugal	9.9
Denmark	5.2
Ireland	3.5
Luxembourg	0.4

As a trading nation, Germany has a clear advantage over the other eleven members with a huge lead of $32 billion (1992) in its merchandise surplus. Holland was second with $14 billion.

There were originally three European Communities, each created by a separate treaty. The first was the European Coal and Steel Community, established under the Treaty of Paris in 1951 and designed to regulate the coal and steel industries of the six original signatory states. Then, in 1957, there were two Treaties of Rome, one for the European Atomic Energy Community and the second giving birth to the European Economic Community, sometimes called the European Common Market. Finally, in 1967, the three communities were merged and have since operated under the same government organs. In 1993, the name European Union replaced that of European Community.

The treaties mentioned here are really the constitution of the EU. France, West Germany, Italy, Holland, Belgium, and Luxembourg were the six original members. Britain, Ireland, and Denmark joined in 1973. Greece entered in 1981, and the most recent members, Spain and Portugal, were admitted in 1986.

These twelve countries differ greatly in population, economic development, political stability, standards of living, business sophistication, and other basic factors. They also have inherited the historic rivalries and antagonisms that have colored Europe's history for centuries. In spite of these divisive ingredients, the EU has achieved a degree of unity and prosperity, which nobody expected in 1957 as the continent still struggled to recover from the devastation of World War II.

At this point it should be strongly emphasized that Germany has been the most dominant member of the EU. Critics say that the German dedication arises out of the nation's ability to outperform the other members and maximize their own economic benefits. This is all true, and U.S. corporate executives and attorneys contemplating business with the Germans should consider this carefully in making their decisions.

The basic original objectives of the EU members can be stated as follows:

1. *Common external tariffs.* Thus, an American automobile exported to any one of the member states pays the same duty.

2. *No tariffs on goods moving from one EU member to another.* An automobile made in Italy can be imported free of duty into the other states, but many services such as those of stockbrokers cannot.

3. *Workers migrate freely from one state to the others.* Thus, an Italian electrician can move to Germany to take a job. Lawyers, on the other hand, face restrictions.

4. *Member states agree to work toward greater economic and political union.* This fourth objective has proved a powerful motivation for growth in the EU, not only in the membership increase from six to twelve but also in major changes both externally and within the EU.

The EU has established five organizations to carry out its objectives. They can be briefly described as follows.

European Council

In June and December of each year, the European Council of the twelve heads of state, familiarly called the EU Summit, meets to solve major problems facing the union. They have no formal status in the decision-making machinery of the union, and their agreements must be formally ratified by the Council of Ministers.

Council of Ministers

The Council of Ministers has the real legislative power of the EU. The four major members (France, Britain, Germany, and Italy) have ten votes each on the council. Spain has eight; Holland, Belgium, Greece, and Portugal have five each; Ireland and Denmark have three apiece; and Luxembourg has two. This makes a total of seventy-six votes, and it takes fifty-four to pass most laws of the EU. A unanimous vote is still required for taxes, treaties between the EU and outside nations, the rights of workers, and the free movement of people.

Each member state serves a presidency of the European Council of Ministers for six months. They serve in alphabetical order of their names as written in their own languages. Thus, Germany rotates on the basis of Deutschland and Spain on the basis of España.

There are about eighty sessions of the council each year. Unlike a national government, the composition of the twelve changes with its agenda. The first team is the twelve foreign ministers, who meet once a month in Brussels to discuss the main issues. Finance ministers and farm ministers also meet every month. Altogether, there are more than a dozen different variations of the Council of Ministers.

Laws enacted by the Council of Ministers are of two classes: regulations and directives. A regulation is applicable throughout the EU and goes into force at once. A directive binds the member states to adjust their respective laws to conform with the directive.

If a member country fails to implement an EU directive and thereby change a specific law, it is estopped from enforcing that law. The European Court of Justice has held that individuals may invoke an EU directive to prevent enforcement of the inconsistent national law.

European Commission

The European Commission in Brussels is the seventeen-member executive branch of the EU, the center of power with a civil service staff of 15,000. It has two very important powers: (1) it administers a wide variety of existing treaties and regulations covering the lives of 360 million Europeans, and (2) it makes recommendations to the Council of Ministers as to new action to be taken by the council.

The seventeen commissioners serve four-year terms and are selected by their respective governments. Germany, France, Italy, Spain, and the United Kingdom appoint two commissioners each, while the other seven countries name one each. They are supposed to make recommendations to the Council of Ministers independently of their twelve respective governments.

One of the seventeen is elected for a two-year term as president. Jacques Delors, a former finance minister of France, has completed his fifth term as president, which expired on January 1, 1995. A Socialist and a Catholic, the very competent Delors has proved to be a strong leader of the commission. He is too strong in the opinion of some fellow commissioners who would like him to consult with them more on spending.

The breadth of power accumulated over the years by the European Commission is best illustrated by listing the following responsibilities of the seventeen commissioners:[1]

President Jacques Delors (France): currency questions

Sir Leon Brittan (United Kingdom): international business and trade, the only commissioner on an intellectual par with Delors, a truly brilliant lawyer

Bruce Millan (United Kingdom): regional policy, a quiet Scot accountant who irritates others by spotting errors in their sums

Christiane Scrivener (France): tax and consumer problems, a charmer who carries the cause of France while Delors can appear neutral

Martin Bangemann (Germany): industry and information, a cultivated, linguist, jovial, but bored with details[2]

Peter Schmidhuber (Germany): budget

Antonio Ruberti (Italy): research and youth

Ranifro Vanni d'Archirati (Italy): interior market and middle-sized business

Manuel Marin (Spain): humanitarian aid and economic development

Abel Mentes (Spain): transportation, energy, and atomic power, a smooth negotiator

Karel van Meirt (Belgium): competition, personnel, and administration, industrious and ambitious

Hans van den Broeck (Holland): foreign and security policy, negotiations for expansion

Padraic Flynn (Ireland): social matters, employment in migration, interior, and justice

Ioannis Paleokrassis (Greece): environment, nuclear security, and fisheries

Henning Christophersen (Denmark): economic, financial, and currency policy

René Steichen (Luxembourg): agriculture

Juão de Deus Pinheiro (Portugal): European Parliament and culture

These commissioners began their current four-year terms on January 1, 1993. Nine of the seventeen are carryovers from the 1989–1993 commission.

European Parliament

This body of 564 members elected in 1994 by some 242 million qualified voters has an impressive name but still limited powers. Its most important function is to review the annual EU budget of some $35 billion. In this connection, it can reject parts or all of the budget submitted by the member governments, which it does every year with great relish. The final decision nevertheless still rests with the twelve states.

The Parliament can discuss and suggest amendments to directives and regulations submitted by the commission, but they are only advisory. Legally, the Parliament could fire the commission, but it has never done so.

Nevertheless, this body spends much time discussing problems, which are legally of no concern. It has passed resolutions on the Arab–Israeli conflict, Angola, Soviet intervention in Afghanistan, and human rights in Turkey, to name a few.

This will probably change in the future. As the EU exercises more central control over the economic and political activities of its member states, greater powers are likely to be vested in the European Parliament.

Each country has an assigned number of seats as follows:

Belgium	25
Britain	87
Denmark	16
France	87
Germany	99

Greece	25
Ireland	15
Italy	87
Luxembourg	6
Netherlands	31
Portugal	25
Spain	64

The members of Parliament are elected for five-year terms, the last elections being held in June 1994. The 567 members who are elected come from sixty-six different parties who combine into nine groups. They sit in session as groups rather than as national delegations. The distribution was as follows:

Socialists	199
European People's Party (mostly Christian Democrats)	148
Liberals	43
Leftists (mostly former Communists)	13
Greens	22
Rightists	14
Rainbow Group	8
Democratic Alliance	24
Independents	96

Pay for members is the same as that provided in their home parliaments. This varies from $2,750 per month for the Greeks to $6,700 for the Italians.

Each of the ten groups elects a representative to serve on a bureau, the committee which runs parliamentary affairs. Each representative receives the equivalent of $10,000 per month (mostly tax free).

The European Parliament meets one week each month in Strasbourg, France. Committees meet in Brussels, and most officials have their offices in Luxembourg. Most Euro-MPs want to settle in Brussels, but France and Luxembourg insist that the Parliament remain a traveling circus. Top officials often travel from Luxembourg to Brussels and back several times a day.[3] It may be some dubious consolation to realize that there is at least one legislative body competing with the U.S. Congress in silliness.

Court of Justice

The European Court of Justice sits in Luxembourg to decide legal disputes arising out of the treaties signed by the twelve members of the EU. Each nation selects a judge to sit on this Court for a six-year renewable term, and the five largest members take turns having a second judge on the Court. This makes thirteen judges and prevents a tie vote.

The Court hands down 200 decisions per year, but the backlog is growing. As a result, the judges persuaded the EU to establish a lower court to handle many minor cases. This Court of First Instance came into existence in September 1989.

Since the Court of Justice must hear cases in nine different languages, a staff of 200 simultaneous interpreters is needed. A private party, such as a Greek farmer suing over the EU agricultural rules, has the right to have his case heard in Greek. The more eloquent lawyers often complain that their brilliant arguments are diluted in translation.

Member states as well as individuals can sue. The Court's primary function is to hear complaints as to noncompliance by EU institutions and member states with the laws of the union.

At present, the Court has no power to enforce its decision. Member nations are obligated to implement judgments within their territorial jurisdiction. As of the end of 1991, some 105 Court rulings were not being applied by the EU governments against which they had been entered.[4] The Maastricht Treaty gives the Court the power to levy fines to enforce its orders.

It should be pointed out that the European Court of Justice does not hear international law cases from outside the EU. Such cases can be brought to the World Court in The Hague, Holland. If cases involve fundamental human rights, they can be heard by the European Court of Human Rights in Strasbourg, France.

Budget

The budget for 1993 was adopted by the twelve members in December 1992, amounting to total expenditures of 65 billion European Currency Units (ECUs; 1 ECU = $1.20). The contributions in billions of ECUs for all members were as follows:[5]

Germany	18.7
France	12.1
Italy	10.3
United Kingdom	7.9
Spain	5.7
Holland	4.1
Belgium	2.5
Denmark	1.2
Portugal	1.0
Greece	0.9

Ireland	0.5
Luxembourg	0.1

This came to about 75 billion ECUs for 1993. The principal sources of these funds in billions of ECUs were as follows:[6]

VAT (value-added taxes) taxes	35.1
Budgets of twelve members	14.0
Customs	13.1
Duties on farm imports from Third World countries	2.2

Over the years there have been several major changes in the treaty relations between the member states. In 1986, the Single Market Act was ratified by all twelve members. It envisaged a single market at the start of 1993 that would remove many restrictions on the movement of goods and services between the twelve. This program went into effect as scheduled with a minimum of difficulty.

Then in December 1991, the leaders of the member states met at Maastricht in Holland to draw up a truly monumental treaty named after the city itself. The Treaty of Maastricht has been ratified by all members and went into effect on October 1, 1993.

As we discuss later in this chapter, the Treaty of Maastricht aims to effectuate a single currency, create a central bank to monitor the monetary system, and bring the twelve members much closer to being truly a "United States of Europe."

SINGLE MARKET

The first major change in the founding treaties of the EU came with unanimous ratification of the Single Market Act of 1986. Although the word "Act" in the title suggests that it may be a mere statute, it was really a treaty. It constituted a massive series of amendments to the basic treaties of the EU. Among other changes, the commission passed a long list of directives, which call for the twelve members to amend their laws to comply with said directives. As of September 1993, only one-half of these single market directives had been implemented by all twelve countries.[7]

Since January 1, 1993, people can drive a carload of goods for personal use across EU borders without paying duties. Trucks can cross without a customs check. Public contracts must now be advertised throughout the EU. Banks with a permit in one country can operate in the other eleven. Capital can also move freely without controls except for Greece and Portugal, which have until 1995 to comply.

On one important feature of the single market, the EU pulled back about six weeks before it was scheduled to go into operation on January 1, 1993.

Passport checks between the twelve members were supposed to be abolished, but the EU quietly postponed indefinitely the effective date. Britain and Denmark were and still are strongly opposed to removing passport checks at their borders. Ireland is tied to British regulations; and several other governments were demanding tighter controls to keep out illegal immigrants, criminals, and terrorists.[8]

Probably the most publicized problem arising out of the single market has been the banana squabble arising between those four members which had no import duties on bananas and those with restrictions. For years Germany, Holland, Belgium, and Denmark had no tariffs on bananas. As a result, the longer, much-favored bananas from Latin America had dominated these four states. Per capita banana consumption in 1991 was as follows:[9]

Europe	22 pounds
United States	25 pounds
Germany	35 pounds (East, 59 pounds)

The Germans led all industrial countries in consumption of the fruit. Bananas were very hard to find during the four decades of East Germany, and the residents are now doing their best to make up for lost time.

While four EU countries had free banana imports, the other eight had a wide variety of duties and other import restrictions to protect their old colonies, which produce smaller, less delicious bananas. Britain still had interests in Jamaica and both the Windward and Leeward Islands; France in Martinique and Guadalupe; Portugal in Madeira; Spain in the Canaries; and Greece in Crete.

As of January 1, 1993, with the new single market, the Latin American bananas could be imported without tariff into four of the twelve and then be shipped into the other eight duty free. This would have been disastrous for the less-efficient banana producers. In February 1993, the Farm Commissioner of the European Commission, René Steichen of Luxembourg, proposed a new rule effective July 1, 1993: Latin American planters could import 2 million tons into the EU at a 15-percent tariff ($117 per ton). Imports thereafter would be at 170 percent, or $995 per ton.[10]

This rule carried by a majority in the commission and in the council. Germany then sued in the European Court of Justice on the ground that the rule contradicts the free trade provisions of the Treaty of Rome of 1957. Ordinarily, a final decision would take two years, so Germany asked for a temporary injunction pending the final decision. The Court has not yet ruled on the merits of the case; but on June 29, 1993, it denied the requested injunction on the ground that Germany failed to show "irreparable harm."[11]

An American firm, Chiquita Brands International (formerly United Brands), is now the global leader in buying, marketing, and distribution of bananas. It announced that the EU action would lead it to cut back an undisclosed amount of shipments and reduce its rental of expensive port facilities. Chiquita sales were $4 billion in 1993, and it lost $51 million.[12]

EUROPEAN MONETARY SYSTEM

A large number of European politicians and businesspeople believe that a true single market cannot be achieved until the EU has a single currency. They argue that such a system would further unify the EU and would reduce trading risks and the costs of exchanging the currencies of the twelve members.

It has been pointed out that an Englishman leaving London with £1,000 and changing this sum in all twelve countries (including the United Kingdom on his return) would pay out about £500 in fees and charges. Thus, after converting back into pounds, he would only have one-half his original sum.

The EU embraced the idea of the European Monetary System (EMS) in 1979. It envisions the day when one single currency will supplant the eleven currencies of the EU (Belgium and Luxembourg both have the Belgian franc). The EMS has been compared to a club within the EU because membership is purely voluntary. As a first step toward the visionary single currency, the EU established a new currency, called the European Currency Unit in 1979. Each currency has a nominal rate in terms of the ECU. These ECU values have been changed over the years to reflect devaluations. On September 17, 1992, an ECU was worth the following amounts of the members' currencies:[13]

Belgian Franc	41.9547
British Pound	0.689533
Deutsche Mark	2.03412
Danish Kronen	7.75901
French Franc	6.82216
Greek Drachma	250.550
Irish Pound	0.759300
Italian Lira	1,632.36
Luxembourg Franc	41.9547
Dutch Guilder	2.29193
Portuguese Escudo	176.844
Spanish Peseta	139.176

By 1991, all members of the EU had joined the EMS club except Greece, which, for good reasons, had decided it did not have the resources and institutions to participate in the system.

The eleven participants were divided into "strong" and "weak" members based on the relative stability of their currencies. Germany, Holland, France, and Belgium/Luxembourg were designated as strong and thus required to keep their foreign exchange rates within a range of 4.5 percentage points of their nominal rates.

For example, after September 17, 1992, the agreed upon nominal value for 100 French francs was DM 29.8225. The Bank of France was required to keep this foreign exchange market rate from going higher than 2.25 percent above this nominal value (DM 30.495). At the same time, the Bank of France could not let the rate fall more than 2.25 percent below the nominal value, or DM 29.150.[14]

Spain, Portugal, and the other weak currencies at the same time could fluctuate ±6 percent from their nominal rates. For example, 100 Spanish pesetas had a nominal value of DM 1.4645, and thus the Bank of Spain had to intervene at a top limit of DM 1.552 and a lower limit of DM 1.377 to keep its currency within this range of 12 percent.[15]

For thirteen years, this system worked reasonably well. There were mutually agreed devaluations from time to time, but the arrangement continued until September 1992. Then the British pound and the Italian lira weakened badly in relation to the mark. The two governments could have asked their fellow members for a devaluation, but instead they decided to withdraw from the EMS.

The nine remaining currencies kept the system operating until August 1993. Then the French franc started to weaken. Both the Bank of France and the German Bundesbank intervened with huge purchases of francs and other weak EMS currencies. On Friday, July 30, 1993, the 100 franc rate fell to the floor 2.25 percent below its nominal rate at DM 29.150. Other currencies, like the peseta and the Belgian-Luxembourg franc, also came under severe speculative pressure.

Over the weekend, the finance ministers and central bank chiefs of the EMS met in Brussels and hammered out a new agreement in an effort to salvage the system. It was agreed to let all currencies except the mark and the Dutch guilder "float" as much as 15 percent in each direction.

When the foreign exchange market opened again on Monday, August 3, 1993, some experts were fearful that the 100 franc rate would plunge down to the new floor of DM 25.665; but it only went down to DM 28.567, about 4.25 percent below the nominal value of DM 29.8225.

On August 6, the European Commission met in Brussels to discuss this crisis. Jacques Delors, President of the Commission, had called the meeting. After four hours, a pledge was made to press on toward the goal of monetary union and stated: "One clear lesson is that without closer coordination of economic policies, it will not be possible to progress toward economic and monetary union."[16]

The effort of the EU to maintain stable foreign exchange rates after 1979 under the EMS borrowed heavily on the experience of the IMF, which tried much the same thing for the entire world until 1973.

EMS might have had a better chance except that the global foreign exchange market is much larger in funds involved today. By 1993, about $1 trillion was traded daily on this vast market. About $300 billion was done in London, $192 billion in New York, and $115 billion in Tokyo. Frankfurt was a poor fourth, with about $57 billion, followed by Paris with $35 billion.[17]

The central bankers of the EU no longer have the resources to control the prices of their currencies. This has passed into the hands of foreign exchange traders, working for banks of other institutions or for themselves. The market is not located in London, New York, Tokyo, or elsewhere but spread out over some 200,000 monitors in foreign exchange trading offices all over the world.[18]

TREATY OF MAASTRICHT

This 250-page treaty was named after the Dutch city of Maastricht where a European summit was held in December 1991. It has been ratified by all twelve governments.

Fundamentally, the Maastricht Treaty is a mass of amendments and additions to the founding treaties of the EU, most significantly, the Treaty of Rome of 1957. It is truly a massive step toward a "United States of Europe"; some would even say a shocking step. It can be divided into two main areas: economic and monetary union on the one hand and political union on the other.

On the subject of economic and monetary union, it was agreed to create in three stages a single currency and a central bank for the EU by 1999 at the latest. The first stage had begun on July 1, 1990, when the twelve governments agreed to coordinate their respective monetary policies.

The second stage began on January 1, 1994, with tighter controls on exchange-rate fluctuations and the establishment of a European Monetary Institute, which will eventually be turned into a central bank.

The third stage can come as early as 1996 when the twelve governments will decide which of the member economics have become strong enough to adopt a single currency. There are three main "convergence" criteria. These criteria are measured by inflation, interest rates, and budget deficits. If a simple majority (seven at present) meets these criteria, the EU can decide by a two-thirds majority to start a single currency and a central bank on January 1, 1997.

If these criteria are not met, the EU will automatically establish the central bank on July 1, 1998, and the single currency six months later on January 1, 1999. Countries must still meet the criteria to participate, but any number of qualifying states can adopt the single currency and the central bank without any further act of the EU.[19]

As to political union, the treaty introduces the concept of "European citizenship." It also states that it "marks a new stage in the process creating an ever closer union among the peoples of Europe, where decisions are taken as closely as possible to the citizens."

Union governments agree to establish common foreign and defense policies in order to increase their influence in world affairs. Such policy will be decided by unanimity, but the twelve can decide unanimously that practical aspects of a specific policy can be implemented by a two-thirds majority.

The twelve government leaders at Maastricht either had a divine vision or allowed the wine steward to fill up their glasses too often. Chancellor Kohl,

normally a cautious man with the bottle, was then and remains an ardent sup-
porter of the treaty. The German people seem to favor Maastricht as a whole
but they are not willing to replace their deservedly sacred mark with a single
currency.[20] All the objective evidence points to such a switch as virtually
impossible.

EUROPEAN ECONOMIC AREA

On October 22, 1991, the EU and the European Free Trade Association
(EFTA, composed of Austria, Switzerland, Liechtenstein, Iceland, Sweden,
Norway, and Finland) entered into the negotiation of an agreement to free the
movement of goods, services, capital, and people among these nineteen countries with 380 million people and 40 percent of total world trade. The organization would be called the European Economic Area.

In May 1992 the EU and EFTA finally ratified the treaty, and it went into
effect on January 1, 1993. When fully operative, the goods, services, and
capital of all nineteen countries will move to each other without duty, discriminatory taxes, or quotas. However, goods imported into a single country
will not automatically be allowed further shipping to another participant in
the European Economic Area. Thus, bananas imported into Germany cannot
move into Switzerland. Workers would be allowed to live, work, and offer
their services in all nineteen countries.[21]

NOTES

1. *The Economist*, London, December 26, 1992, p. 66.
2. *The Economist*, London, March 21, 1992, p. 56.
3. *The Economist*, London, April 13, 1991, p. 48.
4. *The Economist*, London, September 26, 1992, p. 77.
5. *Die Zeit*, Hamburg, May 21, 1993.
6. Ibid.
7. *Financial Times*, London, September 30, 1993.
8. *New York Times*, November 23, 1992.
9. *Wall Street Journal*, New York, January 15, 1993.
10. *The Economist*, London, March 20, 1993, p. 74.
11. *Wall Street Journal*, New York, June 20, 1993.
12. *Wall Street Journal*, New York, March 5, 1993.
13. *Frankfurter Allgemeine Zeitung*, September 18, 1992.
14. *Frankfurter Allgemeine Zeitung*, September 19, 1992.
15. Ibid.
16. *New York Times*, New York, August 7, 1993.
17. *The Economist*, London, December 12, 1992, p. 116.
18. *New York Times*, September 20, 1992.
19. "Survey of European Community," *The Economist*, London, July 3, 1993, p. 14.
20. *International Herald-Tribune*, Paris, July 1, 1993.
21. *Wall Street Journal*, New York, October 23, 1991.

9

Legal Forms of Doing Business

BRANCH OFFICE

A relatively small number of U.S. firms in Germany have decided to operate through branch offices. A branch of an American firm is not a separate legal entity and thus has no rights or obligations apart from the company creating it. By contrast, a subsidiary corporation is considered as a complete legal person, existing independent of its parent. Nevertheless, a branch is viewed as a permanent establishment for German tax purposes.

About half the major U.S. banks operating in Germany do so through branches, which conduct their business much the same as their branches in the United States. Of course, the American bank must obtain permission from the German government and conduct its branch activities in accordance with the host nation's banking laws. Bank of America and Bank of New York rely solely on branches to conduct their business in Germany.

On the other hand, Citibank, Bankers Trust, Chase Bank, and Chemical Bank have established subsidiary banks under German law. For example, Citibank of New York has a fully owned subsidiary in Frankfurt called Citibank AG. In turn, Citibank AG has branches in Berlin, Dusseldorf, Munich, Hamburg, and Stuttgart.

While American banks are about evenly split between branch operations and German subsidiaries, other kinds of U.S. businesses have overwhelmingly favored using a German subsidiary. McDonald's employs a branch office in Munich to administer more than 400 units located throughout Germany. Texas

Instruments, General Electric, Dow, and John Deere also use the branch office approach.

Every U.S. firm establishing a branch office in Germany is required to file with the Commercial Register (*Handelsregister*) maintained at the Local Court in the region where the branch is located. The purpose of this Commercial Register is to give reliable information to third parties about the identity of the foreign enterprise, its objectives, stated equity, board of directors, and the persons authorized to act on behalf of the branch. Without such registration, it would prove difficult to obtain as much as a telephone line from the post office.

The registration application must be accompanied by the following documentation:

1. A certified copy of the charter, statutes, or by-laws and articles of association of the U.S. firm together with certified translations of these documents.
2. A list of the directors of the foreign enterprise giving their full names, professional designations, and home addresses.
3. A statement of the objectives of the branch and the amount of equity dedicated to its operations.

It is recommended, although not necessary, that the application give names, professional designations, and addresses of one or more persons resident in Germany authorized to sign on behalf of the branch operations. The application itself must be signed by all of the directors of the foreign enterprise with signatures authenticated by a notary public.

The Commercial Register will examine the application and the documentation submitted to determine whether the stated objectives require special operating permission (e.g., insurance, banking, air traffic, chemical, pharmaceutical, etc.). In addition, the Commercial Register will, in cooperation with the local Chamber of Industry and Commerce, investigate the branch name to prevent the use of names in Germany that are not admissible or in conflict with existing names. Thus, it is wise for the U.S. firm to check its name against those of companies already registered before filing.

In 1987, a fast-food restaurant opened in Freiburg offering Chinese dishes under the name McChinese. It was to be the first of a chain in Germany. McChinese featured items called "Sea-Mac Rolle" and "Sea-Mac Rice." McDonald's, already established in Germany with "McBacon" and "Big Mac" demanded that McChinese cease using this confusing name. When the firm refused, McDonald's filed a lawsuit. On February 12, 1992, the State Court of Appeals in Karlsruhe found in favor of the plaintiff, pointing out that McChinese was giving the impression to the public that it was the Chinese food branch of the worldwide American firm. The Court cited as further support for its ruling that McChinese could offer no reason for using the syllable "Mc" in its name.[1]

Once an American firm has registered a branch in Germany, there are no additional annual filings. There is no requirement for the branch of a foreign enterprise to file a balance sheet and profit-and-loss account. On the other hand, the branch must establish such separate balance sheet and profit-and-loss account for taxation purposes. Tax returns must be filed annually on the basis of such accounts.

Every substantial change in the American firm must be filed with the Commercial Register, always including certified copies of the respective changes and certified translations. This applies to changes in the charter, statutes, articles of association, name, objectives, stated or paid-in equity, and powers of representation.

An American branch is subject to strict requirements as to its business stationery. It must state the place of its registered office and its legal representatives with their full names, including at least one Christian name on all stationery originating from its German branch office.

A registered branch operation may be closed without formal liquidation. All that is required is a notice of closure of operations with the Commercial Register, again duly notarized. Upon receipt of such notice, the recording of the branch in the Commercial Register will simply be canceled. The branch will set up a closing balance sheet and file its last set of tax returns.

CORPORATIONS

Most U.S. firms in Germany have found the corporate form of business to be the most satisfactory. This can be effectuated by buying an existing German company, as General Motors acquired Adam Opel AG, or creating a brand new corporation, as Ford organized Ford-Werke AG.

German law offers two kinds of corporations: the stock company, *Aktiengesellschaft* (AG for short), similar to American corporations, and the limited-liability company, *Gesellschaft mit beschränkter Haftung* (GmbH for short), which does not exist under U.S. law. The AG form is much older but less popular today than the GmbH. There were 376,429 GmbHs at the start of 1989 and only 2,372 AGs; but the former had combined stated capital of DM 57 billion, while the latter reported DM 123 billion. It should be noted that a GmbH can legally reorganize into an AG and vice versa.

The first stock corporation in the world was created by the Dutch Parliament in 1692. The Dutch East India Company was established to develop colonies in the East Indies. The first in Germany, established in 1765, was Höchster Porzellan Manufaktur AG.[2]

Every stock company in those days, regardless of country, was created by an individual statute of the legislature, obviously a time-consuming and clumsy procedure. Eventually legislatures passed statutes allowing individuals to create their own stock companies by complying with a series of requirements set forth in those statutes. Such a statute did not come in Germany until

Prussia enacted enabling legislation in 1843. There have been many changes since then, and the current Stock Company Act (*Aktiengesellschaft Gesetz* [Akt G for short]) was passed in 1965.

By contrast, the limited-liability company (GmbH) was not used in Germany until 1892 when the Reichstag passed the Limited-Liability Company Act (*Gesetz über die Gesellschaft mit beschränkter Haftung*). With subsequent revisions, it now embraces 85 sections. The Stock Corporation Act contains 410 extremely detailed and inflexible sections requiring conformity with numerous, expensive formalities. Both kinds of corporations must indicate their legal status in their titles, as in Deutsche Texaco AG and Deutsche Wrigley GmbH.

The major difference is that only the AG can sell its stock to the general public and be listed on the stock exchange. The stock transfers of a GmbH are entirely restricted to the books of the corporation. However, German GmbHs can easily convert to AGs if they want to go public.

The American subsidiary has very little reason to sell its stock or go on an exchange. This role is much better reserved for the American parent. No U.S. subsidiary in Germany so far has gone on the stock market, but many parent companies are currently listed.

The corporation laws of Germany are federal rather than state (as in the United States). Thus there is no advantage in incorporating in one German state rather than another; and there is no competition among states as we have in America, where Delaware is the state of incorporation for more than half the Fortune 500 companies and some 204,000 others.

Both kinds of German corporations must draw up articles of incorporation (*Satzung der Gesellschaft*) to govern their activities. Both must file this basic document with the Commercial Register in the Local Court where the company plans to have its main office. Both the AG and GmbH are regarded as legal persons under the law and have the same protection of limited liability for their stockholders. Both pay the same corporate income tax.

A major difference, which greatly affects its popularity, is that the AG must make a much fuller disclosure of its financial results. Also, it must have a minimum paid-in capital of DM 100,000, compared with DM 50,000 for the GmbH.

The total costs of establishing a GmbH with DM 5,000 in paid-in capital will run about DM 1,500, which includes all registration and notarial fees. By contrast, costs for the AG will run much higher because of the expensive formalities involved in its creation.

A German AG must have two boards: a supervisory board (*Aufsichtsrat*) and a management board (*Vorstand*). The supervisory board is appointed by the incorporators and has authority until the first meeting of the stockholders. All subsequent supervisory boards are selected at the meetings of shareholders and usually have regular meetings every quarter.

The supervisory board must consist of at least three members, and the total must be divisible by three. The number cannot exceed nine if the capital is DM 3 million or less, fifteen if it is more than DM 3 million and less than DM 20 million, and twenty-one if the capital is more than DM 20 million.

The supervisory board appoints the management board, which provides the day-to-day administration. The articles may provide for a single member if capital is DM 3 million or less. Otherwise, there must be at least two members. Most corporations use an odd number to prevent paralyzing tie votes. German law prohibits a supervisory board member from serving on the management board and vice versa.

A limited-liability company employing 500 or less workers may or may not have a supervisory board. If employing more than 500, it must have a supervisory board; and one-third must be labor representatives.

The management of a GmbH can be a single manager, who may be named by the articles and hold office for an indefinite period.

In 1994, the corporation laws of Germany were amended to make it easier for a firm to adopt the AG form. Previously, five incorporators were necessary to start an AG. Now a single person is sufficient, and the AGs with fewer than 500 employees no longer need to appoint labor representatives to their supervisory boards. AGs over 500 employees must still have one-third labor representatives on this board.

The new legislation is expected to lead to some 5,000 conversions of GmbHs into AGs. The principal inducements for such changes are (1) ability of AGs to go on the stock market, (2) greater capability of raising capital, (3) reduction of dependence on banks for loans, and (4) easier transmission of corporate shares during life or at death.[3]

Where an American firm has a choice, it is usually more effective to exercise direct control over its German subsidiary rather than use an intermediary subsidiary, in which it does not have complete ownership and control. Xerox provides an example of the difficulties in following the latter method.

Xerox Corporation, based in Stamford, Connecticut, gets its name from a process called "xerography," invented in 1938. Derived from the Greek words for "dry" and "writing," it is a method of transferring images from one piece of paper to another using static electricity. Xerography was discovered by a patent lawyer in New York, Chester Carlson, who was frustrated by the expense and difficulty of copying documents.

In 1974, Xerox had 85 percent of the worldwide plain-paper copier market. Its name was synonymous with copying, but Japanese manufacturers began to cut into this share. Ricoh concentrated on less-expensive machines, which were smaller and less subject to breakdowns. Canon came in to challenge at the higher-priced level. Sharp, Toshiba, and Minolta also jumped into the market. At home, IBM and Kodak entered into the competition. By 1985, Xerox had dropped to 40 percent in market share.

Alco Standard of Valley Forge, Pennsylvania, with revenues of $4.9 billion in 1992 and net income of $104 million, has become a serious competitor of Xerox, not as a manufacturer but as a distributor of Japanese machines.

It now handles Ricoh, Canon, and Sharp machines and has 7 percent of the U.S. copier market, compared with 15 percent for Xerox.

In October 1992, Alco acquired Germany's largest copier distributor, IMM Office Systems Holding GmbH, for about $90 million. IMM, located in Munich, is Germany's largest independent distributor of office equipment, with sales of $440 million in 1992 and profit of $34 million.

In 1956, while still struggling to produce a marketable copier, Xerox entered a joint venture with Rank Organization PLC, a British film company. The venture partners formed an English corporation, now called Rank Xerox PLC, designed to market Xerox products outside North America. Xerox took 51 percent of the stock and exercises full management powers.

Rank Xerox PLC operates in Germany through Rank Xerox GmbH in Dusseldorf, which had to report losses for six years in a row from 1983 to 1988. In a report issued in 1990, these deficits were blamed primarily on Japanese competition.

Fiscal 1989 ended on October 31, just nine days before the Berlin Wall was unexpectedly opened. This brought great hope to the company because it ended the severe restrictions on the use and possession of copiers by the East German government. Before the Berlin Wall was pierced, there were only 311 copying machines for every one million citizens, compared with 16,200 in West Germany. Marxist leaders were understandably fearful of document copiers and rigidly limited them. U.S. business travelers in East Germany were irritated by this shortage. They could get copy service in the better hotels (which were thoroughly monitored by state security). Thus, in the interest of confidentiality, it was wiser to go to the U.S. Embassy library. After the Berlin Wall was opened, one of the first self-service copy shops was started behind Humbolt University in East Berlin. The first student customers reacted like children on Christmas morning to their new technological experiences.

The financial results for Xerox in fiscal year 1990 did not live up to expectations. Revenues climbed only $20 million to $870 million, and profit declined 50 percent to $26 million.

Then in fiscal year 1991 (the first complete year after German reunification on October 3, 1990), Xerox had a good report. Sales rose 13 percent to DM 1 billion, and profit climbed 108 percent to DM 48 million. These results were not to be repeated, for they were followed by a disappointing 1992. Sales grew 10 percent to DM 1.1 billion, but net collapsed to DM 5.8 million.

The Rank investment in the joint venture cost only £7 million in 1956 and is now probably worth about £1.5 billion, a most impressive gain. In June 1993, a London newspaper reported that Xerox was planning to buy up the minority holding of its venture partner within the next eighteen months. Other papers treated it as idle rumor, but the idea makes sense for both corporations and may still take place. Xerox, the world's largest maker of document copiers, could eliminate an unnecessary level of bureaucracy. It would also erase the confusing Rank image, which is known today for films, hotels, bingo games, and the chain of Hard Rock Cafes. Rank, for its part, could use the cash to retire its current debt of approximately £0.5 billion. With the remaining £1 billion available, Rank could strengthen its position in the entertainment industry.

This move would also improve communication between Xerox in Stamford and its German subsidiary in Dusseldorf, Rank Xerox GmbH. At present, there is unnecessary confusion in the German sales organization, which must wait while American instructions are filtered through the British intermediate layer in London. This German subsidiary has some 2,800 workers. Another subsidiary in Berlin, Rank Xerox Service GmbH, with a work force of about 300, has been established to handle business in the former East Germany.

UNINCORPORATED FORMS

While most U.S. firms will not be interested in using the other business forms allowed under German law, they should be acquainted with their legal aspects. It is essential to know the nature of the firms, with which they will be entering contracts. There are three principal kinds of unincorporated businesses in Germany, and they are quite similar to those found in America's legal system. Reform legislation was passed in 1985 requiring elaborate bookkeeping, valuation, and accounting rules for all businesses. Individual proprietorships were included for the first time.

Individual Proprietorship (*Einzelfirma*)

The individual proprietor is the simplest form of business organization in Germany just as it is in the United States. It consists of one person who owns the entire business and assumes unlimited liability for all debts and obligations and must be entered in the Commercial Register.

While the great mass of individual proprietorships are small in Germany, some giant firms have used this form. Friedrich Krupp of Essen, the famous armament maker, was a sole proprietorship from its founding in 1811 until 1903 and again from 1943 to 1968.[4]

General Partnership (*Offene Handelsgesellschaft*)

This is practically the same as a general partnership in the United States, a contract between two or more partners (individuals or corporate). Business must be conducted under the firm's name, which must contain either the names of all the partners (this is rarely done in practice) or the name of at least one partner with the addition of "& Co." or the letters "OHG" (both forms are commonly used). The partnership must be entered in the Commercial Register at the Local Court having jurisdiction over the partnership's domicile.

All the partners in a general commercial partnership are jointly and severally liable for all debts and obligations of the partnership, making this, in effect, an unlimited partnership. Any clause in the partnership agreement to the contrary is invalid with respect to third parties.

Limited Partnership (*Kommanditgesellschaft*)

This is much like the limited partnership in the United States and differs from the general partnership in that a limited partner (*Kommanditist*) is liable only to the extent of his contribution to the partnership. Only the general partner or partners, whose liability to creditors of the firm is unlimited, have the right to manage the partnership and to represent it in dealings with third parties. The name of the firm must contain the name of at least one general partner, along with the letters "KG," to describe the legal nature of the company. The limited partnership must also be entered in the Commercial Register.

Silent Partnership (*Stille Gesellschaft*)

The silent partner remains unrecorded and unknown but furnishes capital to the firm in return for right to share in profits. He or she has no liability beyond contribution and may be a judicial person. The owner of record has full liability.

Combined Limited Partnership and Limited Liability Company (GmbH & Co. KG)

This form differs from the normal limited partnership in that the general partner is a limited liability company (responsible only to the extent of its assets). The limited partners are liable only to the extent of their registered shares.

Corporation-Partnership (*Kommanditgesellschaft auf Aktien* or KGaA)

This form has at least one general partner fully responsible for business debts. Ordinary shareholders are responsible only for their capital contributions.

GERMAN SUBSIDIARY OR BRANCH

Without detailed analysis of all relevant factors, it cannot be determined which of the two alternatives is better. Among the points to be considered, the following are perhaps most important:

1. A branch is usually less expensive to set up and to operate, since there are no no-tarial fees to be incurred in its formation, there is no need for auditors to review its books, and there is no publication of accounts.

2. The recording and maintenance of such recording of a branch is administratively more cumbersome than the recording of a corporate subsidiary. The records of the company as a whole (home office and branch) must be placed on public record; and there is a need for continual updates, whereas the subsidiary public records will be limited to the legal affairs of its own.

3. In respect to commercial aspects, such as marketing and consumer confidence, a subsidiary may be more acceptable to local customers than a branch of a foreign company.

4. It is frequently easier to control the amount of profits subject to German tax through the use of a subsidiary by making use of interest charges, management fees, technical service fees, royalties, pricing policies, and the like. However, such controlling is limited by the power of German tax authorities to adjust the effects of intercompany transactions to the extent that these do not meet arm's-length requirements.

5. A branch operation is sometimes useful if start-up losses are anticipated, since, where the overseas company is resident, it is possible for start-up expenses and losses to be set off currently against the income of the branch from other sources. Care must be taken in this situation if it should be intended to transfer the business of the branch to a subsidiary once the profit threshold has been reached. The transfer of the business may give rise to a taxable capital gain for the branch in the event that goodwill could be deemed to be realized.

6. If the German operations should need to borrow money from independent foreign sources, there may be more difficulty in obtaining a deduction for the interest in a branch, since it will be necessary to show that the funds were actually made available to the German operations. By contrast, a German resident subsidiary will not incur similar problems.

7. If a court gives a judgment against a subsidiary, liability will be restricted to its assets. By contrast, if there is a judgment against a branch, this is (at the same time) a judgment against all assets of a foreign company, enforceable in principle in its home country.

8. Last, in terms of winding down and liquidation, the branch is easier to handle. There is no statutory liquidation period and no need to appoint a liquidator. By contrast, the subsidiary must be terminated by shareholder resolution; a liquidator must be appointed (unless the managers carry on as liquidators); the liquidation must be published three times in the *Federal Gazette (Bundesanzeiger)*; and following the publication, a one-year waiting period commences during which the claims of all creditors must be met or else the company must be put into bankruptcy. During the one-year waiting period, the subsidiary must continue meeting its accounting requirements, establishing annual accounts, having the same audited, and so on, although only one tax return needs to be filed for the entire liquidation period.

GOVERNMENT OWNERSHIP

About 50 percent in value of German business is owned by governments—federal, state, or local. Germans are traditionally more comfortable with government ownership than Americans. There were some 1,000 companies owned in whole or in part by West Germany's federal government in 1949, largely carryovers from the Hitler period. Bonn has tried with varying degrees of intensity to privatize these holdings; but in 1990, it still owned stock in 202 corporations, including ten banks.[5]

Although corporations owned by the federal government are better known and incite more political debate, German states and local governments also have large holdings. For example, the State of Bavaria owns stock in sixty-six corporations (on average, 24.4 percent of the total), with a combined capital of DM 2.2 billion. They, in turn, have 360 subsidiaries.[6]

Best known to Americans among Bavaria's business holdings is the 400-year-old, world-famous Hofbräu Haus in Munich (*Staatliche Münchener Hofbräuhaus*). It was founded by the Duke of Bavaria as a court brewery to supply his staff. With the smallest annual capacity in Munich (200,000 hectoliters), Hofbräu Haus sold about DM 40 million in beer in both 1990 and 1991 and suffered a loss of DM 7 million in each year. Experts say that such a small brewery cannot make a profit in the rough Munich market. The Bavarian Audit Office has recommended privatization, but the state government has no intention of separating itself from this expensive symbol of Bavarian culture.[7]

Volkswagen AG (VW) was 100 percent owned by Nazi Germany when it was organized in 1937. After the FRG came into existence in 1949, the stock of VW was divided between the federal government and the State of Lower Saxony (where the Wolfsburg central office is located). Over the years, Bonn has sold all its stock, and Lower Saxony reduced its holdings to 20 percent.

One of the most glamorous German corporations is Meissen AG, maker of the world-famous porcelain carrying that name. Since 1719, this enterprise has belonged wholly to the state: to the kingdom of Saxony (1719–1920), State of Saxony (1920–1949), East Germany (1949–1990), and since 1990, once again to the State of Saxony. It is one of the most profitable companies in the German public sector. Meissen sales in 1992 were estimated at DM 90 million and profits at DM 420,000. This profit margin of 0.46 percent for such an enterprise is disappointing, but heavy repairs and maintenance have burdened the new firm. Such items had been seriously neglected by East Germany.

Employment has fallen from 1,800 to 1,400, incredibly little by comparison with other East German enterprises. Personnel costs are up 20 percent; and the highly specialized artists now draw DM 3,000 per month, compared with Ostmark 1,000 in the old days. The workweek is 40 hours as opposed to 43.5. Three holidays and four vacation days have been added. The yearly working time has been cut 15 percent.

About 60 percent of Meissen production is dinnerware, and 15 percent is figurines. The balance includes a wide variety of boxes, vases, clock housings, and works of art. The most popular dinnerware in the United States is the five-piece setting—three plates with a cup and a saucer. In one store in Los Angeles in September 1988, these settings ranged from $350 to $1,105.

The history of Meissen porcelain is fascinating because the manufacturing process was a closely guarded secret of China until 1719. Then, a pharmacist in Dresden, Johann Boettger—who was in the service of King August the Strong of Saxony—discovered the formula. He found a way to combine kaolin, quartz, and feldspar to make a hard-paste porcelain; and this enabled the kings of Saxony to establish the first porcelain factory in Europe.

To protect the secret, the factory was transferred from Dresden to an abandoned castle on a hill overlooking Meissen fifteen miles to the north. Much ater, in 1865, the operations were moved into a more modern plant in the center of Meissen.

The State of Berlin is the owner of a competing porcelain maker, Königliche Porzellan Manufactur (KPM). This enterprise was established by King Frederick II (the Great) of Prussia (1746–1786). He lured away Meissen's top artisan by offering him a better salary and perquisites to become manager of his shop in Berlin.

In 1989, KPM converted to a GmbH, a corporation with all the stock owned by Berlin. In 1988, the business lost DM 2.7 million; but in 1989, it earned DM 1.7 million.[8]

In addition to the firms specifically mentioned, the states and local governments own airports, public utilities (electricity and gas), banks, shipyards, housing projects, breweries, trade fairs, gambling casinos, rathskellers, insurance companies, real estate plots, and many others.

In the West, according to a study of the Bundesbank, the three levels of government hold an array of firms worth DM 370 billion.[9] This is enough to pay the combined deficits of these same governments for a two-year period during this painful period of reunification. It is estimated that this public sector accounts for about 50 percent of the GNP in western Germany.[10]

Government ownership and nationalization of business are matters of major concern to Americans and other foreign investors. It should be emphasized that there has been no new nationalization of business in West Germany since 1945, quite in contrast with France and the United Kingdom. This has been true even during the period from 1969 to 1982 when the Socialists under Chancellors Brandt and Schmidt were in power in Bonn.

The government of Chancellor Kohl inherited holdings in 818 companies when it came to power in 1982. During the first eight years, it cut this number down to 202, a truly remarkable performance including the selling of its 16 percent remaining interest in Volkswagen. The government also disposed of all its shares in Veba, Saltzgitter, and Viag. Bonn realized DM 10.5 billion from the sale of these 600 companies.

In 1992, the Kohl administration announced a new plan for privatization of its remaining assets. It has a new and more powerful motivation not even on the horizon in 1982: the huge deficits caused by the high costs of reunification.

There is another reason for more vigorous selling of government-held corporations. The German universal banks are anxious to expand the volume of stock listed. At present, the volume of shares listed in Frankfurt and the smaller stock exchanges is considerably below New York, London, and Tokyo.

The German railway system was built by private entrepreneurs in the early 1800s and then nationalized about 1900.[11] It was divided into two in 1945 upon the division of defeated Germany. Then, with reunification in 1990, the two systems were coordinated (but not merged). They are the biggest money losers in the federal public sector. The Bundesbahn (West) with 204,000 workers, had revenues of DM 25 billion in 1991 and lost DM 5.3 billion. The Reichsbahn (East) had 252,000 workers on its payroll, DM 9 billion in revenues, and a DM 4.3-billion loss.[12] In 1994, they were merged into a new company, Deutsche Bahn AG, a majority of which must remain under the control of Germany according to the Constitution. A minority is to be privatized.

On July 21, 1992, Chancellor Kohl announced a plan to privatize another group of companies, including Lufthansa, the government printing house, construction companies, port authorities, as well as the Frankfurt and other airports.

In 1993, the Constitution was amended to permit the privatization of the Deutsche Bundespost. It was reorganized into three AGs: Telekom, Post Dienst, and Postbank.

Telekom is the darling of all German firms in the public sector with a monopoly in almost all telephone business. It is valued by the Finance Ministry between DM 50 and DM 70 billion. All the other firms scheduled for sale might bring another DM 10 billion.[13] In 1992, Telekom showed a net profit of DM 3.2 billion on sales of DM 50 billion, which placed it among the most profitable firms in Germany. While Telekom might bring DM 70 billion if sold to private investors, it would be in the interest of an orderly market to limit the first offering to 25 percent.[14] Another problem is the German Constitution, which stipulates that public post, railways, and other civil services remain under state control. An amendment to overcome this could prove difficult if the SPD opposes it, as is quite probable.

Lufthansa is currently 52.9 percent owned by the federal government. The plan calls for reducing this to 25.1 percent, enough stock for Bonn to block serious changes. Lufthansa had a loss of DM 373 million in 1992 and DM 53 million in 1993, and this will make the company hard to sell.[15]

The decline in profitability at Lufthansa has been accompanied by a drop in passenger load factor. The averages in recent years have been as follows:

1987	66.5%
1988	65.9%
1989	66.4%
1990	65.2%
1991	61.8%
1992	56.5%

NOTES

1. *Frankfurter Allgemeine Zeitung*, February 25, 1992.
2. *Frankfurter Allgemeine Zeitung*, April 28, 1992.
3. *Wall Street Journal*, New York, June 17, 1994.
4. *Frankfurter Allgemeine Zeitung*, March 26, 1992.
5. *Frankfurter Allgemeine Zeitung*, March 7, 1992.
6. *Frankfurter Allgemeine Zeitung*, November 7, 1992.
7. *Frankfurter Allgemeine Zeitung*, November 23, 1991.
8. *Frankfurter Allgemeine Zeitung*, June 8, 1990.
9. *The Economist*, London, November 24, 1990, p. 73.
10. *International Herald-Tribune*, Paris, May 26, 1993.
11. *New York Times*, July 16, 1992.
12. *Frankfurter Allgemeine Zeitung*, September 25, 1992.
13. *Wall Street Journal*, New York, July 22, 1992.
14. Ibid.
15. *Wall Street Journal*, New York, March 18, 1994.

10

German Accounting

GERMAN VERSUS U.S. ACCOUNTING

It is rightfully said that accounting is the language of business, but unfortunately the Germans and Americans differ greatly on those principles of accountancy underlying their respective business languages. In an essay published in 1879 entitled "The Awful German Language," Mark Twain wrote that an intelligent person ought to be able to learn English in thirty hours, French in thirty days, and German in thirty years. Most readers smile when they read this statement, but non-German accountants are more likely to cry.[1]

The most enlightening illustration of the broad disparity between U.S. and German accounting came on September 17, 1993. Edzard Reuter, the distinguished chairman of the management board of the even more distinguished Daimler-Benz AG, called a press conference in Stuttgart to report on his company's performance for the first six months of 1993. Daimler had sales of DM 41.64 billion, a drop of 13 percent from DM 48.1 billion in the same period in 1992. This did not surprise any of the listeners because all automakers had experienced sharp declines in the first half of 1993. Nor did Reuter create any excitement by announcing that net income had fallen during these six months to a very disappointing DM 168 million. This was still a modest profit for Daimler-Benz, Germany's largest industrial corporation measured by sales, a company with a continuous record of profits since World War II.

Reuter then dropped a bomb. For the very first time in history a German firm was going to report its net income under American standards of accounting. Under such methods (Generally Accepted Accounting Principles or GAAP), Daimler-Benz had a loss of DM 949 million.[2]

In order to show the DM 168 million profit under German methods, a very embarrassed chairman went on to admit to a practice seldom publicly mentioned: "Speaking frankly, we made use of a German accounting rule that allowed us to release reserves."[3]

By drawing on previously accumulated secret reserves, Daimler was able to offset the loss in the six-month period and show a profit of DM 168 million. These reserves did not appear in the balance sheet and had been created silently in earlier profitable years out of unreported net income.

Daimler's financial member of the management board, Gerhard Liener, was also present at this famous press conference. He stated very bluntly, "In a bad year like 1993, all German companies are releasing reserves to improve their net profit." Liener is unquestionably one of Germany's most outspoken top business executives. Once, in an interview with David Waller of the *Financial Times*, Liener casually told the writer what Daimler-Benz profits were going to be in the current year and the next. Waller wrote,

The willingness to let slip highly sensitive information is indicative of a cavalier approach to the mass of shareholders. It can be taken for granted that Germany's big banks and insurance companies, which own large stakes in numerous large German companies, know the figures long before they slip out in interviews and presentations. Other shareholders are not so well served.[4]

Commenting on Daimler's compliance with SEC (Securities Exchange Commission) requirements to get its ADRs traded on the New York Stock Exchange (NYSE), Liener acknowledged that investors get more information under U.S. rules. "There is a big gap between German accounting standards and U.S. principles. U.S. accounting discloses so much more and tells you what is really happening in a company."[5]

At this point, it should be clarified that U.S. law allows the use of reserves under certain conditions, but they must appear in the balance sheet. German regulations, on the contrary, permit the hidden employment of such reserves. Daimler also restated under American accounting principles its earnings for 1990, 1991, and 1992. For 1992 net income was DM 1.45 billion auf Deutsch and DM 1.35 billion auf Amerikanisch.[6] For all of 1993, Daimler reported a net income of DM 651 million under German rules and a loss of DM 1.8 billion with American rules.

By using American accounting methods, Daimler also increased its net worth by 58 percent. As of the end of 1992, German methods produced DM 17 billion while U.S. principles yielded DM 27 billion.[7]

Using hidden reserves was not the only reason for the different results reported under the two sets of rules. Differing methods for treating acquisitions, divestitures, foreign currency changes, pensions, and deferred taxes also had important effects on the final figures.[8]

In good years, Daimler-Benz and most German corporations can use a reverse procedure to show lower profits than those actually earned. They report only part of profits and silently stash the remainder in hidden reserves. In March 1993, Daimler shocked the world of business by admitting to "extraordinary income" of DM 4 billion, which it had previously earned and put in hidden reserves.[9]

Daimler-Benz thus became the first and only German corporation to comply with American standards because it was the only way it could have its American Depositary Receipts (ADRs) listed on the NYSE. The U.S. SEC had repeatedly refused efforts of Daimler and other German firms to be registered without the severe disclosures required of American corporations. As of October 5, 1993, Daimler-Benz became the only German company on the "Big Board." By way of contrast on that date, 168 U.S. firms had listings in Frankfurt.

Earlier outside studies had shown the results of using American accounting principles on German companies. An exercise by Gary Schieneman, a New York analyst, showed that shareholders' equity for Mannesmann AG at the end of 1989 would have been 40 percent higher if calculated under U.S. rules, while net profit would have been 50 percent and 36 percent higher in 1988 and 1989, respectively. In another study, Schieneman showed that Volkswagen net profits in 1989 would have grown from DM 1.04 billion under German rules to DM 1.9 billion by U.S. methods.[10]

This keen desire of Daimler to be traded on the NYSE surprised many people. It was done to facilitate a securities issue planned to raise additional capital for expansion. The automobile giant can secure funds more economically on the huge U.S. market than it can in Germany. It was also counting on some 300,000 American drivers of the Mercedes-Benz to become owners of their stock.[11]

It should not be inferred from this that American accounting is perfect; it has plenty of deficiencies. The two accounting systems have different basic underlying characteristics, which can be summarized as follows:

1. German law grants precedence to creditors over stockholders. This principle firmly enshrined in accounting practice puts companies under pressure to understate profits and assets. American accounting tends to favor the shareholders and thus overstate profits.

2. German accountants do not prepare separate accounts for paying taxes and for public information as in the United States. Thus, German companies have a tax incentive to keep profits as low as possible.

3. There is much less pressure on German companies to boost profits. The vast majority of the 650 companies listed on the German Stock Exchange are controlled by banks or families with long-term profit goals. These shareholders are insiders with access to the management accounts, which tell the full story denied to those who must rely on published figures.

4. German companies do not want labor unions to have access to information that can be used to push wages still higher.

On February 28, 1994, Arthur Levitt, chairman of the SEC, spoke in Frankfurt before the American Chamber of Commerce in Germany. The executives of leading German firms were in attendance, hoping that Levitt would announce some new compromise. There was no change, and German companies will need to follow the tough requirements imposed on Daimler-Benz in 1993.

The Securities Industry Association estimated in 1993 that less than 7 percent of America's $5 trillion of institutional and mutual funds assets are invested in foreign securities.[12] American investors want a good quality of investment information as a basis for making informed decisions. This simply is not available in Germany except for Daimler-Benz. Investing in other German stocks is a stab in the dark.

ACCOUNTING DIRECTIVES
OF EUROPEAN UNION

As pointed out in Chapter 8, the European Union, in its effort to harmonize the twelve member markets, has the power to formulate directives. These are prepared and presented by the European Commission to the Council of Ministers for approval. The twelve national legislatures are then obliged to implement these directives by changing their respective laws to conform.

Over the life of the EU, the Council of Ministers has been trying to harmonize the diverse (shall we say chaotically conflicting) company laws of its member states. The European Commission has labored tirelessly to prepare numerous directives to achieve this goal, but only seven have been adopted by the council. Three of them—the Fourth, Seventh, and Eighth Directives—deal with accounting rules. All three have been implemented by the twelve member states.

The Fourth Directive took fifteen years to develop and appeared in 1978, covering basic accounting rules for limited companies. The Seventh Directive in 1983 also had a long period of gestation; it dealt with consolidated accounts. The Eighth Directive defines the qualifications of persons responsible for carrying out the audits required by the Fourth and Seventh Directives.

All of this may sound like real progress except that the twelve union members could not agree on some basic principles and decided to take the easy way out of their dilemma. The three accounting directives leave many options to the member states. The EU says that it does not plan to pursue further accounting directives for now, although it has set up an advisory forum to make recommendations on accounting problems.

GERMAN ACCOUNTING STATUTES

Until 1985 the rules covering German accounting were scattered through a confusing variety of statutes. Then the Bundestag passed the Balance Sheet Directive Act (*Bilanzrichtlinien-Gesetz*), called BiRiLiG for short. This statute was designed to implement the Fourth, Seventh, and Eighth Directives of the EU by bringing German law into conformity with that of the union.

The Balance Sheet Directive Act thus consolidates most, if not all, statutory requirements concerning the accounting, auditing, and publication of financial statements into the commercial code. In effect, it rewrote Chapter 3 of the code, the main points being as follows:

1. Basic accounting rules apply to all firms, regardless of which legal form of organization is employed.
2. Supplementary provisions apply to stock corporations (AGs), limited liability companies (GmbHs), and partnerships limited by shares (KGaAs), covering
   a. Financial statements.
   b. Management reports.
   c. Consolidated financial statements.
   d. Auditing.
   e. Disclosure and publication requirements.

The Act divides stock corporations (AGs), limited liability companies (GmbHs), and partnerships based on shares (KGaAs) into three classes: small, medium, and large. It goes on to set forth specific criteria for each of these three classes. They are thus separated on the basis of sales, balance sheets, and work forces.

Four financial statements must be prepared in accordance with detailed requirements set forth in the statute:

1. Balance sheet
2. Profit-and-loss statement
3. Annex
4. Annual report

While medium-sized and large firms must have their financial statements audited prior to their ratification by the shareholders' meeting, small units are exempt from such obligation. The audit must be performed by an independent public accountant (*Wirtschaftsprüfer*). Medium-sized corporations may also have their accounts audited by sworn accountants (*Vereidigte Buchprüfer*).

Large corporations must submit for publication, not later than at the end of the ninth month following the balance sheet date, the following documents to the *Federal Gazette* (*Bundesanzeiger*): (1) the audited financial statements together with the management's report; (2) the report of the supervisory board; and (3) if the proposal for the use of the profits and the resolution adopting it is not reflected in the financial statement, such proposal and resolution. Subsequently, the publication in the *Federal Gazette*, together with the documentation listed here, must be filed with the Commercial Register of the Local Court in the place where the corporation is located.

Medium-sized corporations must file the same documentation with this Commercial Register without undue delay after the submission to the shareholders within the nine months following the close of their fiscal year. As soon as practicable following such filing, the management of the corporation must publish a notice which specifies the Commercial Register docket number and the Local Court to which the documentation was submitted.

Small corporations must file the balance sheet and any annex with the Commercial Register on or before the end of the twelfth month following the end of the fiscal year.

NOTES

1. Mark Twain, *The Complete Travel Books of Mark Twain*, Vol. 2, *A Tramp Abroad*, ed. Charles Neider (New York: Doubleday, 1967), Appendix D, p. 326.

2. *New York Times*, September 18, 1993; *Wall Street Journal*, New York, September 20, 1993.

3. *Wall Street Journal*, New York, September 20, 1993.

4. *Financial Times*, London, July 1, 1993.

5. *Wall Street Journal*, New York, October 5, 1993.

6. Ibid.

7. David Hart (ed.), *Membership Directory and Yearbook 1994* (Frankfurt: American Chamber of Commerce in Germany, 1994), p. 92.

8. *New York Times*, September 18, 1993.

9. *Wall Street Journal*, March 25, 1993.

10. *Financial Times*, London, March 19, 1992.

11. *Frankfurter Allgemeine Zeitung*, September 10, 1993.

12. *Wall Street Journal*, New York, February 25, 1994.

11

German Tax Law

GERMAN TAXES IN PROPER PERSPECTIVE

Germany's high taxes must be treated in proper context rather than in the alarmist fashion characteristic of most businesspeople, politicians, and journalists dealing with the subject. Surely German taxes take 43 percent of GDP—compared with those of the United States, which extract 30 percent— but two additional points must be made. First, German accountants do not report as much corporate net income as their American colleagues and thus reduce the actual burden. Second, Germany provides its citizenry with far better services than they would obtain in the United States. Chapter 15 is devoted to the generous social security benefits available in Germany, which make America look modest by comparison. Moreover, education at all levels (including the deservedly praised apprentice system) supplies industry with superb workers, which American schools simply cannot duplicate. Excellent police, fire, and public transportation are other services that impress all foreign tourists.

Like America, Germany has three levels of government: federal, state, and local. Each level has authority to collect certain taxes, and then it shares some of them with the other two levels. As a result, the federal government winds up with about 40 percent of all tax revenues, 35 percent goes to the sixteen states, and the remaining 25 percent goes to local governments.

Most German taxes are basically consumer taxes and are self-explanatory. It is interesting to note that Germany's world champion beer drinkers, who consume about 140 liters per capita every year, pay only a 26-percent tax. By contrast, cognac sippers pay 149 percent for their stimulant, and sparkling wine fanciers are carrying a 50-percent burden. Even coffee drinkers with 43 percent pay more than beer consumers, but tea drinkers are most favored with a rate of only 13 percent. Cigarette smokers are penalized far more than drinkers; they must pay a 253-percent tax. If any of them wants a dog, he or she will have to pay DM 12.5 per month.

Our examination of taxes will focus on those affecting foreign business in Germany.

Corporation Tax (*Körperschaftsteuer*)

Prussia enacted the first modern German income tax in 1820. It was graduated according to social classes with burdens increasing with the descent of the social order. In 1851, this law was changed to impose the same tax on everyone with income beyond a certain amount, regardless of social class. Then, in 1891, Prussia (now the dominant state in the German Empire created in 1871) introduced the graduated income tax. This tax applied to individuals and commercial entities alike (corporations, partnerships limited by shares, mining companies, and certain cooperatives). The top bracket was 4 percent, which applied to all taxable incomes above 100,000 marks. The other states followed the Prussian model with some variations.

At the time of the founding of the German Empire in 1871, attempts were made to transfer the income tax from the states to the federal government, but they were unsuccessful. The states were required to make contributions to the imperial treasury in Berlin.

After World War I (in 1920), income taxes were transferred to the federal government under the Weimer Republic. After World War II (in 1945), they were transferred by the Allied Occupation Powers to the various zones.

Then, in 1949, under the Constitution of the Republic of Germany, income tax powers were vested in the federal government. Administration, however, is entrusted to the states; and their proceeds are shared by the two in a ratio, which changes from time to time.[1]

The corporation income tax yielded DM 31 billion in 1992. Net income of corporations registered in Germany is taxed at a flat rate of 45 percent. However, that portion of net income paid out in dividends to stockholders is reduced to 30 percent. A corporation registered outside Germany pays a rate of 42 percent, and there is no reduction on that portion paid out as dividends. As of January 1, 1995, the corporation tax was increased by a 7.5-percent surtax called *Solidaritätszuschlag*, designed to help pay for the costs of reunification. Corporations registered in Germany are subject to tax on all income worldwide. A corporation not registered in Germany is liable only for income having its source in Germany.

An unincorporated branch of a foreign company, whether in the form of a registered branch or a nonregistered permanent establishment, is taxed under the rules relating to corporations not registered in Germany and is considered an integral part of its nonresident head office. It—or rather the nonresident head office—is subject to German taxation on all income and profit properly attributable to its operations in Germany.

The corporation tax applies to corporations (*Kapitalgesellschaften*), cooperatives (*Genossenschaften*), and certain other legal entities organized under civil law.

There is no distinction in German income tax law between gains on the sale of capital and noncapital assets. Rather, a distinction is made between sales, exchanges, and other conversions of business property versus nonbusiness property. All gains from the sale or other disposition of business property (this would include all assets of a company or unincorporated business) are taxed as business income of the company at normal rates. Losses suffered from the disposal of business assets are treated as ordinary losses. There is no tax on gains from sales of nonbusiness property.

If a company sells its entire business (*Geschäftsaufgabe*), the tax is 50 percent of the regular tax rate on the gain. The taxable gain is the difference between the book value and the price received for the business.

U.S. firms have a choice of operating directly in Germany or using a German subsidiary. Although the overwhelming majority have selected the subsidiary alternative, some, like John Deere and McDonald's, use a branch office. The branch can be attractive when substantial startup losses are expected in Germany, and the U.S. corporation can use these at once to reduce its taxable income and taxes in the United States. With a German subsidiary, the U.S. parent would have to wait until it generates profits before the losses can be deducted. Sometimes the direct support or reputation of the American head office is likely to be a major factor in the commercial success of German operations. Banks are a good example of this situation.

Net Capital Tax (*Vermögensteuer*)

The net worth tax yielded DM 6.7 billion in 1992. Its rate is 1 percent for individuals and 0.6 percent for legal entities. Resident individuals, companies, entities, associations, and accumulations of property (e.g., trusts and estates) are unlimited taxpayers and are subject to net worth tax on net assets both inside and outside Germany, except where certain foreign assets are excluded by tax treaty. Partnerships file returns on partnership assets, but the partners are taxed individually on their respective shares of partnership net assets. Net assets of resident companies can suffer double net worth tax— once at the corporate level and again at the shareholder level on the value of the latter's shares. The tax only applies when the worth exceeds DM 70,000, and worth in excess of DM 120,000 is valued at only 75 percent of actual value for purposes of this tax.

Nonresident individuals, companies, and the like, who have neither their residence, domicile, nor place of management in Germany will be subject to net worth tax only on certain assets situated in Germany. Nonresidents are exempt from net worth tax and need not file a return if domestic property does not exceed DM 20,000.

Trade Tax (*Gewerbesteuer*)

In actuality, this is a second corporation income tax levied by municipalities on firms in their jurisdictions, which yielded DM 44 billion in 1992. It amounts to 5 percent of the net income and 0.2 percent of business capital, subject to certain deductions. This total is then multiplied by a municipal multiple, which varies from 240 percent to 450 percent, depending on the municipality. Thus, the effective rates vary between 12 percent and 20 percent of taxable income. For example, the rate in Frankfurt in 1991 was 19.4 percent. Individual proprietorships and partnerships must also pay this tax, but they have an additional deduction of DM 36,000. This trade tax is deductible as an expense in calculating the corporate income tax.

Value-Added Tax (*Mehrwertsteuer*)

The value-added tax yielded DM 197 billion in 1992. The tax applies to the value added at each level as products move from original owner to the ultimate consumer. The rate is 15 percent on each transfer, but certain commodities such as food carry 7 percent. Imports of goods are subject to the tax. The suppliers of most services, such as lawyers and accountants, must also collect this tax from the customer.

EU regulations require that all members have a uniform 15 percent VAT rate by January 1, 1993. Only Germany and Spain were in compliance by that date. Variations ranged as high as 25 percent in Denmark and as low as 12 percent in Luxembourg.[2]

Income Tax (*Einkommensteuer*)

This tax is by far the leading source of revenue, yielding DM 300 billion in 1992 and applying only to natural persons. For residents, it applies to all sources of income, subject to certain personal exemptions and allowable deductions. If an individual has his or her permanent or habitual residence outside the FRG, only revenue from German sources is subject to the income tax.

Depending on family status, the taxpayer has certain deductions. Rates are progressive and range from 19 percent to 53 percent.

Those taxpayers receiving income in addition to wages and salaries (about 37%) must file tax returns much like those used in America. However, the majority (about 63%) are covered by the employer's withholding tax (*Lohnsteuer*) and do not have to file returns. This is not a separate tax but rather the device used by the government to collect the income tax on wages and salaries from the employers before such income is paid out to the workers.

In 1992, DM 247 billion out of the total income tax revenue of DM 300 billion was collected in this manner. Employers are required to deduct withholding taxes on all emoluments paid to employees insofar as these represent taxable income to the employee. The withholding tax must be deducted in accordance with official tables that are geared to the employee's taxable income earned evenly over the year. Many allowances an employee is entitled to claim for personal tax purposes are included in the deduction by the employer, provided they are documented on a wages–tax card, which an employee must complete annually. Other allowances and reliefs can only be claimed by an employee at the end of the tax year (always January to December regardless of the accounting year of the company) by filing a personal income tax return.

In the employee's hands, the withholding tax borne by deduction is treated as a payment on account of his final liability. However, it is regarded as a final settlement if a personal return is not filed (generally not mandatory for smaller incomes from employment only). It should be noted, however, that the employer is under a legal obligation to withhold the correct amount of wages tax.

Germany also uses a withholding device to collect income tax on dividends and interest payments. It is called a capital yield tax (*Kapitalertragsteuer*), but it is really part of the income tax. It brought in DM 11.2 billion in 1993.

Corporations withhold 25 percent on all dividends paid to their stockholders, which become a credit toward the overall income tax due by the stockholder, including his or her tax due on dividends. This credit applies only to shareholders domiciled or living in Germany, taxable for global income.

Prior to January 1, 1993, there was no withholding tax required by payers of interest; and tax evasion on interest payments was a scandal. Interest payers were not required to report such payments under German law, and only about half the recipients voluntarily declared them. As a result, it was estimated that DM 50 billion in income tax revenues was lost every year.[3]

On June 27, 1991, the Federal Constitutional Court held on the petition of regular taxpayers that this arrangement was unconstitutional and ordered the government to start collecting the full tax on interest by January 1, 1993.

The tax law passed in response to the court's order does not apply to foreigners. It called for a 30-percent withholding by banks on interest starting January 1, 1993. A single person is not taxed on the first DM 6,000, and a married couple gets DM 12,000. It will be difficult to fully enforce such a law because depositors can transfer their accounts to foreign banks, particularly to Luxembourg and Switzerland.

As a rule, an individual is not taxed on gains from the sale or other disposition of nonbusiness property, nor is he or she permitted to deduct a loss from this source for income tax purposes. However, an individual is taxed on gains from so-called "speculative transactions," that is, sales and certain other dispositions of property not held over certain periods (for real property, two years; for corporate stock, six months).

Real Estate Tax (*Grundsteuer*)

This tax brought in DM 9.9 billion in 1992. It is based on the assessed value (much lower than the market value) of the real property involved. The basic rate is 0.35 percent for land and buildings, while specific rates between 0.26 percent and 0.60 percent apply to certain types of realty. This is multiplied by municipal multiples up to 370 percent. The total tax may thus amount to as much as 1.4 percent.

Real Estate Transfer Tax (*Grunderwerbsteuer*)

This tax imposed on the transfer of title to real property yielded DM 3.8 billion in 1992. The tax rate is 2 percent on the value of the consideration (if not determinable, then the lowest assessed value). It is the joint liability of the parties but is generally paid by the purchaser.

Church Tax (*Kirchensteuer*)

This tax, originated by Bismarck, applies to all individual wage and income taxpayers who are members of a recognized church. The rate varies according to district and generally amounts to between 8 percent and 9 percent of the income tax payable. It produced DM 17.3 billion in 1992, DM 8.7 billion for the Lutherans, and DM 8.6 billion for the Catholics.

A foreign national can avoid paying the church tax by not entering any religious affiliation when registering with local authorities or on his or her wages–tax card. Baden-Württemberg levied the tax on corporations until 1965 when the Federal Constitutional Court held that only individuals could be members of a church; legal persons could not.

The church tax provides churches with a substantial part of their budgets. In 1990, the Catholic Diocese of Berlin reported that the church had a budget of DM 126 million in West Berlin, of which DM 76 million (60 percent) came from the church tax.[4] Prior to unification in 1990, there was no church tax in eastern Germany. It had been terminated in the Marxist era.

Gasoline Tax (*Mineralölsteuer*)

The gasoline tax yields 5 percent of all taxes in Germany (DM 55 billion in 1992), compared with less than 1 percent in the United States. It amounts to $2.74 per gallon for the Germans and $0.39 for the Americans. The price of a gallon of gasoline in Germany in June 1994 was $3.55, while Americans paid $1.10. In Japan, it was $4.35 ($2.10 in tax).[5]

Other taxes paid by Germans in 1992 were as follows in billions of marks:[6]

Tobacco tax (*Tabaksteuer*)	19.2
Motor vehicle tax (*Kraftfahrzeugsteuer*)	13.3
Customs (*Zölle*)	6.7
Insurance taxes (*Versicherungssteuer*)	8.0
Cognac tax (*Branntweinabgaben*)	5.5
Inheritance tax (*Erbschaftsteuer*)	3.0
Coffee tax (*Kaffeesteuer*)	1.7
Beer tax (*Biersteuer*)	1.6
Sparkling wine tax (*Schaumweinsteuer*)	0.8
Fire protection tax (*Feuerschutzsteuer*)	0.3
Foreign exchange tax (*Wechselsteuer*)	0.3
Dog tax (*Hundesteuer*)	0.2
Amusement tax (*Vergnügungsteuer*)	0.1
Energy tax (*Leuchtmittelsteuer*)	0.1
Sugar tax (*Zuckersteuer*)	0.1
Lottery tax (*Totallisatorsteuer*)	0.1
Soft drink tax (*Getränkesteuer*)	0.06
Tea tax (*Teesteuer*)	0.05
Sport bet tax (*Sportwettsteuer*)	0.04
Hunting & fishing tax (*Jagd-u. Fischereisteuer*)	0.04
Racetrack wager tax (*Rennwettsteuer*)	0.02
Movie tax (*Kinosteuer*)	0.02
Liquor license tax (*Schankerlaubnissteuer*)	0.01

U.S.–GERMAN DOUBLE TAXATION TREATY

Germany has a Double Taxation Treaty with the United States, the rules of which take precedence over the internal German tax laws. The main purpose of this treaty is to provide relief from the taxation of the same income by both Germany and the United States. This is done by allowing exemptions or reducing the rates or granting credits.

For example, if the U.S. parent corporation holds 10 percent or more of the voting shares of its German subsidiary corporation, it is deemed under the treaty to have a substantial participation in the German firm. As such, the U.S. corporation is exempt from the regular German tax on intercorporate dividends.

This provision and others in the U.S.–German Treaty can greatly affect the profitablility of American firms in Germany. They should be carefully analyzed by companies studying the possibility of doing business in that country.

FEDERAL BUDGET

The 1994 federal budget was approved by the cabinet on September 7, 1993. It called for expenditures of DM 478 billion, a 4.4-percent increase over 1993. Revenues of DM 425.2 billion would leave a deficit of DM 53.2 billion (up from DM 49.8 billion in 1992).[7]

The largest budget expenditure for 1994 was social security, which was expected to cost DM 121.8 billion, a jump of 1.7 percent over 1993. By contrast, military defense for 1994 came to DM 48.6 billion, down 2.5 percent from 1993. This amounted to $29 billion for defense as opposed to $290 billion for the United States.

Federal expenditures have been growing as follows since 1987 in billions of marks:

1987	268
1988	275
1989	291
1990	311
1991	324
1992	425
1993	455
1994	478 (estimated)

In 1989, the last complete year before West Germany absorbed the East, federal expenditures were only DM 291 billion. Gradually starting in 1990, the burden of annexing the old Marxist state appears in the budget; expenditures for that year were up DM 20 billion. In 1991, the jump was DM 13 billion; in 1992, it really soared—by DM 101 billion.

Many Americans do not realize that Germany has been living with a federal deficit for years, long before unification in 1990. These deficits between 1975 and 1992 have been as follows in billions of marks:

1975	29.9
1976	25.8
1977	21.7
1978	25.9
1979	25.6
1980	27.1
1981	37.4
1982	37.2
1983	31.5
1984	28.3

1985	22.4
1986	22.9
1987	27.5
1988	35.4
1989	27.8
1990	30.0
1991	31.5
1992	50.5
1993	49.8
1994	53.2 (estimated)

It will be noted that the deficit shot up in 1981 to DM 37.4 billion from DM 27.1 billion in 1980 and hit DM 37.2 billion in 1982. These deficits were results of the recession then prevailing in Germany.

Germany had a federal debt of DM 690 billion as of December 31, 1993. This, too, had increased rapidly in the years before unity. Following are the figures in billions of marks as of year end in selected years:

1960	27
1965	40
1970	57
1975	114
1980	232
1985	392
1989	490
1991	590
1993	690

STATE BUDGETS

The sixteen states were budgeted in 1991 to spend DM 50.4 billion and collect income of DM 30.9 billion, resulting in a deficit of DM 19.5 billion. Total state debt at the end of 1991 was DM 344 billion.

At this point, some discussion is in order of financial balancing (*Finanz-ausgleich*), which attempts to balance the burden between richer and poorer states. The more affluent states pay into a common pool that is supplemented by payments from the federal government. At present, only two states—Baden-Württemberg and Hessen—are net contributors to the pool.

At one time, the net recipients (they have always constituted a majority) were happy with the system. Even before unity in 1990, some of them began to complain that they were not getting a fair share. They appealed to the Federal Constitutional Court, but they obtained no real improvement.[8]

The unification with five new eastern states made things even worse. If *Finanzausgleich* had been applied at once, all eleven of the old states would have become contributors. It was decided, however, to postpone this until 1995 when, it is hoped, the new eastern states will be in better shape.

The old states quickly agreed to make a small contribution to a newly created German Unity Fund, mainly paid for by the federal government. The finances of the new *Länder* are not getting much better, and by 1995 the old states will probably face a huge contribution (unless there is some reform of *Finanzausgleich*). As of the end of 1991, state debts amounted to DM 349 billion. This was a jump from DM 310 billion in 1989. The western states accounted for DM 346 billion, and the new states DM 3 billion of this 1991 total.[9]

Bavaria has a biennial budget, and on October 7, 1992, the State Finance Minister submitted his 1993–1994 budget to the Bavarian state legislature (*Landtag*). His proposal called for expenditures of DM 53.6 billion in 1993 (up 5.9 percent) and DM 55.6 billion in 1994 (up 3.9 percent). About one-third of these totals would go to education and science. Some DM 420 million in 1993 would be spent on asylum seekers, more than Bavaria spends on housing money benefits.

Under *Finanzausgleich*, Bavaria would pay DM 1.7 billion in 1993 and DM 1.9 billion in 1994 into the fund for the eastern states. As the Bavarian Finance Minister pointed out, in 1995 the eastern states will begin to contribute to *Finanzausgleich*; and Bavaria's share should decline to DM 1.5 billion. He had this to say to citizens complaining about contributions to easterners: "Germans, who spend DM 50 billion yearly for foreign vacations should not lament too loudly since peace and freedom in Europe have their price."[10]

Saxony's cabinet on October 7, 1992, approved this eastern state's budget for 1993. It called for DM 26.9 billion in expenditures, an increase of 3.9 percent over 1991. Only one-third of these expenses would be covered by taxes. About 47 percent of the budget outlay would come from contributions by the federal and old state governments. Saxony as of October 7, 1992, had 120,000 civil servants on the payroll. It was hoped to reduce this number to 102,000 by the end of 1993. The projected deficit for 1993 was DM 2.5 billion.[11]

For purposes of analysis, we will separate the state budgets into eastern and western for 1991, the first complete year of a unified Germany. Expenditures for the ten old states (excluding Berlin) came to DM 279.1 billion, while revenues were DM 264.2 billion, leaving a deficit of DM 14.8 billion. The five eastern states spent DM 10.7 billion more than their revenues. This came to DM 25.5 billion in combined state budget deficits.[12]

In the United States, total state expenditures in 1991 came to $661 billion (an increase of 9.8 percent over 1990), while revenues were $628 billion (up 4.6 percent). This created a deficit for the fifty states of $33 billion, but do not rush to congratulate the governors. About half of them are required by law to balance the budget every year.[13]

LOCAL BUDGETS

As of the end of 1993, local governments had total debt of DM 140 billion, up from DM 121 billion in 1989.[14] The German Association of Taxpayers annually publishes a "Black Book" (*Schwarzbuch*), which lists the outrageous or simply foolish ways that governments spend money. The prize for 1991 was a bridge built over the Blies River in southwest Germany. The town on the German side had agreed to pay DM 100,000 to construct the bridge. After its construction, it was discovered that the bridge was in France.[15]

TOTAL PUBLIC-SECTOR DEFICIT

Total public debt (including federal, state, local, railroad, postal, and Treuhand obligations) came to DM 1,840 billion as of the end of 1993. This was an increase of DM 1,305 billion since 1980, when it amounted to DM 535 billion.[16]

Total transfer payments from western to eastern Germany were DM 201 billion in 1992. They can be broken down as follows in billions of marks:[17]

Federal government	78
Western states and local units	15
Old-age pensions	19
Unemployment insurance	30
Treuhand Anstalt	30
Eastern railway (Reichsbahn)	10
Eastern telephones	9
Reconstruction banks	10

Germany has followed the dubious practice used by the United States and other countries to hide or mask public indebtedness by creating separate off-budget funds for financing government functions. The German Post Office and the two railway systems (Deutsche Bundesbahn in the West and Deutsche Reichsbahn in the East), along with three government-owned banks established by West Germany to make various reconstruction loans after World War II, all have separate debts.

Treuhand Anstalt, set up in 1990 to privatize the companies once owned by East Germany, also has authority to contract debt in its own name. And the German Unity Fund, organized to meet the deficits of the eastern states and local governments, is also authorized to borrow.

The Economist has tried to calculate the total public-sector debt of Germany as of December 31, 1991. Its study fixed the figure at DM 1,194 billion, broken down as follows, in billions of marks:[18]

Federal	590
Western states	346
Eastern states	3
Local governments	135
German unity fund	51
Treuhand	25
Other (post office, railways, and three banks)	44
Total	1,194

This represented 42.2 percent of GNP.

NOTES

1. *Taxation in the Federal Republic of Germany* (Chicago, Commerce Clearing House, 1963), p. 128.

2. *Los Angeles Times*, April 16, 1993.

3. *The Economist*, London, July 6, 1991, p. 85.

4. *Tagespiegel*, Berlin, April 6, 1990.

5. *New York Times*, July 14, 1994.

6. *Der Spiegel*, Hamburg, 20 (1993): 135.

7. *Frankfurter Allgemeine Zeitung*, August 14, 1993, September 8, 1993.

8. *The Economist*, London, April 25, 1992, p. 55.

9. "German Survey," *The Economist*, London, May 23, 1992, p. 5.

10. *Frankfurter Allgemeine Zeitung*, October 8, 1992.

11. Ibid.

12. *Frankfurter Allgemeine Zeitung*, July 3, 1992.

13. *New York Times*, October 22, 1992.

14. *Frankfurter Allgemeine Zeitung*, February 17, 1994.

15. *Wall Street Journal*, New York, October 30, 1991.

16. *Frankfurter Allgemeine Zeitung*, February 17, 1994.

17. *Der Spiegel*, Hamburg, 38 (1992): 25.

18. "German Survey," *The Economist*, p. 5.

12

Product Liability Law

In the United States, it is estimated about 15 percent of the price of machine tools is accounted for by the cost of product liability insurance. During the 1980s, total annual premiums for product liability insurance in America tripled to $20 billion, and some firms found it hard to find insurance at any price. Comparable premiums in Germany are about 20 percent of those paid in the United States.[1]

A 1985 study estimated that total costs of product liability lawsuits (attorney fees, payouts to claimants, and administrative costs of insurers) came to $80 billion, or 2.5 percent of GNP. By contrast, Switzerland, a poor second in this "tort tax," paid out only 0.7 percent. West Germany, in seventh place, had 0.5 percent.[2]

The average size of product liability court awards in the United States has multiplied ten times in real costs since 1960. It should be noted, however, that appeals and settlements after trial on the average reduce the award by 43 percent and that only 40 percent of the cost reaches the victim.[3]

In 1991, the top five awards in product liability cases in the United States were as follows:[4]

$127.7 million (Chicago): Product liability verdict against drug manufacturer Upjohn Co., alleging that the antiinflammation drug Depo-Medrol caused blindness, which resulted in loss of plaintiff's eye.

$91.3 million (Brooklyn): Forty-five-plaintiff consolidated award in case tried against Owens-Corning Fiberglass and other asbestos manufacturers.

$86.5 million (St. Louis): Sum of verdicts against Decom Medical Waste Systems, KML Corp., Bunker Resources, Recycling and Reclamation Inc., and Raymond Adams for accusing plaintiff of bringing AIDS virus into a hospital. Settled, amount sealed.

$84.5 million (Houston): Premises liability award against an apartment complex and its management company in case of children drowned and brain damaged in complex pool. Settled for $17 million.

$75 million (New York): Product liability case consolidating thirty-six plaintiffs against the Manville Trust, Owens-Illinois, and other asbestos manufacturers.

For more than a decade, business groups fought to restrict such suits; and in 1992, President Bush backed a bill to curb product liability by reforming the law at the federal level. It generated intense debate and vigorous lobbying on both sides but was voted down by a few votes in the Senate.[5]

FEWER PERILS IN GERMANY

Product liability law in Germany presents far fewer perils to a business than in the United States, making lawsuits less likely and damage awards less devastating. There are several features of German law contributing to this situation:

1. Jury trial does not exist in Germany. Cases tried by a judge alone are less influenced by emotional considerations and are less likely to result in excessive damages for the plaintiff.

2. Loser in German law case must pay court costs and attorney fees not only for himself but those of his adversary. This discourages frivolous suits by litigants.

3. Contingency fee arrangements (which allow American litigants to pay no legal fees unless the lawyer wins damages) are not allowed in Germany.

4. Generous social security benefits in Germany make injured party less inclined to go into court to recover damages.

5. Germans traditionally are less litigious than Americans.

6. Punitive damages are not awarded in Germany.

7. Damages for pain and suffering are harder to obtain under German law.

8. Lawyer's fees, under German law, are based on the amount requested in the complaint.

9. Court filing fees, under German law, are based on the amount requested in the complaint.

10. The product liability law in Germany is uniform throughout the sixteen states, while in the United States there are separate laws for all fifty jurisdictions and the District of Columbia. Also, juries vary greatly in generosity from state to state and even within the same state. Chicago has long had the reputation for providing extremely sympathetic jurors.

GERMAN LAW BEFORE 1990

German courts started gradually before World War II to develop the idea of product liability under the rules governing tort. Here, the most important statutory basis for product liability claims was Section 823(1) of the civil code. Under that provision, a person who intentionally, or negligently through a wrongful act, violates another person's rights to health, life, or property must pay compensation. In a long series of judgments, the Federal Supreme Court developed the principle that "whoever creates or controls a source of danger, opens a place to the public, or offers services or goods to the public must take all the necessary steps to avoid harm to anyone who uses these facilities."

The courts have said that a manufacturer must ensure that his products are safe. This general obligation entails many individual duties on the manufacturer's part, from the care devoted to the blueprints and production to the placing of the product on the market. Blueprints and production methods must reflect the latest state of science and technology. A manufacturer must organize his enterprise so as to avoid flaws in construction and production as well as to prevent mistakes in the instructions concerning the use of the product. There must be sufficient controls to detect potential errors during production, and there must also be checks on outside components that enter into the end product.

It was not until 1968, in its famous "chicken plague" case, that the Court achieved a judicial breakthrough in product liability by shifting the burden of proof from the buyer to the manufacturer. In that case, the Court held that all a plaintiff need show is a causal relationship between the injury and the defective product; the injured buyer does not need to prove fault on the manufacturer's part. However, it must be proven that the defect was caused by faulty plant organization or by violation of certain duties of care.

In 1975, the Federal Supreme Court extended the concept of product liability to cover individuals having an important and responsible position in the manufacturing process, such as production managers. This means that the burden of proof that falls on the manufacturer also falls on a production manager, who must prove that there was no negligence on his or her part with respect to the defective product. A production manager cannot escape liability by showing that the defect in the product could have been caused by something other than a fault in the organization. Like the manufacturer, the production manager must be allowed to adduce evidence that he or she did everything in his or her power to avoid producing defective products and that even the tightest controls cannot prevent an occasional slipup.

A manufacturer is anyone who produces goods, even if it only consists in assembling prefabricated parts. In this latter case, both the producer of the parts and the assembler may be considered manufacturers, and each of them is responsible for its share in the manufacturing process. The assembler cannot discharge its specific control obligations by sharing the production with another party.

Importers and distributors are not treated as manufacturers under the law. However, when affiliated with the manufacturer, they may have certain duties of care, such as to perform necessary quality tests they know were not done by the manufacturer; to monitor the products put on the market by it; and eventually, to issue warnings to the consumers.

German law recognizes three kinds of defects in products as follows:

1. *Design defect.* The safety of a product must comply with minimum safety requirements imposed by the state of the art at the time when the product is brought on the market. This is not the case if, for example, reasonable consumer protection devices are missing, the materials used do not have the solidity the consumer can reasonably expect, the use of an article is unnecessarily complicated, and even if the design itself induces the consumer to a dangerous use contrary to the instructions. The more dangerous a product can be, the stricter the safety requirements.

2. *Manufacturing defect.* The manufacturing process must be organized and supervised in a manner that, under the current state of technology, individual defects are eliminated to the extent possible. If, because of the type of product or the production process, defects cannot be eliminated fully, an adequate quality control must be provided.

3. *Instruction defect.* If a product, by its nature, implies certain risks, the manufacturer must warn and instruct the consumer. Such instructions must be clear and simple, which means, above all, in the language of the consumer. Such a duty exists even if the product itself is not dangerous but is ineffective under certain circumstances and the consumer, relying on its effectiveness, does not use another device to prevent damages.

PRODUCT LIABILITY ACT (1990)

In 1985, after many years of controversial discussion, the EU adopted a Product Liability Directive which obligated Germany and the other eleven member states to change their national laws to comply with the directive. Germany implemented this directive in 1988 by passing the Productive Liability Act (*Produkthaftungsgesetz*), ProdHaftG for short.

The statute went into effect on January 1, 1990, with the following provisions:[6]

1. The manufacturer is strictly liable for personal and property damages caused by defects of its products, irrespective of negligence being involved. A product is considered defective if it does not provide the safety that can reasonably be expected under the current state of the art.

2. The term *manufacturer* includes the importer who brings products into the Union as well as persons or entities that only affix their trademarks or trade names to a product manufactured by somebody else.

3. Advance agreements aimed at the exclusion or limitation of product liability are prohibited.

4. Any contributory negligence by the injured party will reduce or eliminate damages recovered.

5. Injured party cannot recover more than DM 160 million if the death or personal injury was caused by one product with the same defect.

6. To discourage frivolous suits, the claimant must ask for at least DM 1,125.

7. Damages for pain and suffering are not recoverable.

8. The manufacturer has these defenses:

    a. It did not bring the defective device on the market.

    b. The defect did not exist when the product was brought on the market.

    c. The defect results from complying with mandatory law.

    d. The defendant was only responsible for a component of the product, and the defect relates to the construction of the final product.

    e. The manufacturer can prove that the defect could not be detected given the state of the technological and scientific knowledge available at the time when the product was put on the market. This "developmental risk defense" existed before 1990 and was not changed by the Product Liability Act. The Product Liability Directive of the EU actually granted Germany and other member states the option to abolish this defense. Germany decided not to change.

9. When the manufacturer is unknown, distributors or retailers can be sued.

NOTES

1. *The Economist*, London, February 13, 1993, p. 63.
2. *Forbes*, New York, February 17, 1992, p. 40.
3. *The Economist*, London, December 2, 1989, p. 84.
4. *Forbes*, New York, February 17, 1992, p. 40.
5. *New York Times*, September 13, 1992.
6. *Tagespiegel*, Berlin, January 21, 1990.

13

Antitrust Law

U.S. business has been living with antitrust law since the Sherman Act was passed in 1890. Although Germany adopted antitrust legislation in 1923, it was of little impact on the nation that seemed addicted to cartelization.

After the defeat of Nazi Germany in 1945, the Occupying Powers in West Germany (United States, United Kingdom, and France) imposed a severe antitrust law. To the surprise of many observers, the West Germans retained such legal controls after independence in 1949.

The struggle between those Germans like Professor Ludwig Erhard (then Economics Minister and later Chancellor), who wanted an antitrust law, and the conservatives anxious to return to the cartel system dragged on for eight years after West Germany was created in 1949. Professor Volker R. Berghahn, a Brown University historian, has carefully portrayed this political conflict and the important role played by the United States in tilting victory to supporters of antitrust legislation. Berghahn points out that Washington invited Erhard and many other influential Germans to visit the American industrial scene to see firsthand the benefits of the competitive system.[1] To residents of war-torn Germany, the prosperous U.S. economy must have been extremely impressive.

In 1957, West Germany entered the European Union under the Treaty of Rome. This treaty and subsequent treaties imposed another layer of antitrust regulation on business operations within the EU.

When there is a conflict between EU antitrust law and that of Germany, the former must prevail. A case decided by the European Court of Justice in

May 1993 illuminates the problem. The Federal Supreme Court of Germany had found a French company in violation of the German law prohibiting comparative price advertising. This statute bans ads that are eye catching in drawing attention to the new price of a product by juxtaposing it with the old price. The German government argued that such advertising is frequently misleading because the customer is in no position to check the old price against the new. The European court found that the German law infringed on the Treaty of Rome in that it curbed the free movement of goods among the member states.[2]

GERMAN ANTITRUST LAW

Unification of the German states in 1871 provided ideal conditions for industrial expansion. More factories were established between 1870 and 1873 than in the preceding seventy years of the century. This set a favorable stage for German corporations to form cartels, which agreed to limit production and fix prices. In 1879, a protective tariff law was enacted to eliminate or at least reduce the flow of foreign goods into the German market. This also proved a boost to cartelization. From 14 cartels in 1877, the number jumped to 80 by 1875, to 200 by 1895, and about 275 by the turn of the century.

The Germans felt that huge monopolies make for efficiency and economy. During the 1920s, several more were created. In 1925, the super cartel was formed by eight of the already-cartelized top chemical and dye firms (Interessengemeinschaft Farbenindustrie AG, usually called I. G. Farben). This giant holding company monopolized the chemical business not only in Germany but in central Europe and, with the passage of time, in a good part of the world.[3] It was the fourth-largest corporation of the world after GM, USX, and Exxon. I. G. Farben was the parent of the "Big Three" chemicals: BASF (Badische Anilin-und Soda Fabrik), Hoechst, and Bayer. It reached full strength under Hitler.

I. G. Farben turned out a huge variety of products, from tires for the planes of the Luftwaffe to Zyklon B gas used to exterminate prisoners in the concentration camps. It also invented military nerve gases, which Hitler did not use out of fear of Allied reprisals.

Many German firms used slave labor during World War II, but I. G. Farben was the most notorious. It had 25,000 workers furnished by Auschwitz and other concentration camps. After the war, the firm paid out DM 30 million by way of compensation to Jewish groups.

The U.S. military government reported in 1945 that "without I. G. Farben the German prosecution of World War II would have been impossible and unthinkable,"[4] a naive overstatement, but reflecting the awesome image of the cartel. The occupiers were determined to break up the industrial concentration of Nazi Germany, and I. G. Farben was high on the list for dismemberment. By 1951, it was broken up into twelve parts, including BASF, Hoechst, and Bayer.[5] These three have since regained and even surpassed their prewar status. Each one is now larger than its former parent at the zenith.

The remaining assets were transferred to a new corporation in Frankfurt with the title of I. G. Farben in Abwicklung (in liquidation). Its stock is listed on the Frankfurt Stock Exchange as "I. G. Farben Liquidations Anteilscheine" (Liquidation participating shares), called "Liquis" for short.

The assets of the new company consisted mainly of contested claims against foreign properties that once belonged to the original I. G. Farben. Its stock price varied with the changing prospects of recovering on these claims. Quoted as low as DM 1.50 at one time, Liquis were selling at DM 12 just before the fall of the Berlin Wall on November 9, 1989. Then the stock shot up to DM 32 because of hopes of recovering plants and undeveloped land in East Germany that were nationalized after 1945 by the Soviet Union and later transferred to the East German government. These assets were carried on the I. G. Farben balance sheet at DM 1 billion.

The firm has taken legal steps to recover on its claims in the East, but speculators are now much less optimistic. The company has predicted that the proceedings will probably last until 1997.[6] In July 1994, the Liquis were quoted at DM 6.

As previously mentioned, the Germans astonished the world by becoming serious converts to American antitrust legislation after Allied Occupation ended in 1949. Their key statute, Law against Restraints on Competition of 1957 (*Gesetz gegen Wettbewerbsbeschränkungen*), GWB for short, has been amended four times, the last in 1980.

The term *cartel* (*Kartell*) in the legal tradition of Germany was limited to agreements imposing horizontal restraints upon competition concluded between enterprises on the same level of production or distribution to coordinate their impact on the market and thus achieve a common purpose. Assume that the 1,300 German breweries would enter a contract to reduce their production by 50 percent in 1996 to reduce the supply and raise the price of beer. That would be a cartel in the traditional sense of the term.

German antitrust law covers far more than cartels. It extends to "concerted practices" (actions by which enterprises impose horizontal restraints on competition without entering a contractual obligation). Also, it applies to vertical restraints on competition as well as other unfair practices. An example of a vertical restraint would be 100 breweries signing contracts with Bavarian hop growers, under which the latter agree to limit their sales to the 100 brewers. Furthermore, monopolies, oligopolies, mergers, and acquisitions are also included in German antitrust legislation.

It was the huge, efficient German cartels in steel, chemicals, and other products that first dominated public attention and led to regulatory legislation by the Reichstag and still later by the Bundestag.

The agency responsible for enforcing German antitrust laws is the Federal Cartel Office (*Bundeskartellamt*) in Berlin, usually referred to by its English abbreviation as the FCO. Its chief executive is a president, appointed for a term of eight years.

The Law against Restraints on Competition (GWB) declares cartel agreements to be null and void and thus unenforceable. However, it does provide for numerous exceptions as follows:

1. Export and import cartels.
2. Agreements relating solely to business terms and rebates with no price-fixing.
3. Cartels formed because of a substantial decline of demand in an industry.
4. Rebate cartels with no price fixing.

In all cases of exemptions, the participating firms must file a copy of their agreement with the FCO, which may intervene in case it finds anything contrary to law.

Mergers and acquisitions must be reported to the FCO in advance where one of the merging enterprises has annual sales of DM 2 billion or where two of the firms have sales of DM 1 billion each. The FCO may presume a market-dominating position and disallow the merger if any of the following occurs:

1. An enterprise with annual sales of more than DM 2 billion merges with any enterprise that has domination of its market.
2. An enterprise with annual sales of more than DM 2 billion merges with an enterprise that operates in a market consisting of medium-size enterprises.
3. The combined enterprises would have total annual sales of DM 12 billion, and at least two of the combining enterprises have annual sales in excess of DM 1 billion each.

There is also a group of smaller mergers and acquisitions, which must notify the FCO after they have been consummated. This is required if one of the following criteria exists:

1. The participating companies, together, have reached, in the last full fiscal year, worldwide sales in excess of DM 500 million.
2. The participating companies, in the last full fiscal year, have employed 10,000 or more persons.
3. The participating companies, alone or jointly, have reached a market share of 20 percent in the markets affected by the merger.
4. The participating companies have a market share of 20 percent or more in other markets.

Completion of an intended merger, which is subject to premerger notification, prior to approval by the FCO is prohibited and void. Intended mergers that do not require premerger notification may voluntarily request a preliminary examination and avoid the risk of a cease-and-desist order after completion. However, for a premerger notification (in contrast to a postmerger notification), a fee is payable, based on the complexity of the merger proposal but not exceeding DM 100,000. Both kinds of merger notification must contain extensive details about the participating companies and their relative market positions.

Probably the most important case thus far to come before FCO was the Daimler-Benz acquisition of Messerschmitt-Bölkow-Blohm GmbH in 1989 for $854 million. This merger lifted Daimler to the largest firm in Germany, the third in the EU, and tenth in the world. It now had combined sales of $48 billion and a work force of 380,000.

The FCO turned down the proposed merger on the ground that it would lead to a market-dominating position in German defense production. However, the decision was one that could be appealed to the Economics Ministry in Bonn. The Minister reversed the FCO subject to the following conditions:[7]

1. Messerschmitt must divest itself of its 12.5-percent holding in the stock of the arms manufacturer, Krauss-Maffei AG.

2. Messerschmitt and Daimler must both give up their activities in marine technology.

3. Daimler must take over from the government its 20-percent stake in Deutsche Airbus GmbH. (This had great weight in securing approval of the Ministry because Bonn was anxious to shed its costly burden.)

Another major decision of the FCO was announced in 1992 involving Allianz AG, Europe's largest insurance company, which wanted to increase its stockholding in Dresdner Bank from 19.1 percent to 22.3 percent.[8]

In 1989, Allianz and Dresdner, Germany's second largest bank, agreed to sell each others' services, cementing the relationship by taking a 10-percent stake in each other. Allianz increased this to 19.1 percent by 1992 and then wanted to go up another 3.2 percent.

The FCO rejected this proposal on the ground that Allianz through intermediate holdings in firms—which, in turn, owned shares in Dresdner—really had far more influence than the 19.1 percent directly owned shares indicated. One study stated that Allianz had a total control of 47 percent.[9]

The president of FCO stated that "Allianz wishes to be sure that Dresdner cannot have an affair with a stranger. But we cartel officials are more for free love."[10] The case is now being contested in the courts, where it could take years to be decided.

American companies also have been blocked in acquisitions by the FCO. In 1992, Gillette made a move to acquire Wilkinson Sword Europe GmbH, located in Solingen, Germany. The FCO refused to approve the proposed merger, pointing out that Gillette had 62 percent of the German razor market and Wilkinson 34 percent.[11]

Fried. Krupp GmbH, a major steel producer both in Germany and Europe, pulled off a hostile takeover of a competitor, Hoesch AG, in 1992, a rare feat in Germany. The deal was finally blessed by the FCO.

Krupp and Hoesch were about equal in sales in 1990—DM 16 billion each. Both had about 47 percent of their sales in steel, but Krupp had net income of DM 217 million and Hoesch DM 103 million.

Krupp began quietly to buy up Hoesch stock and by September 1991, announced that it held 24.9 percent, a move called a "friendly partnership" by Krupp. Hoesch called it a "hostile takeover, a bomb being dropped that shook the eastern Ruhr Valley."[12]

At first, Hoesch hinted that it would fight but soon found that Krupp had lined up an additional 30.4 percent of Hoesch stock in the hands of various German banks and institutional investors. Moreover, Herbert Zapp, a management board member of Deutsche Bank, was also chairman of the Hoesch supervisory board (and Deutsche Bank supported the merger).

The merger became final in May 1992 and created the second-largest steel firm in Germany after Thyssen. Krupp acquired more than 50 percent of the stock of Hoesch for an exchange of 1.3 shares of Krupp plus DM 6 for each share of Hoesch.

After the approval of the FCO, there was a separate proceeding by the European Commission to determine compliance of the Krupp-Hoesch fusion with the antitrust law of the Union. The Commission stated that the deal did not create or strengthen a dominant position, since there were still many competitors in the market. It went on to point out that Krupp and Hoesch combined would still be considerably smaller than the four largest steel producers in the EU.[13]

One of the conditions imposed by the FCO in approving the Krupp–Hoesch merger was the divesting of Krupp's vehicle spring manufacturing division before the end of 1993. As the agency pointed out, Krupp and Hoesch combined produced more than 60 percent of the vehicle springs on the market, which would raise the danger of the combined enterprise having a dominant market position.

However, just before the deadline, Krupp-Hoesch served notice of cancellation of this agreement, arguing that market conditions had changed. The firm had a bad slump in demand from the automobile industry in 1993 and lost DM 50 million in the vehicle spring division. It also stated that if Krupp sold its facility, the Hoesch unit could not survive.

The FCO in Berlin announced on February 28, 1994, that it would not accept this unilateral cancellation. It ordered Krupp-Hoesch to sell the division or FCO would appoint an independent trust to do so on its behalf. Krupp-Hoesch said it will appeal to the Court of Appeals in Berlin. Several months will be needed to obtain a decision.[14]

The FCO reported in June 1993 that the reunification of Germany had greatly increased the number of mergers and warned that they were often hindering competition in eastern Germany. During 1989 and 1990, a total of 2,962 mergers were registered at the FCO. This jumped to 3,750 in 1991 and 1992.[15]

More than 1,300 of these mergers involved enterprises from the East acquired by western firms, sometimes to stem competition in the new states. During 1991 and 1992, FCO blocked four planned mergers, bringing the agency's total to 101. It complained that too much concentration had developed among grocers, disposal firms, and television stations.

Another interesting action involving a U.S. firm came before the FCO in 1982. The agency prohibited Philip Morris of New York, from acquiring a 50-percent interest in Rothmans Tobacco Holding, London, to the extent that the effects would be felt in West Germany. It was the first time that an FCO decision based on the effects doctrine involved two companies incorporated outside Germany. Although the order had no effect on the actual takeover abroad, the FCO maintained that it has the statutory power to prevent effects in Germany, and the parent companies' merger abroad would result in a merger of the German companies. The Berlin Court of Appeals largely upheld the FCO's order.

During an appeal to the Federal Supreme Court, the parties restructured the acquisition to result in only 30.8 percent of the nominal shares, with only 24.9 percent of the voting rights going to Philip Morris. The FCO, in analyzing the agreements and underlying circumstances, found that Philip Morris had in fact obtained a stronger position than reflected by 24.9 percent of the voting rights and again prohibited the entire merger. The Federal Supreme Court decided that the initial prohibition procedure of FCO did not cover the restructure. The new prohibition has been withdrawn by the FCO, which felt unable to obtain evidence from abroad. The international aspects are thus still unsettled.

Exxon, through its German subsidiary, Deutsche Esso AG, along with four other major oil companies, was ordered by FCO to reduce retail gasoline prices by $0.03 per liter in the Hamburg area in 1990. Regular leaded gasoline was lowered from $0.89 to $0.86 per liter.[16]

Another important German law affecting competition is the Law against Unfair Competition, (*Gesetz gegen den unlauteren Wettbewerb*), UWG for short. This statute primarily covers unfair advertising. It bans comparative advertising and "free gifts." Also, it prohibits claims of exclusivity or superlatives or any other claims, the truth of which cannot be supported by evidentiary fact.

Similar regulations apply to special sales drives, even down to comparative pricing in shop windows and on sales racks. Products advertised must be available in sufficient quantities to satisfy consumer demand.

The law is particularly effective because of the system of enforcement. Every business can take legal action against unlawful advertising of a competitor. In addition there are nonprofit associations with the main objective of enforcement of advertising law. They do a thriving business.

Any violation of advertising laws can be the subject of a motion for cease and desist or a temporary injunction to prevent repetition. Normally, these cases are settled very quickly.

This Law against Unfair Competition also prohibits use of a place name on a product if the item is produced elsewhere. Thus, German sparkling wine cannot be called Champagne, which is a French province renowned for its bubbly. The German wineries thus concocted the name *Sekt*, a very uninspiring title for wines that are truly delightful.

This same law has kept Anheuser-Busch from selling its Budweiser in Germany. As pointed out in detail in Chapter 22, the original Budweiser is sold in Germany by a Czech brewery in the city of Budweis south of Prague. This Budweiser beer is about 600 years older than that of St. Louis and sells about one-fourth of its highly regarded output to the discriminating German public.

The law provides for fines against firms and their officers of up to DM 1 million and an amount equal to triple the additional profit because of the unlawful conduct. The decisions of the FCO may be appealed in court.

EUROPEAN UNION ANTITRUST LAW

As mentioned earlier, the Treaty of Rome of 1957 and subsequent agreements spell out the basic principles of antitrust law of the European Union. These principles have been applied by the European Commission and interpreted by the European Court of Justice (see Chapter 8 for descriptions of these two institutions). This body of law applies to German business and that of the other eleven member nations.

The European Commission has the following powers:

1. To curb firms that so dominate their fields as to abuse their market positions.
2. To block national subsidies that give one company an unfair advantage over others elsewhere in the EU.
3. To regulate joint ventures.
4. To approve or disapprove major mergers and acquisitions across national boundaries.

One of the seventeen members on the European Commission is designated as Commissioner for Antitrust Policy. The current holder of this position is a Belgian, Karl van Miert.

Between September 1990 and March 1993, a total of 137 mergers were referred to the commission. The results were as follows:

Found not subject to EU regulation	15
Approved within one month	113
Approved after full investigation	2

| Approved after full investigation with conditions | 6 |
| Blocked | 1 |

The speed of the Commission's action surprised everyone. Only three were contested, but *The Economist* characterized this in its headline as "Getting Away with Merger."[17]

A major case involving a U.S. firm was decided in 1992 when the European Commission placed restrictions on a joint venture between Ford and Volkswagen involving minivans in Portugal. The most controversial restriction involved the use of VW engines in Ford minivans. (Ford could not use VW engines in more than 25 percent of its minivans over a three-year period.) The Commission also required the two firms to establish distinct distribution channels, avoid pricing cooperation, market the vans separately, and have some differences in styling.[18]

Mention was made earlier of Gillette's problem with the German FCO, which prohibited acquisition of Wilkinson Sword. The European Commission went further and ordered Gillette to divest itself of its 22-percent stake in Eemland Holdings N.V. in Holland, which owns Wilkinson Sword.[19]

In 1992, the Commission fined Parker Pen Holdings Ltd. in the United Kingdom and Herlitz AG of Germany for breaking EC competition rules, which forbade companies fixing their trading conditions. Parker had entered an agreement in August 1986, which prohibited Herlitz from exporting Parker's pens from Germany without Parker's consent. Parker was fined 700,000 ECUs ($962,000), and Herlitz was fined 40,000 ECUs.[20]

Sony of Japan and Daimler-Benz of Germany both ran into trouble with the European Commission in that they bought land for their Berlin offices for bargain prices on Potsdamer Platz. After the Berlin Wall fell in 1989, Potsdamer Platz (which was the center of Greater Berlin before 1945 and was transformed into a wasteland by the Wall) became a highly desirable commercial location. The city of Berlin was anxious to attract prestigious multinational companies to build in this area.

In July 1990, Daimler-Benz purchased 62,000 square meters for DM 92.9 million as a site for the headquarters of its Debis subsidiary. The EU Commission found that this price of DM 33.8 million was too low and that this constituted a subsidy in violation of Commission regulations. Daimler was ordered to pay the undercharge to Berlin.

Sony bought the equivalent of seven football fields on Potsdamer Platz in 1991 for its European headquarters, as well as a hotel, shops, and restaurants. The price was not disclosed, but it was estimated at DM 102 million. Here again, the Commission found the price well below a fair market quotation, thus amounting to a subsidy from Berlin. Sony, as of February 1993, said that if it is ordered to pay more for the site, "Our company has to review totally the original plan, which means withdrawal of the project is probable."[21]

A very interesting case decided in November 1990 was a proposed joint venture between Renault of France and Volvo of Sweden to assemble cars, trucks, and buses. The Commission approved on the grounds that competition would not be disturbed. As everyone now knows, Volvo's stockholders refused to ratify the deal and both parties became disengaged.

Another significant case involved Solvay (Belgium) and ICI (United Kingdom), Europe's two major producers of soda ash (a key ingredient in glass). They were adjudged to have agreed not to compete with each other by dividing up the European market. In December 1990, Solvay was fined $40 million and ICI $23 million.

NOTES

1. Volker R. Berghahn, *The Americanization of West German Industry 1945–1973* (New York: Berg, 1986), pp. 155–181.
2. *Financial Times*, London, June 8, 1993.
3. Marshall Dill, Jr., *Germany: A Modern History* (Ann Arbor: University of Michigan Press, 1961), p. 309.
4. *Der Spiegel*, Hamburg, 49 (1991): 138.
5. David Marsh, *The Germans: A People at the Crossroads* (New York: St. Martin's, 1989), p. 15.
6. *Frankfurter Allgemeine Zeitung*, August 26, 1992.
7. *International Herald-Tribune*, Paris, September 9, 1989.
8. *Financial Times*, London, April 22, 1992.
9. *Financial Times*, London, April 2, 1992.
10. *Financial Times*, London, April 22, 1992.
11. *Frankfurter Allgemeine Zeitung*, July 24, 1992.
12. *New York Times*, November 11, 1991.
13. *Wall Street Journal*, New York, May 26, 1992.
14. *Financial Times*, London, March 2, 1994.
15. *Financial Times*, London, June 29, 1993.
16. *Wall Street Journal*, New York, October 22, 1990.
17. *The Economist*, London, June 12, 1993, p. 84.
18. *Wall Street Journal*, New York, December 2, 1992.
19. *Wall Street Journal*, New York, November 12, 1992.
20. *Wall Street Journal*, New York, July 16, 1992.
21. *Wall Street Journal*, New York, February 3, 1993.

14

Labor Law

FAVORABLE CLIMATE

Since the founding of the FRG in 1949, German workers, both blue-collar and white-collar, have gained rights beyond those attained in any other country. This is the result of a variety of important factors:

1. The federal government has expanded the rights of workers by new statutes, such as the Works Council Act of 1972 and the Codetermination Act of 1976. There is a law requiring an employer to pay an insurance premium of 0.5 percent of payroll to guarantee back pay if the employer goes bankrupt. Also, under law, the employer must pay the salary of a pregnant woman for six weeks prior to her confinement.
2. The labor courts have turned out a large volume of case law, further protecting the workers.
3. The labor unions have extracted major concessions at the bargaining table. Some employers under contract pay a Christmas bonus, usually amounting to a month's salary, and a vacation bonus (which may run as high as DM 300 to DM 500). Other employers grant these benefits voluntarily.
4. Labor and management have cooperated responsibly in a manner seldom found elsewhere in the world. Employers seem less inclined to engage in anti-union measures.

All of these have contributed to a high degree of labor peace in the last five years for which figures are available (1988–1992). The leading nations of the world lost the following numbers of strike days per 1,000 workers:[1]

Switzerland	0.4
Japan	4.0
West Germany	5.6
Austria	6.0
Holland	9.6
France	64.0
United States	69.4
Sweden	100.6
United Kingdom	125.6
Italy	251.4
Spain	678.4
Greece	840.0

German manufacturing workers are among the best paid in the world. A recent study conducted by the *Wall Street Journal* shows the following annual compensation based on April 1, 1992, exchange rates:[2]

Germany	$36,857
Canada	$34,935
Japan	$34,263
Italy	$31,537
France	$30,019
United States	$27,606
United Kingdom	$26,084

By contrast, the same survey showed the following compensation levels for chief executive officers (CEOs):

United States	$717,237
France	$479,772
Italy	$463,009
United Kingdom	$439,441
Canada	$416,066
Germany	$390,933
Japan	$390,723

LABOR UNIONS

Between 1970 and 1987, the percentage of unionized nonagricultural workers in most industrialized countries declined, whereas it increased from 39 percent to 42 percent in Germany. In the United States, the fall was from 31 percent to 17 percent. Japan, the United Kingdom, France, Italy, and Holland all dropped but not as sharply as America.[3]

German unions, however, are facing a problem common to all industrialized nations in that the percentage of manufacturing workers in the work force is declining, while the percentage in services is growing. Service employees are less willing to unionize. Between 1960 and 1990, the percentage of manufacturing workers in the German work force dropped from 57.3 percent to 42.3 percent, while the service percentage grew from 40.2 percent to 56.8 percent.[4]

Labor unions in Germany differ greatly from those in the United States. While they are much stronger, there is also a much more cooperative and less adversarial relationship between unions and management. Furthermore, the German government has shown a disposition to work far more harmoniously with both unions and management than is the case in America.

Until 1933, German workers were organized as craft unions, which negotiated solely for their members. This resulted in a complicated system of labor agreements. It was quite common for people doing the same work to receive different pay.

During World War II, industrial unions began to replace craft unions. In 1990, there were sixteen industrial unions in West Germany, which formed the German Labor Union Federation (*Deutscher Gewerkshaftsbund*), DGB for short. Total membership was 7.9 million at the end of 1990.

When the two German states were merged in 1990, the DGB moved swiftly to organize the workers of eastern Germany. There had been 9.6 million members in thirteen Marxist industrial unions, set up along much the same jurisdictional lines as the DGB. Membership in one of these East German unions was compulsory. They had no real power except as a political instrument to strengthen the loyalty of workers to the state.[5]

Eventually, about 3.9 million (less than half) of the eastern union members joined the DGB, bringing membership to 11.8 million by the end of 1991. The following year proved disastrous for workers in the East. Unemployment increased by over 1 million, and DGB membership shrank to 10.3 million by December 31, 1993.

The sixteen unions and their individual memberships were as follows as of the end of 1992:[6]

IG Metall (Metal)	3,394,282
Öffentl. Dienste, Transport u. Verkehr (Public Service and Transport)	2,114,522
IG Chemie—Papier—Keramik (Chemical, Paper, and Ceramics)	818,832
IG Bau Steine Erden (Construction)	695,712
Handel, Banken und Versicherungen (Commerce, Banking, and Insurance)	629,727

Deutsche Postgewerkschaft (Postal)	611,244
Eisenbahner Deutschlands (Railroad)	474,530
IG Bergbau und Energie (Mining and Energy)	457,239
Nahrung—Genuß—Gaststätten (Food and Catering)	394,686
Erziehung und Wissenschaft (Teachers and Scientists)	346,040
Textil—Bekleidung (Textiles and Garments)	288,198
IG Medien (Media)	236,306
Holz und Kunststoff (Wood and Synthetics)	204,763
Gewerkschaft der Polizei (Police)	197,451
Gartenbau, Land—und Forstwirtschaft (Garden, Farm, and Forest)	120,190
Leder (Leather)	31,890

COLLECTIVE BARGAINING

The Nazis (1933–1945) abolished all rights of collective bargaining for German workers. After the surrender in 1945, the Allied military commanders introduced new laws, once again granting the right to organize unions and engage in collective bargaining.

Article 9 of the German Constitution guarantees both employees and employers the right to form associations for negotiating collective bargaining agreements. Employer groups are powerful and well organized. Their nationwide top association for labor contracts is the Federal Organization of Employers' Federations (*Bundesvereinigung der deutschen Arbeitgeberverbände*), BDA for short. There are employer associations for every branch of business.

The courts have given Article 9 a still broader interpretation, ruling that no worker can be forced either directly or indirectly to join a union. Also, a worker must not incur any disadvantage as a result of so joining.

In 1972, Germany adopted a Works Council Act (*Betriebsverfassungsgesetz*) which provides for a shop council (*Betriebsrat*) in all companies that regularly employ at least five employees. In companies up to twenty employees, the functions of the shop council are performed by one employee. In larger companies, the membership increases to more than thirty-one in cases of more than 9,000 workers.

The principal duties of the shop council are as follows:

1. Ensuring that all laws, collective bargaining agreements, and other rules are observed.
2. Recommending to management measures that will serve the interests of the plant and its workers.

3. Being informed in advance by employer of his general planning as to personnel.

4. In companies with more than twenty employees, consenting to new hiring or transfer or regrouping of employees.

5. Being notified at least one week in advance of employer's intention to fire a worker.

In addition to labor's participation in decisions at the shop level, as outlined previously, the shop council also has rights to representation on the supervisory board in three classes of companies as follows:

1. Corporations with more than 500 employees must have one-third of the supervisory board members elected by the employees. The board may consist of three members, but any larger number must be divisible by three. In the case of a three-member board, the labor representative must be an employee of the company. With larger boards, at least two must be employees.

2. Corporations with more than 2,000 employees must have labor representatives in half the seats on the supervisory board. This group of companies numbers about 650 of some 300,000 German corporations. About forty U.S. subsidiaries are covered. The Codetermination Act of 1976 (*Mitbestimmungsgesetz*) spells out the legal requirements. The method of selecting labor representatives on the supervisory board is quite complicated, but at least one must be an employee (salary earner) picked by the executive staff. This usually ensures a one-member majority sympathetic to management.

3. Coal and steel corporations are covered by a separate Codetermination Act of 1951. Here also, the workers and shareholders have an equal number of representatives on the supervisory board. A majority of labor members must be elected by the unions. The labor and shareholder representatives then elect a neutral chairperson of the supervisory board to avoid a deadlock.

There is no right to strike spelled out in the German Constitution. However, Article 9 has been interpreted by the courts to grant the right to strike by the workers and the right to lockout by the employer. Even without this case law, the European Social Charter (a treaty) has been signed by all members of the European Union. West Germany signed this agreement in 1965, thereby explicitly granting Germans the right to strike and the right to the lockout (including nonstrikers).

EMPLOYMENT CONTRACT

German law distinguishes between salaried employees (*Angestellte*) and wage earners (*Arbeiter*). Salaried employees (white-collar workers) perform predominantly mental work, such as office employees, and their salary is usually calculated by the month. Wage earners (blue-collar workers) include all others, and their wages are usually on an hourly basis. This distinction applies to representation on the shop floor, collective bargaining agreements, and codetermination seats on the supervisory boards.

Germany also has another class of employees, known as supervisory employees (*Leitende Angestellte*). An employee with general power to represent the firm (*Generalvollmacht*) or to sign contracts on behalf of the firm (*Prokurist*) is generally classified as a supervisory employee. These criteria leave many borderline positions, which must be decided on a case-by-case basis in the courts.

Employment contracts in Germany do not need to be in writing, except those involving apprentices or collective bargaining agreements that contain a provision requiring that they be reduced to writing. In all other cases, an oral agreement alone will be binding on both employer and employee. Nevertheless, it is recommended that all labor contracts be put in written form in the interest of clarity to avoid future disputes.

A probation employment contract (widely used in Germany) must be put in writing, but it cannot normally exceed six months unless part of a collective bargaining agreement. During the probationary term, the contract may be terminated on short notice by either party without giving a reason (two weeks).

EAST–WEST WAGE PROBLEM

When Monetary Unification became effective on July 1, 1990, the wages previously paid to East Germans in east marks were then paid in marks on a basis of 1:1. The average easterner thus received about 33 percent of what his western counterpart took in his pay envelope. Unfortunately, he was only about 15 percent as productive.

West German labor unions were understandably anxious to bring eastern wage levels up to those in the West as quickly as possible. In March 1991, steel and metal companies in the East signed a union contract with IG Metall under which wages of eastern workers would be gradually raised to the level of their western counterparts by July 1, 1994. As of March 1993, eastern wages had reached 60 percent of those in the West. The next step in this upward wage adjustment called for a 26-percent increase on April 1, 1993, for metal workers and 21 percent for steel. A few weeks before this pay raise was to go into effect, the steel and metal employers unilaterally scrapped the increases on the grounds that they could not afford them. This sparked a strike by more than 40,000 members of IG Metall, who voted 85 percent in favor (75 percent was the required minimum). About 300,000 western workers walked out in sympathy.

There had not been a strike in the East in sixty years, since the Nazis banned strikes and other union activities. On May 3, IG Metall called a strike in fifty plants. After eight weeks, a settlement was reached granting the 26-percent increase by December 1, 1993, instead of April 1, as originally agreed. That brought the workers to about 80 percent of western rates. Final equality at 100 percent will now come on July 1, 1996, two years later than called for in the 1991 contract.[7] The terms apply to 450,000 workers; but the new contract says nothing about productivity, which is still only about 40 percent of the level prevailing in the West. However, there is an escape hardship clause that the individual employer may invoke if IG Metall agrees to cooperate. This would enable the firm to pay less than the wages called for in the agreement.[8]

APPRENTICESHIPS

As of June 1993, only 4.9 percent of Germans aged 16 to 24 were unemployed, compared with 5.6 percent for the population as a whole. It was the only country in the EU where unemployment for young workers was lower than that for the entire work force. In France, youths had 23 percent, while overall unemployment was 10.8 percent.[9] One powerful cause of this fortunate situation in Germany is its highly respected apprenticeship system, which had 1.6 million youngsters on its payrolls as of the time when the survey was made.

The European apprenticeship system began in the eleventh century, but it reached its highest development in Germany after 1949. There are now some 400 different careers recognized by the German government. To fully practice one of them, the student must hold a diploma from a specialized school. These apprenticeship schools are run by the combined support of government, employers, and unions.

For example, a young Berliner finished school in 1992 at the age of 19. He applied for and was accepted as an apprentice metal worker with Siemens, the giant manufacturer of electronics and computer products. He is one of 1,100 young people learning some twenty trades at Siemens. His three-year course combines classes in theory and on-the-job training. He is paid about DM 1,000 per month and will earn three to five times that amount when he completes his course. A recent survey of 10,000 German apprentices showed that 95 percent found their learning programs interesting. Budget figures show that the federal government annually spends about DM 7.6 billion on apprenticeship programs. It is estimated that industry invests DM 14,000 per year in each apprentice on its payrolls.[10]

At the end of 1992, there were 1,388,000 (down 3 percent from 1991) undergoing training in the West and 278,000 in the East (up 18 percent over 1991).[11] In the West, the average apprentice earned DM 920 per month in 1992 and DM 620 in the East. The best paid were scaffold mechanics, who made DM 1,686 in the old states and DM 1,349 in the new. Masons, carpenters, and stucco mechanics were also well paid. Lowest on the scale were barbers for men—DM 265 in the West and DM 210 in the East.[12] Auto mechanic was most popular for boys, with 74,000 enrolled, while 62,000 girls selected office work.[13]

The apprentice must pass an examination at the end of his three years. If he passes, he becomes a journeyman (*Geselle*). Then, after three to five years' work as a journeyman and passing another exam, he becomes a Master

(*Meister*). In 1991, some 59,000 apprentices took their first exams; and 77 percent (45,000) passed. In the West, 39,000 (92 percent) of all candidates passed the exam. Women made up 11 percent of the graduates (12.6 percent in the old states).[14]

One problem is the increasing difficulty in filling apprenticeship positions in Germany where more and more students want to go to the universities. About 25 percent of all students now go on to higher education. They must first obtain the *abitur*, which is the certificate granted after a thirteen-year curriculum designed for university candidates. University education is free in Germany, and for the first time there are now more students in universities than in apprenticeship programs.[15] Most students can postpone their final exams for their university degrees as long as they want. Some take up to fifteen years.

German universities in the West are all high grade, and the quality differences between them are small. Fortunately for German youths, there are no universities comparable to some utterly unqualified American institutions allowed to prey on students with little or no supervision. Universities in eastern Germany suffered four decades of Marxist rule and are currently somwhat inferior to those in the West. However, they are being rehabilitated, and it is to be hoped they will soon be on a level with the Western institutions.

FOREIGN WORKERS

Labor shortages in West Germany from the 1950s to the early 1970s led to large-scale migration from less prosperous countries. West Germany concluded bilateral social security agreements with twenty governments, including that of the United States. Alien workers have the same rights as their German counterparts, earn the same wages, and have the same social security benefits.

In March 1992, there were 1,966,000 foreign workers in western Germany. They made up 6.5 percent of total employment and were broken down as follows by national origins (in thousands):[16]

Turkey	649
Yugoslavia	357
Italy	159
Austria	93
Spain	55
Poland	49
Portugal	43
United Kingdom	41
France	41

United States	30
Czechoslovakia	26
Morocco	21
Romania	20
Vietnam	17
Iran	14
Other	245

Including families and dependents, there were over 4 million foreigners in Germany at this time.

Just before the reunification in 1990, there were some 87,000 foreign workers in East Germany, 58,000 of whom were Vietnamese.[17] By late 1992, there were only 20,000 left, 15 percent of whom were estimated to be still employed in their old jobs. The government is trying to have all of them repatriated by the end of 1994.[18]

NOTES

1. *Focus*, Munich, 23 (1993): 120.
2. *Wall Street Journal*, New York, October 12, 1992.
3. *The Economist*, London, August 18, 1990, p. 57.
4. *The Economist*, London, January 23, 1993, p. 63.
5. *Der Spiegel*, Hamburg, July 23, 1990, p. 81.
6. *Frankfurter Allgemeine Zeitung*, June 18, 1993.
7. *The Economist*, London, May 22, 1993, p. 64.
8. *Financial Times*, London, May 15, 1993.
9. *New York Times*, August 12, 1993.
10. *New York Times*, February 6, 1993.
11. *Handelsblatt*, Dusseldorf, May 31, 1993.
12. *Frankfurter Allgemeine Zeitung*, January 30, 1993.
13. *Berliner Morgenpost*, May 27, 1990.
14. *Frankfurter Allgemeine Zeitung*, October 10, 1992.
15. *Los Angeles Times*, January 1, 1993.
16. *Der Spiegel*, Hamburg, 52 (1992): 90.
17. *Frankfurter Allgemeine Zeitung*, April 20, 1990.
18. *Der Spiegel*, Hamburg, 43 (1992): 145.

15

Social Security Law

The German social security system has become a model for other European countries. Almost all systems in Europe were well established before the United States timidly began to enter this field in 1935. German social security actually embraces three kinds of programs:

1. *Social insurance.* Employers, or employers and employees jointly, make fixed contributions to four programs. They both pay in for health insurance, unemployment insurance, and retirement pension insurance. Employers alone contribute to worker's compensation.
2. *Social benefits.* The state alone, without any contributions by the employer or employee, makes benefit payments to various groups needing help.
3. *Social supplementary benefits.* These are made by the state alone to persons who, even with payments from social insurance and social benefits, are living below an adequate level of income.

Germany, under the inspiration of Chancellor Otto von Bismarck, pioneered in social security. In 1881, just ten years after unifying thirty-nine states into the German Empire, Bismarck wrote an Imperial Proclamation announcing social security for the Germans and then persuaded Kaiser Wilhelm I to issue it in the latter's name. Despite his conservative philosophy, Bismarck clearly saw two strong reasons for such programs. First, the economic lot of the average German worker had greatly deteriorated with the industrialization of the country. Second, workers had become attracted to socialism and labor unions, which Bismarck wanted to weaken.

The Imperial Proclamation was followed by the enactment of the Health Insurance Act in 1883 and then the Industrial Accident Insurance Act of 1884. In 1889, a Retirement Pension Insurance Act also became the law of the land. The Unemployment Insurance Act did not go into existence until 1924.

HEALTH INSURANCE

Germany rightfully boasts that its health insurance program covers practically all its residents (99.8 percent). By comparison there were 35 million Americans uninsured in 1993. There are no German insurance companies as we know them. The program is administered by 1,100 different sickness funds (*Krankenkassen*) which are nonprofit associations administered by management and labor groups. All workers, with very few exceptions, must become members and pay about 6.5 percent of their wages before taxes, up to DM 4,875 per month. The employer pays an equal contribution. Premiums for the unemployed are paid for by the unemployment funds. Full-time, part-time, and self-employed workers are covered together with their entire families for life.

The sickness fund pays for all medical and dental care, medication, hospitalization, maternity benefits, nursing care at home, as well as cash benefits. Some funds even pay for a two-week stay at a spa every two years.[1]

The patient is free to choose his or her doctor and hospital. Office care is provided by self-employed doctors and hospital care by the hospitals, both public and private.

Cooperation by doctors, hospitals, sickness funds, employees, and employers is the key to success of German health insurance. They work to hold the system together and keep government intervention to a minimum.

In 1991, health spending in Germany amounted to 8.3 percent of GDP, compared with 13.4 percent in the world-leader United States, far ahead of second-place Canada (10 percent).[2]

On a per capita basis, the health expenses of the United States in 1989 were $2,354, far ahead of Germany at $1,232.[3]

On Unification Day, October 3, 1990, the West German social security programs became applicable in eastern Germany with some modifications. For example, the health insurance fee in eastern Germany is payable on employee income up to DM 2,250 per month, compared with DM 4,875 in the West.

Under the German health system, a few costs are carried by the patient. For the first fourteen days in the hospital, he or she must pay DM 6.80 per day; after that, it is free. The same rate applies for a therapy program at a spa. There are also set rates for contributions by the patients for medical supplies such as dentures and, in some cases, drugs. The health insurance program also pays a sickness benefit based on lost earnings of the patient. This is limited to DM 4,875 per month in the West and DM 2,250 in the East. Thus, a person in a higher income level is likely to take out a private insurance policy to cover this gap, as well as other benefits, like a private room.[4]

Joining one of the 1,147 sickness funds is mandatory for 88 percent of the population. Only Germans who earn more than $50,000 per year are not required to buy health insurance, but most of them—about 6.3 million—join a sickness fund anyway. It is estimated that less than 0.2 percent of the German population has no health insurance, compared with 13.6 percent in the United States.[5]

Typical amounts paid to the doctors by sickness funds are as follows:[6]

Consultation, office or phone	$ 5.00
Consultation at night	12.50
House call	17.80
House call at night	45.00
Diagnosis of pregnancy and test for hemoglobin	20.00
Attendance at normal birth	93.75
Attendance at breech birth	143.75
Examination of a baby	$20.00 to 22.50
Simple electrocardiogram	15.60
Chest X-ray for lungs	28.13

Rising costs have been a problem in recent years, but German politicians are understandably reluctant to raise the fees paid. Accordingly, in 1990 new laws were passed to curtail costs. Sickness funds were ordered to pay only for generic drugs when available. Dental benefits were curtailed, and hospitals were directed to increase efficiency.

Costs kept rising, however, and the government enacted a draconian new law to meet the problem, effective January 1, 1993. The pharmaceutical industry was ordered to reduce prices 5 percent on most nongeneric drugs sold in the West and a price freeze through 1994. Patients would need to pay more for drugs but no more than $4.20 per prescription. In the East, all medicines must be sold at a 20-percent discount. By 1996, hospitals and doctors must work out new fees based on the procedure, not on the length of stay, which is often longer than necessary. A doctor's fees will rise only to the extent that income from fees increases. In all, the government said, the new law would save $6.5 billion in 1993 and fees paid to the sickness funds will not need to be raised any faster than inflation (about 3 percent annually).[7]

German physicians in private practice average $135,000 per year, about 20 percent less than their U.S. counterparts. They are never tempted to turn down a destitute or unemployed patient because the government pays insurance fees for such people. Also, the poor are not tempted to resort to expensive emergency room treatment because that is the only way they can gain access to a hospital.

Hospital patients must pay only $6.80 ($6.25 in the East) per day on rooms with much lower daily rates than in the United States. Even in the highly technical University Hospital in Bonn, a teaching institution, the daily rate is $400. As mentioned earlier, after fourteen days the patient pays nothing.

Prior to January 1, 1995, there was a failure to cover the cost of prolonged nursing care. A patient was covered for the first four weeks, but only if connected with an illness or accident. The new law plugs this gap by enacting a new state-run insurance plan financed by a payroll tax of 1 percent (split equally by employer and worker).[8]

UNEMPLOYMENT INSURANCE

This program did not go into effect until 1924, the latest of the four German social insurance programs. It is administered by the Labor Office (*Arbeitsamt*), which has branches throughout the country. Practically all workers are covered. Here again the worker and employer pay an equal fee (6.3 percent) up to DM 6,500 per month in the West and DM 3,000 in eastern Germany. Upon losing his or her job, the employee draws monthly benefits equal to 63 percent of his or her net income (68 percent for married worker with a child). Benefits are limited to fifty-two weeks, but then unemployment assistance is paid (56 percent, with 58 percent for a married person with a child).

If the worker is responsible for losing his or her job, he or she must wait twelve weeks before receiving payments. Students can also receive unemployment insurance if they were employed before they became students or if they have completed their required military service (or as a substitute, civilian service).

In 1987, Germany began to pay Short Work Money (*Kurzarbeitergeld*) to a worker on a reduced workweek (which can be as little as no hours per week) to bring the pay up to 63 percent of normal (68 percent for a married person with a child). This can be paid for two years. Short Work Money has been used extensively in eastern Germany since reunification in 1990, thus keeping down the number of workers counted as unemployed even though some were not working at all.

The law also allows for Bad Weather Money (*Schlechtwettergeld*) in the construction industry when climatic conditions force a shutdown or reduced hours. Payments made are similar to Short Work Money.

When a business fails, its workers can receive tax-free Bankruptcy Money (*Konkursausfallgeld*) for 3 months. These payments are equal to net wages. In addition, the Labor Office also pays in the affected workers' contributions to their social insurance programs.

By comparison, many American workers are covered by unemployment insurance and the program is limited to twenty-six weeks. If times are bad, Congress may authorize another thirteen weeks in a bill, which the President may or may not sign. When the worker's unemployment insurance runs out, he or she must apply for a state relief program (which varies greatly in the individual states). Unemployment benefits in the United States are about 50 percent of wages.

OLD-AGE INSURANCE

The Reichstag incorporated old-age insurance into law in 1889, and it went into effect in 1891. The worker and the employer contributed equally to the pension fund, 0.85 percent of the wage (1.7 percent together). The average worker paid in the equivalent of about DM 80 per year. At age 70, the worker drew a pension of 18 percent of his or her active wage, or DM 85 per month.

A century later, in 1990, the worker and employer still shared equally in the old-age contribution, 18.7 percent in all or 9.35 percent each. In 1990, the pensioner could retire at age 65 after forty-five years at an average of DM 1,667 per month, or 70 percent of his or her wage. This was twenty times the purchasing power enjoyed by his or her great-great-grandfather a century before in 1891. The employer is obliged to withhold the tax on the worker. The 9.35-percent tax paid by the worker applies to a monthly wage of up to DM 6,500 in the West and DM 3,000 in the East.

A worker retiring at age 65 with thirty-five years of coverage receives 65 percent of the average wages or salary in the last three years. If the pensioner has been covered for less than thirty-five years, the pension is correspondingly reduced. Those working beyond age 65 can increase the pension 0.5 percent per month for each year worked, up to 75 percent. A disabled worker can draw a pension at age 60.

Since the start of 1986, all mothers born after 1920 are credited with one year of old-age pension coverage for each child they have reared. Fathers are entitled to this "baby year" if they have reared the child alone before 1986. Parents with children born after 1985 must notify their old-age pension fund within three months after birth if the father is to be credited rather than the mother. Whoever claims the credit gets about DM 25 per month in additional pension for each child reared.

Men receive higher pensions than women, and salaried employees receive more than blue-collar workers. On January 1, 1990, the highest monthly pension paid for a salaried man was DM 3,800; but it was DM 3,000 for a woman. As for blue-collar workers, the maximum was DM 2,900 for men and DM 1,700 for women. The amount paid also varies with the number of years worked, up to a maximum after forty-five years.

As of July 1, 1993, the average pensioner in the West received an increase of 3.8 percent, while the easterners enjoyed 14.24 percent. On June 30, 1990, eastern German pensioners had payments between 29 percent and 37 percent of those paid in the West. By January 1, 1994, this level had climbed to 95 percent.[9]

WORKER'S COMPENSATION

Contributions to this program are made only by the employer to associations set up in all branches of trade and industry (*Berufsgenossenschaften*).

The amount contributed is fixed by the association on the basis of risk and past safety record. It averages about 1.66 percent of the payroll.

Workers become eligible in case of occupational disease or accident in connection with the job or while commuting to and from work. Usually one is entitled to full pay for six weeks. If his or her earning capacity is still impaired, he or she is entitled to worker's compensation amounting to 80 percent of wages earned during the last month on the job. If earning capacity after thirteen weeks is permanently reduced by 20 percent or more, he or she is entitled to a pension. A worker totally unable to work receives a pension equal to two-thirds of his or her last annual earnings.

SOCIAL BENEFITS

Now we can examine the major social benefits paid for by the government with no contribution by either employees or employers.

Child Benefits

These are paid regardless of need of the family. In 1988, benefits of DM 50 per month were being paid for the first child (7,513,000 such cases). DM 100 was being paid for 3,625,000 cases involving a second child. A third child brought DM 220 (1 million) and each additional child DM 240 (363,000). For families with higher incomes, the second child payment is reduced to DM 70 and for each additional child to DM 140.

Child benefits are paid until the age of 16 unless the child is engaged in a higher education or an apprenticeship program when payment continues until age 26. If the child has no apprentice training or higher education and is unemployed, payments can be made until age 21.

Youth Benefits

These are paid when parents fail to meet their constitutional obligations of care and education of their children.

Education Promotion Benefits

These are available after nine years of schooling to those students pursuing some form of advanced education. The *Bundesausbildungsförderungsgesetz* (BaföG) of 1971 (Act to Promote Education) provides for a wide range of payments to help students, including night school. For example, a student living with parents gets DM 590, and one living elsewhere gets DM 725 for two semesters in a university program. Tuition, of course, is free in German universities.

Housing Benefits

These payments go to renters whose incomes are not sufficient to rent suitable quarters and to owners who cannot afford to meet all their costs. In 1986, 12 percent of the tenants and 1.5 percent of the owners were drawing an average monthly housing benefit of DM 152. In 1990, a case came to light in Berlin in which a family of four paid DM 3,000 a month for a sparsely furnished 25-square-meter apartment in the Kreuzberg section. The father was a carpenter who paid DM 1,813.66, and the Social Office (*Sozial Amt*) paid DM 1,187.34 as a housing benefit.[10]

Benefits for War Victims

War veterans suffering injuries receive pensions and health benefits. These are also paid to their surviving dependents. In 1989, some 1,400,000 people were beneficiaries of this program.

SOCIAL SUPPLEMENTARY BENEFITS

This element of the German social security system (*Sozialhilfe*) is designed to fill the gaps that exist for many less fortunate people after they have exhausted their rights under the social insurance and social benefits programs. In 1986, there were 3,020,000 recipients under this arrangement drawing DM 23 billion. About 13 percent of those benefited were foreigners. The most important reasons for these supplementary benefits were insufficient pensions (16 percent), unemployment (31 percent), nonpaying fathers (13 percent), illness (6 percent), and inadequate income (7 percent).

NOTES

1. *Los Angeles Times*, September 16, 1993.
2. *The Economist*, London, March 27, 1993, p. 113.
3. *New York Times*, February 17, 1992.
4. *Los Angeles Times*, December 30, 1992.
5. David Hart, "German Health Care—A Model for U.S. Reform," *Commerce Germany*, Frankfurt, American Chamber of Commerce in Germany, 1 (1993): 54.
6. *New York Times*, January 23, 1993.
7. Ibid.
8. *Frankfurter Allgemeine Zeitung*, June 1, 1994.
9. *Frankfurter Allgemeine Zeitung*, March 18, 1994.
10. *Berliner Morgenpost*, April 25, 1990.

16

German Banking System

Germany is famous for its tendency to legislate the details of everyday life, but one is surprised how comparatively free the nation's financial institutions remain from regulation. One is struck repeatedly by the much more restricted position of their American counterparts. The first hasty conclusion might be that German bankers have done a much better job in selecting lobbyists, and one would be quite right; but there are signs that this advantage is diminishing.

Despite this relative freedom, the German financial system has worked reasonably well for the German people, not so much because the financial institutions are so well designed but because the bankers are thoroughly imbued with the need for monetary stability. The bankers are so orientated because the entire population knows either firsthand or from older citizens that the absence of such stability can produce withering inflations, as in 1924 and in World War II. It was a painful learning process, but it has yielded enormous benefits.

COMMERCIAL BANKS

Commercial banks are so called because of their two vital functions. First, they accept deposits and honor withdrawals by the depositors. Second, they make loans for business purposes. Under German law commercial banks are allowed to go far beyond the limits imposed on U.S. commercial banks. The main differences are these:

1. German banks can branch nationwide.
2. German banks can buy stock in other corporations.
3. Only banks can underwrite security issues.
4. Banks are under less legal pressure to disclose financial data about themselves, such as hidden reserves.

For these and other nonlegal reasons, German commercial banks have far greater control over the economic system and bank customers than is true in the United States. As a result, German banks can influence corporate mergers, intervene in business matters, and discourage competition from foreign commercial banks far more effectively than their American counterparts. Last, German bankers are not any more intelligent than their U.S. competitors, despite what most of them think on this subject.

Banks in Germany are under the supervision of two agencies, the Bank Supervisory Authority (*Bundesaufsichtsamt für das Kreditwesen*) in Berlin and the Bundesbank, the German central bank in Frankfurt. The Bank Supervisory Authority operates under the provisions of the Banking Act of 1961 (*Gesetz über das Kreditwesen*), KWG for short, which, with few exceptions, applies to all banks.

Partnerships and corporations, but not individual proprietorships, are legally qualified to apply for a banking license. The Bank Supervisory Authority must issue a written license before a bank can start operations. Generally, a license must be issued if

1. the financial funds required to engage in the banking activity are available within Germany, in particular, in the form of equity capital
2. the applicant has appointed at least two full-time managers who are qualified to manage a bank and who are considered reliable.

A person will generally be considered qualified to manage a bank if he or she has held a managerial position in a bank of comparable size and business for at least three years. German citizenship is not required, but the Bank Supervisory Authority insists that the applicant must be sufficiently fluent in the German language.

Not long ago, U.S. banks dominated global commercial banking. Citibank, Bank of America, and Chase Manhattan were always at the top on the basis of assets, but this picture has changed dramatically since 1980. As of December 31, 1992, Citibank placed twenty-seventh in rank with $221 billion in assets. This was less than half of Japan's Dai-lchi Kangyo, the world's largest, with $473 billion. Germany's biggest bank, Deutsche Bank, with $305 billion, was tenth.

German banks rate first in number of bank offices per million residents. As of July 1989, the comparative figures were as follows:[1]

West Germany	1,020
France	889
United Kingdom	803
Sweden	678
Japan	553
Canada	487
Italy	475
United States	452

However, the United States had more individual banks than Germany, as the following list shows:[2]

United States	12,300
Germany	4,500
France	2,032
Italy	1,133
Japan	692
United Kingdom	559
Canada	65

The 4,500 banks in Germany divided themselves into the following classes:

Commercial	337
Big Three	3
Regional and local	185
Private	83
Branches of foreign banks	60
Savings	746
Credit co-ops	3,416
Mortgage banks	36

In July 1993 the Federal Supreme Court struck down as illegal a fee that German banks had been charging for deposits and withdrawals by their account holders. Generally the charge was one mark for each deposit and each withdrawal (unless through an automatic machine). The court's opinion held that a bank could not collect a fee for a service that a statute required it to perform.

As mentioned earlier, German commercial banks perform more functions than U.S. banks; thus, they are called universal banks.

In addition to the four kinds of banks mentioned previously, Germans—like most Europeans—can also use their nearest post office for banking functions. They offer savings and checking accounts and will even accept small overdrafts; otherwise, no loans can be made.

German banking is influenced by different habits for paying for goods and services than those found in the United States. German customers pay for 90 percent of their obligations in cash, compared with 12 percent in America. Only 7 percent in Germany is by check, as opposed to 14 percent in the United States. Customer credit cards issued by retailers account for only 1 percent in Germany, compared with 61 percent in the United States. Bank credit cards pay 2 percent of the bills of Germans; it is 13 percent in America.[3]

Credit cards got off to a slow start in Germany, largely because the banks and their antidebt customers were not enthusiastic. This has now changed, and business is better. As of September 15, 1992, Eurocard—with four million holders—had 57.2 percent of the market; Visa was second with 1.6 million, followed by American Express (1 million) and Diner's Club (360,000).[4] Only 75,000 of the 4 million Eurocard holders were in the East.[5]

In addition, there are 12 million customer credit cards issued by department stores, hotel chains, airlines, and auto rental companies. There are also 35 million Eurochecque Cards, which allow the holder to have checks accepted up to DM 400 each.

Private banks in Germany, as in other countries, do not take customers walking in off the street. They accept only clients who meet their high standards, most important of which is a large minimum balance. The oldest private bank still in existence is Berenberg Bank, dating back to 1590 in Hamburg. Private means that all the capital is subscribed privately and not through a public offering.

The first commercial banks in Germany, as in most countries, were private banks in the sense that they used the private capital of their owners (individual proprietors or partners) rather than selling stock in a bank corporation. Private banks in Germany can no longer be organized as individual proprietorships but only as partnerships or corporations.

A century ago, there were still 2,500 private banks in the German Empire. This had dropped to 710 in 1933. By 1957, only 245 remained; by 1992, there were 50 survivors.[6]

Over two-thirds of today's private banks are small, with assets less than DM 1 billion. The largest private bank with DM 6 billion in assets is Bankhaus Sal. Oppenheim Jr. & Cie in Cologne, founded in 1789. Of course, private banks publish no annual reports for the public. Purists argue that only twenty-five of the eighty are authentic private banks in the sense that they do not have partial ownership by commercial banks. Big German banks have acquired interests in prestigious private banks to keep wealthy customers from being lured away to such institutions. Even major foreign banks like Midland and Lloyd's of London and Crédit Lyonnais of Paris have made such investments.

German banks still use the overdraft as the preferred method of lending. The customer and his or her bank agree on an overdraft facility up to a certain amount needed by the customer. The borrower then draws up to that figure even though the money is not in his or her account and usually pays interest only on the amount of total overdrafts. Obviously, this method gives the bank far greater control over the loan than it has when it actually puts the loan proceeds in the customer's account. Total overdraft loans in Germany climbed from DM 17.5 billion in 1980 to DM 30.2 billion in 1990.[7] The overdraft loan is still used occasionally in U.S. banks.

Germany established its present bank deposit insurance program in 1966. It is completely private, voluntary, and managed by the banks themselves. The banks pay an annual premium of 0.03 percent of their total deposits, and each depositor is fully protected. Fortunately, there have been very few bank failures in Germany in recent years.[8]

Deutsche Bank, the largest in Germany, reported assets of 556 billion marks at the end of 1993 (up 11 percent over 1992). It ranked as the tenth largest bank in the world as of the last day of 1993. The other two banks in the German Big Three were Dresdner Bank (380 billion marks in assets as of the end of 1993) and Commerzbank (255 billion marks).[9]

All three of these banks had their head offices in Berlin until the surrender in 1945 but moved to Frankfurt when West Berlin became an island in the middle of East Germany. They will probably stay in Frankfurt.

The Big Three today have extensive branch networks in both the East and West, as well as in all major foreign cities. They were all very profitable in 1993. Deutsche Bank reported net income of 2.2 billion marks in 1993, up from 1.8 billion marks in 1992. Dresdner had a net income of 1.0 billion marks, up from 0.9 billion marks; and Commerz had a net income of 0.5 billion marks, up from 0.4 billion marks.

German banks as a whole in 1991 owned 11.6 percent of all equity of German corporations. They also held enough proxies from individual shareholders to control about half of all German shares listed on the stock exchanges. As a result, bankers from the Big Three have seats on the supervisory boards of about half the 100 biggest firms. Supervisory boards under the law must have a minimum of two meetings, and most boards stick with the minimum.

An interesting study by Jeremy Edwards and Klaus Fischer published in 1991 compared the sources of investment finance for nonfinancial German firms between 1970 and 1989. Retained earnings provided 62 percent of the total, and bank loans provided 19 percent.[10]

Between 1980 and 1991, the German banks increased their share of international lending from 4.0 percent to 6.1 percent, while U.S. banks retained the same share of 9.4 percent. Japanese banks jumped from 6.2 percent to

15.1 percent, and British institutions dropped from 26.2 percent to 16.3 percent. Total international lending grew from $51 trillion in 1980 to $56 trillion in 1991.[11]

BUNDESBANK

England created the first central bank in 1689 when an established commercial bank was granted central bank powers. It was already carrying the appropriate name, Bank of England. Germany was relatively late in establishing the Reichsbank in 1873 in Berlin, but Germany did not become a united nation until 1871. The United States had been united for 125 years before founding the Federal Reserve Bank in 1914 and did not grant effective powers to the bank until 1935.

Germany's Reichsbank collapsed with the Third Reich in 1945. It was not until 1950 that West Germany formed a new central bank, Deutsche Bundesbank (German Federal Bank). In 1990, the bank's jurisdiction was extended to eastern Germany.

The principal functions of the bank are much the same as those of the Federal Reserve Bank as follows:

1. Sole power to issue paper money.
2. Serves as bank for the federal government.
3. Provides refinancing, clearing, and collection services to commercial banks.
4. Controls money supply so as to maintain stability of prices.

The Bundesbank has won high marks for its performance. Many students of banking argue that independence from political control has been the major reason for the fine record compiled by the Bundesbank.

The Bundesbank has a headquarters in Frankfurt's suburbs, which fascinates most visitors. It is highly modern in every detail. The total work force of the Bundesbank is about 17,000, of whom only 2,000 are in the Frankfurt head office. The rest are distributed among the regional branches.

A president heads up this huge agency, appointed by the chancellor for an eight-year term. He is assisted by a vice president and three directors. Hans Tietmeyer is now president of the Bundesbank. He served in the Kohl Ministries of Economics and Finance before going with the Bundesbank.

The policy-making arm of the Bundesbank is the fourteen-member Central Bank Council, which meets every other Thursday. The council includes the five executives in Frankfurt and nine members selected by the Bundesbank branches in sixteen states. The council often invites members of the government in Bonn (such as the chancellor, finance minister, or others) to attend the meetings. They are merely consultants and have no vote.

The policy actions taken by the Central Bank Council are announced immediately after meetings. This enables all concerned (banks, businesses, politicians, and general public) to work together to achieve the results desired. In the United States, the decisions made by the Federal Open Market Committee are kept quiet for six weeks.

The Bundesbank has substantially the same powers over the money supply as the Federal Reserve Bank. They can be described as follows:

1. Open-market operations.
2. Fixing discount and Lombard rates.
3. Fixing minimum reserves.
4. Conducting foreign-exchange operations to protect the mark.

Changes in the two basic bank rates are the most efficient tools available to the Bundesbank, while open-market operations are less important. The Bundesbank usually reports tremendous annual profits, particularly from interest on its security holdings and from foreign-exchange operations.

In 1993, the Bundesbank reported interest income of DM 24.5 billion and interest expense of DM 3.3 billion. Other expenses brought the Bundesbank net profit down to DM 18.8 billion, compared with DM 14.7 billion in 1992.[12] As required by law, the bank paid DM 18.2 billion to the government.

The Bundesbank is also required by law to set annual goals for monetary growth and then exercise its powers to achieve such goals. In December of each year, the Central Bank Council sets a money-growth target for the next calendar year. It uses M3 as its key measurement. M3 is largely currency in circulation and bank deposits.

During the past two years, M3 has increased far beyond the targets set by the Bundesbank. For 1994, the goals were between 4 percent and 6 percent. M3 shot up 21 percent in January, 15 percent in April, and 11 percent in June.

To curb expansion of M3, the Bundesbank raised its discount rate ten times from mid-1988 to July 1992 (from 2.5 percent to 8.75 percent). The discount rate is the interest charged by the Bundesbank to buy the notes of member commercial banks. After July 1992, the bank reduced the rate ten times to 5 percent as of April 14, 1994.

The Lombard rate does not exist under the Federal Reserve system, but it is a very important device for the Bundesbank and other central banks. It is the interest rate at which the central bank will refinance the commercial banks by loaning them on the collateral security of bonds. The Lombard rate normally is held 1.5 percent above the discount rate. It peaked at 9.75 percent in July 1992 and was then gradually reduced to 6.5 percent as of April 14, 1994.[13]

These rate reductions by the Bundesbank over the past two years in the face of excessive M3 growth contradict traditional monetary theory. But the bank has been able to accomplish this because, fortunately for Germany, inflation has been declining—from about 5 percent on January 1, 1993 to 3 percent in June 1994.

DEUTSCHE MARK

On June 21, 1948, the new Deutsche Mark was introduced by a decree requiring citizens of the Western Zones of Occupied Germany to register the amount of Reichsmarks (RM) they had in their possession as well as bank accounts, securities, war bonds, and other intangible assets. Each German was allowed to exchange RM 400 for DM 40 (10 RM = 1 DM) and another RM 200 in two months. All other intangible holdings were declared worthless. Farms, other real estate, and tangible personal property were not affected.

Obviously, this was a draconian measure for the great majority of Germans who had their savings in the nullified forms of property. Home ownership at that time was seldom achieved by the average German. Even today, it is much less frequent in Germany than in America. The new mark, although it had no gold or silver backing, was accepted by the people. Goods reappeared in the stores, labor productivity improved, morale rose, and West Germany slowly began to prosper.

The new mark was fixed by the IMF at 30 cents, but this rate proved too high. On September 19, 1949, the rate was reduced to 23.8 cents, which held for almost twelve years, until March 6, 1961, when the mark was revalued to 25 cents. The 25-cent rate prevailed for the next eight years, until October 27, 1969.

From the creation of the mark in 1948 until August 15, 1971, all changes in its value in relation to the dollar were made within the fixed-rate system, which had been set up by the Bretton Woods Agreement of 1944. The treaty, administered by the IMF starting in 1947, set fixed dollar rates for the currencies of the member states. More important, the members could convert their paper money into U.S. dollars and then into gold at the U.S. Treasury at a rate of $35.00 per ounce of gold. In effect, the IMF was operating on a modified gold standard.

This system worked well as long as the U.S. Treasury had enough gold to redeem U.S. dollars presented for redemption by West Germany and other member nations of the IMF. By August 15, 1971, our gold had declined to the point where it could not pay for all the dollars being offered for redemption; and President Nixon halted further operations.

This was a severe but not a mortal blow to fixed foreign-exchange rates. The IMF persuaded member countries to hold on to the system for another nineteen months, until March 19, 1973, without the gold redemption feature. Finally, on that date, fixed rates were ended by the IMF; and currencies were "floated" in the market to find their price as determined by the laws of supply and demand. Of course, central banks like the Federal Reserve and the

German Bundesbank could intervene by buying to support or selling to depress their respective currencies, but they were no longer obligated to keep them within fixed limits.

Since floating rates began on March 19, 1973 (1 DM = 35 cents), the German currency has gone as low as 28 cents on March 8, 1985, and as high as 71 cents on August 24, 1992. It closed at 64.56 on December 30, 1994. When the mark was in the dumps in 1965, U.S. authorities feared the impact of low-priced marks on our balance of trade. Thus, the United States met at the Plaza Hotel in New York on September 20, 1985, with the six largest industrial nations to discuss foreign-exchange rates. The other members were the United Kingdom, West Germany, Japan, France, Italy, and Canada, which, with the United States, make up the Group of Seven (G-7). They entered the Plaza Agreement to restrain the strength of the dollar.

On that date, the mark was worth 35.16 cents. The G-7 has continued to operate as a unit in this area, and the dollar has been in general decline. During the period since the Plaza Agreement, U.S. authorities have been content to see the dollar fall in relation to the mark and other currencies because they want U.S. exports to be cheap and imports to be more expensive. This has kept the deficit in merchandise trade from growing even more than it has.

NOTES

1. *Frankfurter Allgemeine Zeitung*, November 7, 1989.
2. "World Banking Survey," *The Economist*, London, May 2, 1992, p. 5.
3. *Tagespiegel*, Berlin, November 7, 1989.
4. *Frankfurter Allgemeine Zeitung*, September 29, 1992.
5. *Frankfurter Allgemeine Zeitung*, October 10, 1992.
6. *Frankfurter Allgemeine Zeitung*, September 5, 1992.
7. *Der Spiegel*, Hamburg, 22 (1991): 123.
8. *The Economist*, London, March 10, 1990.
9. *Frankfurter Allgemeine Zeitung*, April 2, 1994.
10. *The Economist*, London, December 7, 1991, p. 91.
11. "Survey: Financial Centers," *The Economist*, London, June 27, 1992, p. 4.
12. *Frankfurter Allgemeine Zeitung*, April 22, 1994.
13. *Financial Times*, London, April 15, 1994.

17

German Stock Markets

EIGHT STOCK EXCHANGES

As mentioned in Chapter 16, only commercial banks can underwrite securities in Germany. They also have seats on German stock exchanges. U.S. and other foreign-owned banks organized under German law also enjoy these powers. Thus Citibank of New York's German subsidiary, Citibank AG in Frankfurt, as a German corporation, can underwrite securities and act as a broker and dealer on the Frankfurt Stock Exchange. The Frankfurt branch of Citibank, merely an office of an American corporation, cannot perform these functions.

The eight German stock exchanges are organized under the Stock Exchange Act (*Börsengesetz*). They are located at Hamburg, Frankfurt, Berlin, Munich, Dusseldorf, Stuttgart, Bremen, and Hanover. Hamburg, founded in 1558, is the oldest; but Frankfurt (1585) now dominates, with about two-thirds of the total trading. Berlin (1686) was the dominant market until World War II.

The German fragmentation is highly inefficient, and the eight exchanges are facing stiff competition from London and Paris. London is stealing German business and on some days handles blue-chip German stocks equal to one-third of that of all German exchanges.

Slowly but haltingly, the eight markets are moving toward unity. Deutsche Börse AG was created in 1992 to own the Frankfurt Stock Exchange as well as the Deutsche Terminbörse, a futures and options exchange founded in 1989, and Germany's clearing and settlement houses. The members of the Frankfurt Stock Exchange own 68 percent of the stock in Deutsche Börse, and the seven other independent German exchanges mentioned previously hold 10 percent.[1]

The *Börsengesetz* and the rules of the exchanges set the requirements for listing stocks in Germany. To be listed, a corporation must be sponsored by a member bank and file a prospectus, which includes the following information:

1. The history and corporate purpose of the company.
2. The development, nominal value, and classes of capital stock and their respective rates.
3. Substantial holdings of outside parties and references to intercompany agreements (in particular, on controlling interests and profit and loss absorption agreements).
4. Members of management and a description of their functions.
5. Provisions of the articles of association that concern the convening of shareholders' meetings and voting rights of the shareholders.
6. The publication of announcements to be made by the company.
7. Paying agents and depositories.
8. The most recent financial statements of the company or, where applicable, consolidated financial statements dating back no more than thirteen months.
9. Should the balance sheet be older than nine months, a current financial statement and relevant data covering the current fiscal year must be attached.
10. Explanations regarding all balance sheet items of substance and, in the case of long-term liabilities, the average terms and an indication of any liabilities not shown on the balance sheet.
11. Substantial holdings in other companies.
12. A description of business operations and current business activities and prospects.

As of December 31, 1992, there were 1,259 stocks listed on the eight markets, 665 domestic issues and 594 foreign. The latter were distributed as follows:[2]

United States	167
Japan	74
United Kingdom	51
Italy	45

German investors have traditionally avoided stock purchases, preferring to put their money in bonds, bank accounts, or insurance. In 1993, only 5 percent of all Germans owned stock, compared with 21 percent in the United States.[3]

In 1993, some DM 271 billion were invested in German mutual funds. Only 16 percent of that was in stocks, while 76 percent was in fixed-income securities. By contrast, in America the DM 3.4 trillion in such funds were 34 percent in equities and 38 percent in fixed-income instruments. In Britain, the split of DM 244 billion in mutual funds was 97 percent stocks and 2.7 percent fixed-income securities.[4]

Another impediment is the small German ratio of total listed stock to the GNP. It is only 18 percent in Germany, 67 percent in the United States, and 97 percent in Britain (the world's highest).[5]

As of the end of 1992, the total value of all stocks listed in New York was $4.7 trillion, compared with $2.3 trillion in Japan and $348 billion in Frankfurt. London was $839 billion.[6]

It is sometimes asked why a U.S. company would want to list its stock on a foreign stock exchange. There are several benefits:

1. Advertising value.
2. Wider distribution of stock and thus less likelihood of an outsider takeover.
3. Selling additional stock.
4. Reach investors who want the secrecy of a foreign bank.

American investors thinking of buying German stocks should realize that they face problems not found in buying U.S. shares. The principal risks are as follows:

1. Lack of information. German law is lax on what corporations must disclose, and Germany has no SEC to force disclosure.
2. Risks involved with foreign-exchange rate changes.
3. Government intervention in business.
4. As discussed later in this chapter, insider information is very common in the German market, and the government is not too anxious to regulate this practice.
5. German banks can act as dealer for themselves and broker for a customer in the same transaction. They can also act as broker on both sides of the same securities transaction.
6. Stockholders living in the United States have more difficulty in keeping themselves informed than those in Germany.

Over the years, the Frankfurt Stock Exchange has enjoyed impressive gains. Using the *Frankfurter Allgemeine Zeitung* (FAZ) Index with December 31, 1958, as 100, here is the story:[7]

12/29/1950	19.73
12/31/1960	240.75
12/31/1970	187.43
12/30/1980	222.56

12/28/1990	603.06
12/30/1992	602.97
12/30/1993	847.57
1/4/1994 (All-Time High)	855.67
12/30/1994	784.43

COMPARATIVE PERFORMANCE
OF GERMAN STOCKS

In 1993, the German stock market exceeded the expectations of investors. The FAZ Index climbed 40.6. The seven cuts made in interest rates by the Bundesbank during 1993 were a major force in this upward movement. During 1993, the discount rate dropped from 9.5 percent to 6.75 percent, while the Lombard rate fell from 8.25 percent to 5.75 percent.[8]

However, the 40-percent gain in the market during 1993 did not result in the same increase for dollar-based investors. The dollar strengthened against the mark in the course of the year, and thus the U.S. investor only realized a gain of 37 percent. That was still far better than the 10-percent increase the investor would have received on the NYSE.

U.S. INVESTORS IN GERMAN STOCKS

U.S. investors have not shown great interest in German stocks over the years. The following are the net purchases by Americans in billions of dollars between January 1, 1990, and March 31, 1994:[9]

United Kingdom	38.6
Japan	34.8
Mexico	11.6
Hong Kong	9.7
Germany	6.8
Canada	5.5
Italy	4.9
Holland	4.3
France	3.9
Spain	3.7

There are six basic methods of investing in foreign stocks available to Americans:

1. Stock certificates bought on stock exchange in home country of corporation.
2. Stock certificates purchased on U.S. stock exchanges.
3. Foreign mutual funds with holdings in foreign stock.

4. U.S. mutual funds, which own foreign stock.

5. ADRs registered with the SEC and traded on U.S. stock exchanges.

6. ADRs not registered with SEC and traded on the over-the-counter (OTC) market.

(However, the second method is not available in the case of Germany because no German stocks are listed.)

German companies (for reasons discussed in Chapter 10) have been reluctant to disclose their financial information and follow U.S. accounting rules, as required by the SEC for listing either stock certificates or ADRs on American exchanges. In October 1993, Daimler-Benz became the first and so far the only exception when its ADRs became listed on the NYSE.

ADRs came into existence in 1927, when J. P. Morgan invented the instrument. Bank of New York, Citibank, and Morgan Stanley along with Morgan are the major players in this lucrative business. There are about 1,000 foreign corporations (up 100 percent since 1985) from forty-five countries who have ADRs in the United States. The bank buys a block of the stock, keeps it on deposit in the home country, and then sells ADRs to American investors. The ADR certifies that the issuing bank is holding a specified number of shares in trust for the holder of the instrument. Australia, Japan, and Britain account for over half the 1,000 ADRs on the market.[10]

Only about 25 percent of the 1,000 companies available by ADRs are registered with the SEC and listed on the NYSE, the American, or the National Association of Securities Dealers Automated Quotations (NASDAQ). These firms must comply with SEC requirements as to financial disclosure and accounting standards. The remaining 75 percent of the available ADRs are traded over the counter and thus not required to file with the SEC. Some twenty German corporations fall into this group, including Hoechst, Bayer, BASF, Deutsche Bank, Dresdner Bank, Allianz, Siemens, Volkswagen, and Schering. Kaufhof Holding—a major department store chain, one of the few large companies in Germany to post a rise in profit in 1993—entered its ADR on the OTC market in October 1993.[11]

Obviously, the U.S. stock exchanges are anxious to get more ADRs listed on their boards and thus divert funds that American investors are now pouring into foreign stock exchanges. They are particularly upset over the fact that Germany only has Daimler-Benz listed in ADRs and no stock certificates listed in America.

In March 1994, Arthur Levitt, chairman of the SEC, made a two-day visit to Germany to encourage its leading industrial corporations and banks to seek a U.S. listing. Levitt was the first chairman to visit that country.

ADRs can represent a fraction of a foreign share, a single share, or multiple shares. Usually, the owner of an ADR sells the receipt just as he or she would the shares themselves. For an extra fee, he or she can convert the ADR into the specified number of shares it represents. ADRs can be sponsored or unsponsored by the issuing corporation. An issuer sponsors its ADRs when it agrees to provide them with financial reports. Unsponsored ADRs are created by the bank, which passes the fees on to the investor. The investors usually receive less information than those with sponsored ADRs.[12] The ADRs of Commerz Bank, Volkswagen, and Kaufhold Holdings are sponsored, while those of Deutsche Bank and most German companies are unsponsored.[13]

By announcing in advance that it was going to list its ADRs on the NYSE in October 1993, Daimler-Benz stimulated widespread interest in its stock. The price in Frankfurt on June 1, 1993, was DM 552; it climbed to a high of DM 737 on September 21, 1993, just about two weeks before the New York listing.[14] By December 30, 1994, the shares had reached DM 762.

GERMAN REGULATION OF SECURITIES

As of July 1, 1994, Germany still had no agency comparable to the SEC in the United States; and the securities industry was probably less regulated than in any other major nation. There are state regulatory authorities but with very limited and ineffectual powers.

However, this situation has changed. In late 1993, the Ministry of Finance introduced the Finance Market Development Act (*Finanzmarktförderungsgesetz*), which has been enacted into the statutory law of Germany. The statute's main provisions are as follows:[15]

1. Creates a Federal Security Supervisory Office (*Bundesaufsichtsamt für das Wertpapier Wesen*) along the lines of the SEC to enforce the provisions of the law. This came into existence in January1995.
2. Establishes disclosure rules as to issuance of securities.
3. Sets up rules of conduct for brokers and dealers.
4. Bans insider trading, punishable by up to five years in prison.
5. Requires investors to report to the new agency all acquisitions of stock amounting to 5 percent of the firm's total. Further disclosures are obligatory at 10 percent, 25 percent, 50 percent, and 75 percent levels.

Many observers are puzzled at the obvious change of heart in Germany's bankers, who have denounced America's SEC for years but are now tolerating reforms comparable to those of the United States. The reason is quite simple. The Germans knew that such changes were necessary to get the Economic Community to establish the future European Central Bank in Frankfurt, which is now assured.

INSIDER TRADING LAW

In November 1991, the Council of Ministers of the EU passed an Insider Trading Directive, requiring all twelve member states to make insider trading illegal by June 30, 1992. The Finance Market Development Act mentioned above brings Germany into compliance with this directive.

As of July 1, 1994, the German stock exchanges still operated under a voluntary code, which banned insider trading. There have been comparatively few cases, but there have been commissions of inquiry appointed at each German stock exchange to investigate complaints. Klaus Kuhn, the chairman of the supervisory board of AEG, a diversified electrical concern, became the country's first publicly acknowledged insider trader in 1986. He admitted trading his company's shares prior to its takeover by Daimler-Benz.

In the ten days before Daimler announced its takeover bid, the price of AEG stock rose 30 percent.

The commission of inquiry at Frankfurt investigated and, after seven months, reported a "slight violation" of the rules but refused to divulge details. Under pressure, Kuhn admitted publicly that he bought 700 shares of AEG during acquisition talks. He sold them for a profit of DM 16,000 after the takeover bid. His punishment consisted of paying this profit to AEG.

German banks have long required staff members likely to handle sensitive information to sign a contract of employment that incorporates the code of practice. Under the code, anyone caught dealing on the basis of inside information has to pay back any profit made. As there was no legal redress, the only deterrent is the scandal of public disclosure.

As the Finance Minister of Hessen, Ernst Welteke had authority to regulate the Frankfurt Stock Exchange located in his state. Welteke said, "The current sanctions against insider trading are minimal. They are not at all enough. At the moment it is just a matter of common sense that you don't do it—or at least you don't get caught."[16]

NOTES

1. *New York Times*, October 8, 1992.
2. *Frankfurter Allgemeine Zeitung*, February 9, 1993.
3. *Frankfurter Allgemeine Zeitung*, August 21, 1993.
4. *Frankfurter Allgemeine Zeitung*, March 10, 1994.
5. *The Economist*, London, July 17, 1993, p. 102.
6. Ibid.
7. *Frankfurter Allgemeine Zeitung*, July 1, 1994.
8. *Wall Street Journal*, New York, January 3, 1994.
9. *Wall Street Journal*, New York, July 26, 1994.
10. *New York Times*, January 15, 1994.
11. *Financial Times*, London, October 20, 1993.
12. *Wall Street Journal*, New York, February 12, 1990.
13. *Frankfurter Allgemeine Zeitung*, July 1, 1989.
14. *Der Spiegel*, Hamburg, 40 (1993): 139.
15. *New York Times*, July 11, 1994.
16. *Financial Times*, London, June 15, 1993.

18

U.S. Commercial Banks
in Germany

In 1994, there were only nine U.S. commercial banks still operating subsidiaries or branches in the highly competitive banking system of Germany. This figure does not include firms in other fields such as investment banks that have obtained German banking charters as vehicles for transacting their business activities (Salamon Brothers, Morgan Stanley, Merrill Lynch, and Goldman Sachs). It also excludes Ford Bank and Opel Bank, which use bank charters to conduct retail and wholesale financing for Ford and GM automobiles. IBM and American Express also have banks to facilitate their business in Germany.[1]

Although there are only nine American commercial banks in business in Germany today, there were twenty at the peak in 1985, fighting to gain enough business to justify their presence. For example, Continental Bank of Chicago once had branches in Frankfurt and Munich, but it has closed both and now handles its German operations from the London branch. First National of Chicago followed the same strategy with its branches in Frankfurt and Dusseldorf. Continental's branch in Frankfurt reported a loss of DM 17 million for 1989, its last year in operation.

American branch closings overseas have not been confined to Germany. The number of U.S. branches overseas declined from 917 in 1984 to 849 in 1988. Thirty-one of 132 American banks withdrew completely from such operations during that period.[2]

In addition to the U.S. banks, there were ninety other foreign banks in

Germany in 1993. Japan had nineteen, and the member nations of the European Community operated forty-nine.

A sickening statistic for foreign banks recurs year after year in connection with German banking. The share of foreign banks in the German market remains at about 5 percent, a low only duplicated by Japan among advanced economies.[3] Foreign banks in the United States, by way of contrast, hold about 20 percent of total banking assets.

Hans-Georg Engel, vice president of J. P. Morgan GmbH in Frankfurt and chairman of the Association of Foreign Banks in Germany, said in 1991, "With only very few exceptions, the profit situation of foreign banks in Germany is less than satisfactory."[4]

The nine U.S. commercial banks still in Germany seem to have been tough enough, smart enough, and yes, willing to spend enough money to establish themselves in the rigorous Germany banking system. The operations of these nine American banks were as follows:[5]

Citicorp (New York)

    Citibank AG (subsidiary)

    Citibank (branches)

    Citibank Privatkunden AG (subsidiary)

J. P. Morgan (New York)

    J. P. Morgan GmbH (subsidiary)

    Morgan Guaranty Trust (branch)

Bankers Trust (New York)

    Bankers Trust GmbH (subsidiary)

Chase Manhattan (New York)

    Chase Bank AG (subsidiary)

    Chase Manhattan (branch)

Chemical Bank (New York)

    Chemical Bank AG (subsidiary)

    Chemical Bank (branch)

Bank of America (San Francisco)

    Bank America (branch)

Bank of New York (branch)

Bank of Boston (branch)

NBD Bank (Detroit) (branch)

Five of these nine banks have established German subsidiaries. Under the German banking law these subsidiaries can engage in both investment and commercial functions, thus competing in both fields with the so-called universal banks of Germany. Branches of U.S. banks still must follow the restrictions on investment banking imposed by U.S. law.

A German subsidiary of a U.S. bank can itself open branches as needed. Citibank AG, for example, has branches in Berlin and Dresden. During 1991, it had to close branches in Dusseldorf, Hamburg, and Stuttgart, thereby reducing its total work force from 600 to 420.[6]

Today, Citibank of New York has only one German branch, located in Frankfurt. In 1984, it terminated branches in four cities: Cologne, Nürnberg, Hanover, and Mannheim. At the time, a spokesman stated that Citibank had "misjudged" both the level of demand for its services in Germany as well as the strength of the competition from German banks.[7]

Citibank has been criticized by both its German and American rivals for its undue aggressiveness in rushing to open unprofitable branches not only in Germany but in other countries like Switzerland. While such criticism is justified, Citibank did give a psychological lift to the West Germans when needed during the Cold War. Citibank became the first and only U.S. bank to open a branch in West Berlin, a showplace in Europa Center far splashier than required. Later, the branch was quietly moved to a modest suite in less pretentious Reuter Platz, and it is still there.

In 1988, Citibank became the only U.S. bank to acquire control of a large German bank specializing in consumer credit, which was based in Dusseldorf. Then in 1991, the name of the bank was changed from KKB Bank AG to Citibank Privatkunden AG (private customers). Over the next three years, Citibank raised its capital from DM 650 million to DM 1 billion.[8] The bank at the end of 1992, had DM 14 billion in assets and 4 million customers scattered through Germany served by 304 offices. These customers held bank accounts, life and property insurance policies, and Citibank Visa credit cards. Profit for 1992 came to DM 105 million, compared to DM 69 million in 1990.[9]

Citibank Privatkunden has also extended its services to Belgium, France, Greece, and Spain through the strong Citibank facilities already in place in those countries. As of February 1993, Privatkunden had 186 offices in these four countries in operation and 3.3 million customers. Plans for further aggressive expansion are in place.[10]

KKB Bank was listed on the stock exchange; but minority stockholders proved a problem, complaining about low dividends. For this and other reasons, Citibank paid off these shareholders at DM 1,150 and took the stock off the exchange in 1992.[11]

Citibank Privatkunden was slow in moving into eastern Germany after reunification in 1990, largely because it ran into problems involving land claims. Finally in 1991, it opened a branch in eastern Berlin. It had forty offices in the East by the end of 1993.

Citibank has also organized two German insurance companies, which supply policies to customers of Privatkunden. In 1985, it founded a life insurance subsidiary called Citi Lebensversicherung AG in Dusseldorf. At the end of 1992, the insurer had 19,000 policies with a total face value of DM 523 million.[12]

In May 1992, Citibank founded a new property insurance subsidiary named Citi Versicherung AG, also in Dusseldorf, with an original capital of DM 4 million. This corporation handles all kinds of property insurance and has the same management board as Citi Lebensversicherung.[13] During its short first year of 1992 (May to December), Citi Versicherung wrote over 20,000 accident policies.[14]

U.S. banks in Germany suffer by reason of disadvantages arising out of the banking system in which they are competing. In addition, the American institutions have made serious mistakes of their own.

Among the structural features of German banking that hurt U.S. banks are

1. Germany has nationwide branch banking, and several banks have built up huge chain systems. Deutsche Bank has more than 1,900; Dresdner, 1,500; and Commerz, 900. Meanwhile, U.S. banks generally can, at best, serve their customers in only a few German cities. Citibank Privatkunden, with more than 300 branches, is the one exception.

2. German banks, especially those with large branch networks, take in huge savings and checking deposits at low interest costs. U.S. banks, on the other hand, again with the exception of Citibank Privatkunden, must pay much higher rates on the German money market to obtain funds; thus, their interest margins on loans are considerably smaller.

3. U.S. banks are generally not members of clearinghouse associations and thus must pay German members to clear their checks. This considerably increases costs of doing business.

4. German banks have more freedom from government regulation than their U.S. rivals. The combined supervision of the Bundesbank and the Bank Supervisory Office is much lighter than the U.S. equivalents—the Federal Reserve and the Comptroller of the Currency (or state banking authorities for state-chartered banks). German banks have nothing to duplicate the U.S. Federal Deposit Insurance Corporation (FDIC), which wraps additional regulatory layers around American banks.

5. Members of the managing boards of German banks have traditionally sat on several supervisory boards of their customers. Deutsche Bank, Dresdner Bank, and Commerzbank (the Big Three) have management board members on about half the 100 largest corporations. No other bank, American or German, can hope to seduce away such customers.[15]

6. German banks can buy stock in their customers, which is not permitted under American banking law. The banks owned 11 percent of all stock of German corporations in 1991. With voting proxies on stock held for customers plus their own holdings, the banks control about half of all German shares. This creates a tie to the customer that rival banks can seldom overcome.

7. In 1990, western German banks moved with incredible speed to set up their respective branch networks in the East. The weakened state-owned banks caved in

to the western Big Three and practically gave branches away before July 1, 1990, the day the mark became the currency in East Germany. Foreign banks, for the most part, did not try to follow, seldom leaving Berlin.

8. German banks can make loans in the form of purchases of the borrowers' stock. Often, the loan is not repaid and the bank's stock holding becomes more or less permanent. Control by the bank is virtually unbreakable by rival institutions.

9. Germany has no equivalent of the SEC; and under German principles of accounting, banks are able to keep secret far more financial data than American institutions. Thus, banks have hidden reserves and rarely report full operating profits, extraordinary income, or profit from trading on their own account. Consequently, banks, as well as other corporations, minimize their assets and profits and squirrel the latter away into hidden reserves.

Aside from the disadvantages just listed, U.S. banks in Germany have made mistakes that were avoidable. The most serious were as follows:

1. Most Americans going to manage banks in Germany had little knowledge of the country and its banking system. Some did not even have the necessary linguistic skills.

2. Rotation periods for American bankers sent to Germany were too short. They were reluctant to stay more than three years for fear they would lose out on promotions back in the home bank.

3. Some banks, especially Citibank, opened branches recklessly without adequate feasibility studies. In the 1960s particularly, an aura of unwarranted optimism seemed to infect the judgment of top management of U.S. banks contemplating moves into Germany.

4. U.S. banks did not take competition from German branches in America with sufficient seriousness and lost many good customers.

5. German bank customers put great emphasis on permanence of their banks. The Big Three in Germany are all more than 100 years old. The record of U.S. banks in Germany in starting and closing is, at best, pitiful.

6. American commercial banks have had frightening bank failures, which severely shook prospective German customers. There were 122 closings in the United States in 1992, with total assets of $44 billion, while there was only one in Germany, with DM 208 million.[16]

The nine American commercial banks active in Germany all have trading departments, which buy and sell securities on behalf of their customers. They also trade for the bank itself, known as "proprietary trading." J. P. Morgan has 2,000 people in its trading department worldwide, and bank analysts believe it usually derives 50 percent of its net income from trading. Citibank has seventy trading rooms throughout the world.[17] Citibank revenues from trading in 1993 were a record $2.9 billion; but in the first quarter of 1994, these revenues were only $71 million, compared with $457 million in 1993.

Trading revenues of Citibank in the first quarter of 1994 were reported as $66 million from foreign exchange (119 different currencies) and $5 million from securities. By comparison, in the first quarter of 1993, foreign-exchange revenues were $240 million and securities $217 million.[18]

Banks make profits from foreign-exchange transactions for their customers simply by buying at a lower rate than they sell, strictly a banking service. They also trade for their own accounts, which can be risky. Most banks do not like to talk about proprietary trading because investors in bank stocks do not regard it as a stable and reliable source of earnings.

For that reason, Chemical Bank will not let profits from trading for its own account grow to more than 20 percent of all trading net income. J. P. Morgan is an exception and has always been very strong in trading for its account. Such operations exceed market-making for its customers.

NOTES

1. *Commerce Germany*, Frankfurt, American Chamber of Commerce in Germany, 1 (1994): 6.

2. *International Herald-Tribune*, Paris, July 6, 1990.

3. *The Economist*, London, October 17, 1992, p. 72.

4. *Commerce Germany*, Frankfurt, American Chamber of Commerce in Germany, 10 (1991): 8.

5. *Commerce Germany*, Frankfurt, American Chamber of Commerce in Germany, 1 (1994): 6.

6. *Frankfurter Allgemeine Zeitung*, July 10, 1992.

7. *Financial Times*, London, July 3, 1986.

8. *Frankfurter Allgemeine Zeitung*, October 21, 1992.

9. *Frankfruter Allgemeine Zeitung*, May 14, 1992.

10. *Frankfurter Allgemeine Zeitung*, February 18, 1993.

11. *Frankfurter Allgemeine Zeitung*, November 20, 1992.

12. *Frankfurter Allgemeine Zeitung*, March 10, 1993.

13. *Frankfurter Allgemeine Zeitung*, May 6, 1992.

14. *Frankfurter Allgemeine Zeitung*, March 10, 1993.

15. *Der Spiegel*, Hamburg, February 25, 1991, p. 116.

16. *Frankfurter Allgemeine Zeitung*, September 16, 1993; *Wall Street Journal*, New York, June 28, 1993.

17. *New York Times*, August 4, 1993.

18. *Financial Times*, London, April 20, 1994.

19

General Motors and Ford in Germany

DEVELOPMENT OF GM

General Motors as a corporation did not come into existence until 1908, but the first of its constituent companies began in 1892. In that year, R. E. Olds converted his father's naval and industrial engine factory into the Olds Motor Vehicle Company. In 1895, the first Oldsmobile, a four-seater with five horsepower and a speed of 18 miles per hour, sold for $1,200.

Buick began in 1900, and soon there was a bevy of car manufacturers in the overcrowded industry. Will Durant, a director of Buick, saw the need for a merger and created GM in 1908. Oldsmobile and Buick became part of the consortium at the outset, followed later by Cadillac, Oakland (Pontiac), Chevrolet, and others, bringing the total to thirty.

In 1921, GM accounted for 12 percent of all U.S. car sales; and by 1941, it had 44 percent. After 1950, the smaller European cars started to cut into the American market; and by 1957, imports had 8 percent of the market. This trend has continued, and their market share in 1992 was 24.3 percent.

GM followed the same acquisition policy overseas, picking up Vauxhall in England in 1925 and Adam Opel AG in Germany in 1929—both well-established car makers. Opel had been founded in Rüsselheim about twenty-five miles from Frankfurt in 1862 by Adam Opel (1837–1895) to manufacture sewing machines. Then, in 1886, Opel began to make bicycles; and in 1898, his five sons initiated automobile production.

By 1928, Opel held the top position on the German auto market, a 44-percent share (43,000 units). In 1929, GM bought 80 percent of the Opel shares and then the balance in 1931, for a total price of $33 million.

The Germans seized Opel during World War II, and GM did not regain control until 1948. For a short while after the surrender, the Soviets eyed Opel as possible reparations even though it was not in their occupation zone but in that of the Americans. By 1949, production was up to 40,000, about the same as when GM bought Opel in 1929.

Opel has had growing sales in recent years and reached DM 29 billion in 1992; but sales fell 20 percent to DM 23 billion in the recession year of 1993. Opel had been profitable every year between 1987 (DM 479 million) and 1992 (DM 202 million), but it reported a loss of DM 571 million in 1993. In 1993, output decreased 21 percent to 856,000 units. Its share of the German market in 1993 fell to 16.1 percent from 17.1 percent in 1992. Opel declared no dividends to GM for 1993, while in 1992, they had amounted to DM 300 million.[1]

After staggering losses three years in a row (1990–1992), GM reported a profit of $2.4 billion in 1993 on sales of $138 billion, a profit margin of 1.8 percent. Market share in the United States came to 33.5 percent in 1993, up from 33.1 percent in 1992.[2]

FORD BACKGROUND

As a personality, Henry Ford (1863–1949) is so fascinating that one can easily be distracted from his most relevant activities in developing the world's second-largest automotive empire after General Motors. Henry was an engineering genius, but he was twenty-seven before he started in this field as an employee of the Detroit Edison Company. He rose to be chief engineer, but in his spare time he constructed experimental gasoline engines. In 1899, Ford was fired because his superiors felt he was giving too much time to his hobby. Working independently in a small shed, he developed two four-cylinder eighty-horsepower racing cars that won several races.

With $28,000 of capital raised from friends and neighbors, Henry established the Ford Motor Company in Detroit in 1903 in a converted wagon factory. Here, he developed his original Model A, a two-cylinder eight-horsepower design. The company produced 1,708 of them in the first year of operations.

In 1908, Ford introduced his Model T, and 10,000 units were produced in 1909. The car was a huge success over eighteen years, selling 20 million before being terminated in 1927 (second only to 21 million VW Beetles). GM introduced its new Chevrolet in that year, a more stylish and powerful car than Ford's Model T. Fortunately, Ford was ready with his new Model A, a six-cylinder car. It took six months to retool, but by the end of 1926, the new model was in production.

Henry relied on the application of three basic principles, two of which were not original with him. First, he used the assembly line to produce cars. Second, Ford applied standardized, interchangeable parts in assembling his automobiles.

Henry Ford's third principle (his own idea) was to produce a car at the lowest possible price to make it available to the largest number of buyers. By contrast, the European and other American manufacturers originally saw the car solely as the plaything of the rich.

Ford's Model T was invented in 1908 and cost $850 when the average worker earned $500 per year. His competitors were charging between $2,000 and $3,000. Ford concentrated on cost cutting and passing this on to the customers at continuously lower prices. The Model T revolutionized the automobile industry; and the price, by 1927, had been reduced to $290.

In 1904, the firm went multinational by starting Ford Motor of Canada with an assembly line just across the Detroit River in Windsor. In 1906, an English operation was established.

By the 1920s, Ford was selling in Germany, but the high protective tariff against imported automobiles was a major barrier. He decided to get inside that wall in 1926 by assembling his Model T in Berlin and importing American-made parts, which carried proportionally lower duties than a finished car. Ford-Werke AG, a wholly owned subsidiary of Ford, was created under German law.

Actual production began in early 1926, with a total of thirty-seven workers. Ford's historic decision to switch from the Model T to the Model A brought all his assembly lines to a halt for the necessary retooling. Detroit was shut down for only six months, but Berlin was idle for eleven. By 1929, the Berlin plant was literally bursting at the seams, but its maximum daily output was only sixty cars. Konrad Adenauer, the West German Chancellor from 1949 to 1963, was then mayor of Cologne. He offered enough inducements to convince Ford that the new plant should be in Cologne. At that time, Ford tried to acquire the small car division of BMW, but these negotiations failed.

When World War II broke out in 1939, the Cologne plant was seized by the government and converted to the production of trucks. Under strict secrecy, it was even used to assemble 1,500 trucks out of parts captured from the American armed forces. Allied bombers and artillery missed the Cologne plant; and the assembly line was ready to resume operations on May 8, 1945, the day before the official surrender of Germany.

About this time, Ford entered into negotiations to buy up Volkswagen, which had begun operations just before World War II. However, the merger talks were unsuccessful. Cologne remains headquarters and employs 25,000 of the company's 49,000 workers who assemble the Scorpio and Fiesta. The plant at Sarlouis in Germany turns out the Escort and Orion, while a facility at Genk in Belgium produces the Mondeo and the Transit truck.[3]

Ford-Werke had sales of DM 21 billion in 1993 (down 3.7 percent) and lost DM 132 million (DM 469 million in 1992). Its market share in Germany was 9.3 percent in both 1993 and 1992. However, Ford had been profitable for six years (1986–1991).

Although Ford has established a solid dealer network in eastern Germany since the Berlin Wall fell in 1989, it has refrained from investing in manufacturing facilities like GM, Mercedes, and VW. Ford's strategy is to manufacture outside of the East and ship its products into this market.

GM AND FORD IN GERMANY

GM's German subsidiary gradually pulled ahead of Ford's after 1987 on the highly competitive auto market of Germany. By 1992, Opel had a substantial lead in production, sales, market share, and profits over Ford-Werke. It also performed well against Mercedes, BMW, and Volkswagen, the leading German car makers. Furthermore, Opel has maintained its position against French, Italian, and Japanese rivals, who do not produce cars in Germany but export to the Germans in respectable quantities.

In 1987, both Ford and GM had sales of DM 17 billion in Germany, but GM grew more vigorously over the next five years. It climbed 70 percent to DM 29 billion in 1992, while Ford's growth to DM 22 billion was only 29 percent. GM has also outperformed Ford-Werke in profits. Both lost money in 1985, but Ford regained profitability in 1986 and Opel in 1987. While Opel profits climbed from DM 479 million in 1987 to DM 1 billion in 1991, the first full year of booming sales after reunification, Ford declined from DM 810 million to DM 141 million in 1991. By 1992, the boom was over and Opel profits fell 81 percent to DM 202 million; Ford went into the red to the tune of DM 469 million.[4] In 1993, Opel had sales of DM 23 billion and a loss of DM 500 million. Ford reported sales of DM 21 billion and a loss of DM 100 million.

Among Germany's six automakers, only BMW managed to turn a profit in 1993 (DM 500 million on sales of DM 29 billion). Volkswagen lost DM 1.9 billion on sales of DM 75 billion, Mercedes-Benz lost DM 1.1 billion on sales of DM 64 billion, and Porsche lost DM 200 million on sales of DM 1.9 billion.[5]

A variety of reasons account for GM's outperformance of Ford in Germany. Among the most significant are as follows:

1. Opel was more aggressive in launching sleek new models. This helped counteract the German slogan: "Every yokel drives an Opel."
2. Opel was more vigorous in cutting costs.
3. Opel began running its plants around the clock.
4. Opel, in 1989, became the first major European manufacturer to introduce cata-

lytic converters across its full range of models. This had great appeal to the German customer, perhaps the most pro-environment in the world.

5. Opel shook up its cozy relationships with suppliers by aggressively signing up new suppliers both inside and outside Germany, thereby slashing the cost of parts.

6. Opel reacted more quickly and more effectively to the fall of the Berlin Wall in 1989, which revealed 17 million car-hungry Germans anxious to switch from their pathetic Trabants and Wartburgs to modern automobiles. Opel immediately sent teams eastward to set up dealerships in every town with more than 10,000 people. By 1993, Opel had 373 dealers in the East.

7. Opel published 1 million copies of a book for eastern Germans on how to buy a car.

8. Opel moved to build two assembly plants in Eisenach in eastern Germany, while Ford decided to refrain from production in the East. Instead, it would sell cars made in the West to the easterners.

9. Eastern workers in Eisenach have proved easier to train in the more efficient Japanese methods than western workers in Rüsselheim. It is thought that easterners were convinced that their Marxist methods were ineffective and thus were more willing to learn the new.

10. Labor costs are still lower in the Eisenach plants, although the differential will disappear over the years to come.

11. In 1986, General Motors of Europe, responsible for Opel operations, moved its headquarters out of Rüsselheim and thus weakened its close ties with Opel. In Zurich (the new location), management of Opel became less personal and more efficient.

In May 1990, five months before reunification, Opel entered a joint venture with Automobilwerke Eisenach GmbH (maker of the much-derided East German Wartburg) to assemble Opel Vectras in its Eisenach plant. Opel invested $16 million and took 80 percent in the joint venture firm, Opel-AWE GmbH. Shortly after Unity Day on October 3, 1990, cars started rolling at the annual rate of 10,000.

Opel also decided to build a bigger, brand new assembly line in Eisenach. Construction on virgin land reduced the likelihood of title and pollution problems. Work began in February 1991 under the administration of a newly created subsidiary, Opel Eisenach GmbH. It invested DM 1 billion and twenty months later, in October 1992, Astras began to drive off the assembly line. The plant reached its 125,000 annual capacity at the end of 1993, with 2,000 workers on three shifts. By contrast, before 1989 in Eisenach, 10,000 workers turned out 100,000 rattle-trap Wartburgs per year under Marxist conditions.

This new plant in Eisenach has drawn favorable attention, being hailed by Opel and neutral sources as the most modern in Europe. The average time to build a car is eighteen hours, compared with thirty hours in the older German plants.[6]

GM has decided to use Opel to spearhead its expansion into international car markets outside of the United States. Louis Hughes, executive vice president of GM Europe, said in May 1994 that the firm has made a strategic decision to further internationalize and expand the Opel name and Opel products around the world.[7]

Opel is assembling its Astra in Hungary, Taiwan, South Africa, and Turkey and has planned such facilities in Poland, India, Thailand, and Indonesia. The Corsa is in production in Brazil and is in planning for Mexico; the Vectra is being produced in Turkey, Brazil, Egypt, and Malaysia. Opel also has plans for the car in Indonesia and Thailand.

While Chrysler does not assemble cars in Germany, it does have 220 distributors and sold 5,000 units in 1993. Chrysler ranked seventh on sales on the global market in 1993.

AUTO MARKET

In 1993, fifteen auto manufacturers dominated the world market. They ranked as follows on the basis of sales in billions of dollars:[8]

1.	General Motors (United States)	133,622
2.	Ford Motor (United States)	108,521
3.	Toyota Motor (Japan)	85,283
4.	Daimler-Benz (Germany)	59,102
5.	Nissan Motor (Japan)	53,760
6.	Volkswagen (Germany)	46,312
7.	Chrysler (United States)	43,600
8.	Honda Motor (Japan)	35,798
9.	Fiat (Italy)	34,707
10.	Renault (France)	29,975
11.	Mitsubishi Motors (Japan)	27,311
12.	Peugeot (France)	25,669
13.	Mazda Motor (Japan)	20,279
14.	BMW (Germany)	17,546
15.	Volvo (Sweden)	14,272

Three of the auto giants are German: Daimler-Benz, Volkswagen, and BMW (Bayerische Motoren Werke). Two others, GM and Ford, have German subsidiaries, which are major producers in the German market. The rest all sell their cars in Germany.

For 1993, world sales of automobiles came to 33 million. The country totals in millions were as follows:

United States	8.4
Japan	4.1

Germany	3.1
Italy	1.8
United Kingdom	1.77
France	1.72
South Korea	0.9
Spain	0.7
Turkey	0.44
China	0.43

In 1952, there were 3.4 million motor vehicles on 353,000 kilometers of highway in West Germany. By 1990, the number had multiplied ten times to 34.9 million (30.1 million cars and 4.8 million commercial vehicles), but the highway system had grown only 40 percent.[9] It is no wonder that German drivers face horrifying gridlocks on weekends and vacations.

The average price of new cars in Germany has been climbing every year. In 1975, it was DM 10,700; and by 1989, it reached DM 27,100, an increase of 153 percent.[10] The chief cause of this jump has been the comparatively rapid rise of labor costs in the German automobile industry. Total hourly costs in Germany were DM 26.84 in 1980, the third highest after Sweden (DM 28.60) and Belgium (DM 28.14). By 1991, Germany had climbed 65 percent to DM 44.47, ahead of Belgium (DM 35.12) but still second to Sweden (DM 46). During this same eleven-year period, U.S. costs (fourth highest in 1980) had climbed only 44 percent and ranked third.[11]

East Germans in 1988 had little opportunity and even less income for buying western automobiles. As of September 1, 1988, there were 3.6 million cars registered in East Germany, broken down as follows:[12]

Trabant (East German)	1,958,000
Wartburg (East German)	674,000
Lada	349,000
Skoda	307,000
Moskwitsch	169,000
Dacia	74,000
SAS	58,000
Polish Fiat	38,000

On July 1, 1990, economic unification brought the mark to the eastern Germans, and they went slightly berserk in buying western cars, both new and used (330,000 in all). Following is a list of the kinds of cars registered in the new states in the first two months, July and August 1990:[13]

Volkswagen	79,000
Opel	70,000

Ford	48,000
Audi	25,000
BMW	14,000
Renualt	12,000
Fiat	11,000
Mazda	8,000
Mercedes-Benz	8,000
Toyota	8,000

EXPORTS FROM GERMANY

Germany exported 2.2 million cars in 1991, or 52 percent of all produced. Their destinations were as follows:

Italy	18.4%
France	11.2%
Britain	8.1%
United States	7.4%
Japan	4.5%
Other Europe	44.3%
Other Asia	3.2%
Other	2.9%

German cars have long been popular in the United States; but the increasing dollar value of the mark has excessively pushed up their prices, thereby reducing sales. America in 1982 bought 246,000 German cars. This total climbed steadily year by year until it reached 445,000 in 1986. German sales declined rapidly to 212,000 in 1989. By 1992, the figure was 220,000.

Much has been written about the difficulties in selling foreign cars in Japan. In 1992, a total of 4.4 million was sold in that country, but only 181,000 were made abroad. This gave foreign manufacturers only 4.1 percent of the market. By comparison, this figure was 24 percent in the United States and 35 percent in Germany.

In 1992, German manufacturers dominated imports into Japan. VW supplied 42,000; Mercedes, 29,000; and BMW, 25,000, for a combined 54 percent of all imports. GM sold 9,000, Ford sold 3,000, and Chrysler sold 1,000, a total of 7 percent.[14]

IMPORTS INTO GERMANY

In 1952, the Germans bought 8,000 imported cars, or 4.2 percent of their total purchases. This increased to 35.2 percent in 1991. In western Germany, it was 33 percent; and in the East, 50 percent. Commercial vehicles imported in 1952 registered 600 (0.7 percent of the market) and grew to 118,000 in 1991 (37 percent). The share was 33 percent in the West and 40 percent in the East.

New car registrations in Western Europe were as follows in 1992 (in millions of cars):[15]

Germany	3.9
Italy	2.3
France	2.1
United Kingdom	1.5
Spain	0.9

New car registrations (in millions) by maker in 1992 were as follows in Western Europe:[16]

Volkswagen	2.32
Peugeot	1.64
General Motors	1.64
Fiat	1.55
Ford	1.52
Renault	1.43

Japanese costs of manufacturing have long given these cars a great advantage in Germany as well as in other markets. A study done in 1993 by McKinsey Consulting gave the following comparative costs with the average Japanese car made in Japan equal to 100:[17]

Mercedes-Benz	140–150
BMW	140–150
Volkswagen	140
Ford	130–135
Opel	130–135
Volvo	125–130
Fiat	120–125
Peugeot	120
Renault	120
Nissan (in United Kingdom)	110–115
Japanese (in Japan)	100

Japan sold 557,000 motor vehicles in Germany in 1991, a 20-percent increase over 1990. By contrast, total Japanese exports were down 1.3 percent to 5.75 million units in 1991.[18]

DAIMLER-BENZ

Many Americans still think that Henry Ford invented the automobile. Actually, the Germans were the inventors; in fact, they invented it twice. Carl Benz, an engineer in Mannheim, assembled and drove the first car in 1885. Carl's invention was a three-wheeled carriage in which a gasoline motor replaced the horse. His historic drive was quickly terminated, however, when his ignition wire broke. Nevertheless, Carl Benz, then 42 years old, received a patent on January 29, 1886, for the first practical automobile.

Another German engineer, Gotfried Daimler, sixty miles away in Stuttgart and operating without knowledge of Benz, assembled a four-wheeler in 1886. It was more substantial but still primitive. Daimler and Benz never met; but forty years later in 1926, these firms merged to found what is now Germany's top industrial corporation.

During World War II, Daimler-Benz and all other German auto manufacturers were nationalized by Hitler and converted to war production. Two weeks of intense Allied bombing in September 1944 destroyed 70 percent of Daimler's facilities. After the war, Daimler-Benz enjoyed a very prosperous growth with seven plants in Germany as well as facilities in Argentina, Brazil, Mexico, India, South Africa, Belgium, and Ireland.

Until 1984, Daimler-Benz received 95 percent of its revenues from motor vehicles (53 percent cars and 42 percent trucks, vans, and buses). Six years later in 1990, vehicles only accounted for 67 percent of sales (40 percent cars and 27 percent commercial units). The remaining 33 percent now comes from a wide variety of products.[19]

Daimler's diversification took place only after a bitter management conflict. In 1984, Werner Breitschwert, Daimler's chairman of the management board and a plodding engineer, wanted to keep the company focused on making superbly engineered cars. Opposing him was Alfred Herrhausen, the powerful and dynamic chairman of Deutsche Bank's management board, which bank was the leading stockholder of Daimler-Benz. He was also chairman of Daimler's supervisory board and wanted to push out Breitschwert, replacing him with Edzard Reuter, Daimler's management board member for finance. Both Herrhausen and Reuter strongly advocated wide diversification of the company.

In 1987, Reuter and Herrhausen won and Breitschwert took early retirement. Reuter became chairman of the management board and bought up AEG, a large electronics manufacturer, as well as two aircraft makers and an engine producer. Then Reuter reorganized his giant conglomerate into four major divisions as follows:[20]

1. *Mercedes-Benz AG*, a brand new corporation to handle the auto business. It had 209,000 employees and sales of DM 64 billion in 1993, compared with DM 97 billion for Daimler-Benz as a whole.

2. *Deutsche Aerospace AG*, a new company to manage the aerospace and defense operations of Daimler. It employed 86,000 and had sales of DM 18 billion in 1993, but lost DM 0.6 billion.

3. *AEG AG*, the acquired electronics firm, which had 58,000 workers with sales of DM 11 billion in 1993 and a loss of DM 1.1 billion.

4. *Debis AG* (Daimler-Benz Interservices), which provides financial and information services to the producing companies of Daimler and outside firms. It had 8,000 workers and $3.6 billion in sales in 1992.

This reorganization boosted total employment of Daimler-Benz to 366,000 in 1993.

As pointed out in Chapter 10, Daimler shocked the world in September 1993 by publishing its financial results for the first half of 1993 under American accounting principles and under the traditional German rules for the first time. This showed a loss of $556 million under U.S. accountancy and a profit of $65 million using the German system.[21] For 1993 as a whole, Daimler lost $1.05 billion under U.S. rules and made $371 million by German rules.[22]

On June 26, 1994, the Daimler board of supervisors named a successor to Edzard Reuter, to take over in May 1995. The new chairman of the management board will be Jürgen Schrempp, who has held the same position since 1989 with Daimler's subsidiary, Deutsche Aerospace.

An interesting story surrounds the name Mercedes on the prestigious automobile that carries it. In 1893, a speed nut, Emil Jellineck, in Nice, bought a car from Daimler with a top speed of 24 kilometers per hour. Emil complained bitterly that it was too slow, and Daimler built one for him which could reach 42 kilometers per hour.

Jellineck entered the car in a race in Nice under the name of his ten-year-old daughter Mercedes. Her picture shows she was no beauty, but nevertheless, the car won. Her father recommended that Daimler call its car after his child. Daimler did so, and the name was registered as a trademark in 1902.[23]

VOLKSWAGEN

Dr. Ferdinand Porsche, who produced the first and most famous "People's Car," was chief designer for Daimler's Austrian subsidiaries from 1906 to 1911. During this time, he designed sixty-five cars, mostly powerful and luxurious models. He continued to dream of a vehicle that would be low cost and affordable for the ordinary consumer. In the 1920s, he produced the forerunner of what later was called the Beetle but could not find private financiers for his project.

Porsche finally sold Hitler on his car in 1934, Volkswagen AG was established in 1937, and production was started at a new plant in Wolfsburg. In September 1939, the outbreak of World War II terminated the government's effort to supply the Germans with a low-price car. The factory was converted to making vehicles for the military.

Dr. Porsche never participated in his dream. After the war, he was imprisoned for two years on charges of war crimes. While he was later acquitted, his health was ruined and he died in 1951.

The badly battered assembly line in Wolfsburg was in the British Zone of Occupation from 1945 to 1949. In 1949, it became the property of the newly formed Federal Republic of Germany and the State of Lower Saxony, in which Wolfsburg is located. The razed factory was offered to Henry Ford II, but he declined. Heinz Nordhoff, a prewar executive with Opel, was appointed chairman of the management board. He rebuilt the factory and began to put cars on the road. It has now sold over 21 million, the most popular car in history. It even outsold the Model T Ford, which numbered 20 million units between 1907 and 1927.[24]

VW shipped its first boatload to the United States in 1949 and could only sell two cars. In 1950, sales were 330. The Nazi associations hurt the car in America for several years. Finally, in 1959, an American advertising agency took over publicity, and the "people's car" began to appeal to large numbers of U.S. buyers. In that year, Doyle Dane Bernbach gave it the name *Beetle*. The firm also coined such phrases as "Ugly is only skin-deep" and "Think small" to turn drawbacks into selling points. Annual production of the Beetle peaked at 400,000 in 1968, but by the early 1970s, the car was considered outdated. The last Beetle from Germany was sold in the United States in 1977. It is still made in Mexico, where it sells for $7,000 (the cheapest car on that market). However, it cannot be registered in the United States or Europe because it no longer meets safety and emission standards.[25] VW has replaced the Beetle with a variety of models: Golf, Passat, Polo, Jetta, Caravelle, Corrado, and Scirocco.

VW made a major mistake when it decided to make cars in the United States, starting in 1978. Two plants were put in operation—one in Michigan and the other in Pennsylvania. The Michigan facility was sold to Chrysler in 1981. The Pennsylvania factory had serious quality problems since the Rabbits built there had spongy suspensions and slipped out of gear on the highway. The cars were later improved, but that came too late. Output never rose to a break-even level, and VW lost $144 million in the United States alone in 1983. The Pennsylvania plant was closed in 1988.[26]

Prospects are not good for VW in the United States, the world's largest market. From 217,000 in 1986 to 85,000 in 1991, Volkswagen has suffered a heavy decline in American buyers.

Analysts consider VW headquarters in Wolfsburg, a one-company city of 128,000, a costly white elephant. About 60,000 workers out of 250,000 are employed at this huge, rambling, and extremely inefficient plant.

In 1960, the government-owned VW was 60-percent privatized when that much stock was sold to the public. The remaining 40 percent was held, 20 percent by the federal government and 20 percent by the State of Lower Saxony. Bonn has since privatized its 20-percent holding, but Lower Saxony still owns 20 percent.

At the annual stockholders meeting in June 1994, Ferdinand Piech, chairman of the management board, faced severe criticism. He had promised at the 1993 meeting that VW would break even in 1993. Instead, the firm lost DM 1.9 billion in that year.

BMW

BMW (Bayerische Motoren Werke AG) is clearly the most efficient automobile manufacturer in Germany. With headquarters in Munich, it fortunately had the leadership of Eberhard von Kuenheim, who served as chairman of the management board from 1970 to 1993. He resisted the strong expansion course followed by Daimler-Benz and VW. Kuenheim has also declined to invest in East German car and truck plants like Daimler and VW. Bernd Pischetsrieder took Kuenheim's position in 1993.

BMW was incorporated as an airplane manufacturer in 1917 during World War I. General Franz Josef Popp, former Inspector General of the Austrian-Hungarian army, was appointed chairman of the management board, a position he held until 1941. After 1918, BMW turned to the production of train brakes. (The Treaty of Versailles banned aircraft production in Germany.)

In the early 1920s, BMW developed a line of motorcycles, the R32. Ernst Henne, riding a R32, broke the world speed record in 1929. His new time was 173.35 miles per hour, and the record held until 1937.

BMW did not get into the auto business until 1928 when it acquired the ailing Fahrzeugwerke in Eisenach. A year later, the Dixi (a luxury car) was produced. It won racing prizes but created financial problems for BMW, which even discussed a merger with Daimler-Benz in some detail. Fortunately, however, BMW was able to develop a smaller six-cylinder Dixi, which proved a most effective competitor with Daimler. The merger talks were terminated.

Another Dixi, the DA2, was introduced later in 1929 with improved handling, better brakes, and more attractive interior. BMW sold 5,390 Dixi DA2s in 1929, "a mini car at a mini price," followed by 6,792 in 1930. Thus, BMW survived the Great Depression, which forced 17,000 German firms into bankruptcy.

When Hitler assumed power in 1933, BMW and all other German car manufacturers were required to make airplane engines for the new Luftwaffe (in 1939, they were taken over completely by the government). Also in 1939, an edict of the German Ministry of Aviation required BMW to take in by merger the Brandenburgishe Motoren Werke, and a new plant was constructed by the government for BMW tucked away in the woods near Munich. Moreover, the buildings at this factory were constructed at a distance from each other to minimize air-raid damage.

In 1941, the Nazi government ordered BMW to halt all auto production and concentrate on military aircraft. After the war, the Allied Occupation Command ordered the dismantling of many BMW facilities. Few West Germans were in a position to buy a car; but in 1948, the firm developed a very successful motorcycle, the R24. Production reached 10,000 in 1949 and 17,000 in 1950, 18 percent of which were exported.

BMW's original car-making facility in Eisenach was now in East Germany. After World War II, the plant was nationalized and converted to producing frumpy Wartburg cars, the larger of the two auto disasters turned out by East Germany. Meanwhile, BMW turned its Munich aircraft-making plant into producing some of the most prized and most expensive cars in the world.[27]

After the Berlin Wall fell in 1989, the East Germans invited BMW engineers to tour the Eisenach plant, hoping they would take back their nationalized property. Kuenheim declined to make a claim for the factory and even waived monetary damages, to which German law entitles BMW. Kuenheim explained that the Eisenach plant did not come close to meeting BMW environmental standards, that it had four times as many workers as needed, and that it looked like "the picture of one of our plants in 1928, with no renovation since."[28]

BMW has enjoyed a steady growth of both sales and profits in recent years. In 1991, revenues climbed 9.8 percent over 1990 to DM 29 billion. Profits at DM 782 million in 1991 were up 12.5 percent. This was a superb performance. It must be emphasized that BMW is small with 550,000 cars produced in 1991 in relation to 7 million at GM, 4.5 million at Toyota, and 3 million at Volkswagen.[29]

More important, however, is the fact that BMW in 1992 produced and sold more cars than Mercedes-Benz for the first time in history. BMW sold 590,000 worldwide, while Mercedes reported 530,000. The Munich-based firm also outsold its rival in the crucial U.S. market—64,000 to 62,000. Even so, BMW's American sales in 1992 were off 32.9 percent from its peak of 96,000 in 1986.

One major reason for BMW taking the lead on the U.S. market is that it offers a broader range of affordable cars. BMW sells seven models that cost less than $40,000, while Mercedes offers only two. The highest-priced BMW, the 850 CI sports coupe, has a price tag of $83,000, while the most expensive Mercedes, the 600 SEC coupe, costs $132,000.[30]

PORSCHE

It is the smallest automaker in Germany, but it has by far the longest name: "Doktor Ingenieur honoris causa Ferdinand Porsche AG." The firm is named after the distinguished engineer, who designed the original Beetle for VW before World War II.

In fiscal year 1985, Porsche profits reached a peak of DM 120 million; but in 1992 they had shrunk to DM 17 million. In 1992, a loss of DM 65 million was reported—its first. Sales were DM 2.6 billion in 1992, down from DM 3.1 billion in 1991.[31] They fell another 28 percent to DM 1.9 billion in 1993. At its peak in 1987, Porsche turned out 50,000 cars; but this dropped to 22,000 in 1992. About half were sold in Germany. Of the 11,000 exported, 4,100 went to the United States, which had once bought 9,000 per year.[32]

Two families, Porsche and Piech (both descendants of Doctor Ferdinand), own all the common stock and 40 percent of the preferred. The supervisory board is made up entirely of members of the two clans. They have fought in public over the years, but Ferry Porsche (son of Ferdinand), now 86, is still chairman of the supervisory board. Ferdinand Piech, now chairman of VW's management board, is a member of the family and was formerly a member of the Porsche supervisory board.

The present chairman of the Porsche management board is Wendelin Wiedeking, a forty-two-year-old production engineer who was selected by the supervisory board in September 1992. He is the fifth chairman since 1980.

NOTES

1. *Wall Street Journal Europe*, Brussels, June 29, 1994.
2. *Value Line*, New York, June 17, 1994, p. 105.
3. *Frankfurter Allgemeine Zeitung*, June 30, 1994.
4. *Wall Street Journal*, New York, June 9, 1993.
5. *Frankfurter Allgemeine Zeitung*, July 5, 1994.
6. *Financial Times*, London, June 9, 1993.
7. *Financial Times*, London, May 26, 1994.
8. *Fortune*, New York, July 25, 1994, p. 174.
9. *Die Zeit*, Hamburg, August 31, 1990.
10. *Berliner Morgenpost*, September 13, 1989.
11. *Frankfurter Allgemeine Zeitung*, September 26, 1992.
12. *Berliner Morgenpost*, October 3, 1990.
13. Ibid.
14. *Financial Times*, London, June 28, 1993.
15. Ibid.
16. *The Economist*, London, March 13, 1993, p. 74.
17. *Der Spiegel*, Hamburg, 8 (1993): 119.
18. *Frankfurter Allgemeine Zeitung*, January 31, 1992.
19. *The Economist*, London, April 27, 1991, p. 65.
20. *New York Times*, August 3, 1993.
21. *New York Times*, September 18, 1993.
22. *Wall Street Journal*, New York, April 13, 1994.
23. *Frankfurter Allgemeine Zeitung*, June 29, 1989.
24. *The Economist*, London, May 23, 1992, p. 70.
25. *Frankfurter Allgemeine Zeitung*, November 27, 1992.
26. *Wall Street Journal*, New York, June 26, 1992.
27. *Wall Street Journal*, New York, April 18, 1990.
28. Ibid.
29. *The Economist*, London, January 4, 1992, p. 60.
30. *Wall Street Journal*, New York, January 20, 1993.
31. *Wall Street Journal*, New York, September 30, 1992.
32. *New York Times*, April 27, 1992.

20

Coca-Cola and Pepsico

Coca-Cola (Coke) and Pepsico (Pepsi), after a century of "cola wars," have reached something of a stalemate on the domestic market. In 1993, Coke took a 41 percent share and Pepsi 30 percent.[1] Outside the United States, Coca-Cola has been much stronger, leading about 47 percent to 15 percent.

Their subsidiaries on the German front, however, filed quite different battle reports in 1991. Coca-Cola GmbH in Essen used German reunification to win an astounding victory over Pepsi Cola GmbH in Offenbach, scoring a 20-percent market share to 2.5 percent for Pepsi. Coke increased sales by an incredible 66 percent in 1991 over 1990, from $2.3 billion to $3.9 billion. Meanwhile, Pepsi fell 10 percent, from $570 million to $510 million.

Coca-Cola not only badly mauled Pepsico but at the same time turned in an incredible 66-percent increase in sales over 1990, the highest reported by any U.S. subsidiary in Germany. Procter & Gamble was second, with a growth of 24 percent.[2]

Coke was first sold on the German market in 1929. Sugar shortages in World War II almost forced a closing, but the German subsidiary developed its own soft drink called Fanta using available components. This enabled it to keep going until the hostilities ended. Fanta is now marketed by Coca-Cola in the United States and other countries.

Coke's spectacular performance in Germany in 1991 arose out of two groups of factors: astute moves by Coca-Cola, on the one hand, and inept decisions by Pepsi, on the other. The principal successful achievements by Coke were as follows:

1. Coca-Cola streamlined and consolidated its 105 German bottlers into about 30 highly efficient factories. Some of these bottlers are breweries, including Becks, the leading exporter of German beer to the United States.

2. Coca-Cola had been selling a small amount of its products in East Germany long before the Berlin Wall fell on November 9, 1989. Genex, the state-owned mail-order house, sold Coke for hard currencies. So did Intershops, the government's chain of some 200 department stores. Coca-Cola was also available in luxury hotels, bars, and restaurants, which took payment only in convertible funds.

3. Coke commercials televised from West Germany had acquainted the East German viewers with their product.

4. The East Germans in 1991 increased their consumption of Coke by an astounding 252 percent, compared with 10 percent by the West Germans. Cases sold went up from 21 million to 74 million in eastern Germany and from 482 to 531 million in the West.

5. Coke's competitors, "Hit Cola" and "Klub Cola," produced by East Germany's state-owned bottlers, were so awful in taste that they cannot be either described or imagined. When thousands of easterners poured through the newly opened wall into West Berlin in 1989, bananas and Coke were often their first purchases.

6. When the Berlin Wall fell, Coke immediately shipped its products into the East, even though it had no distribution system in place.

7. West Berlin employees of Coca-Cola were sent out on the streets to give away free cans and bottles to the East Berlin visitors.

8. Coke has invested $450 million in East German bottlers and delivery systems, some brand new and others previously owned by the Marxist state. Originally, the policy was to acquire all needed facilities out of the plants originally built by the East German government (1949–1989). It was soon discovered that some of these properties would have involved troublesome and delaying claims by former owners. Accordingly, Coca-Cola bought only properties with clean titles from Treuhand Anstalt, the German agency responsible for privatizing the former communist enterprises. It built brand new plants where necessary to complete its network in the East.

9. Coca-Cola quickly assembled and trained a sales organization to move its products in eastern Germany.

10. Coke installed 8,000 vending machines, taps, and coolers throughout eastern Germany by early 1991.

According to Jürgen Schlebrowski, appointed manager of Pepsi Cola GmbH in 1992, profits for 1991 in Germany were budgeted at DM 30 million but actually turned out to be a loss of DM 1 million. He attributed the decline mostly to faulty management decisions made under his predecessor.[3] The chief blunders seem to have been the following:

1. Pepsi wanted to improve profits and decided to raise prices to the level of Coke. This backfired because many German consumers switched to Coke when the prices of the two drinks were equal.

2. Pepsi planned to buy out some of their franchised dealers and let the central bottling facility of Offenbach take over deliveries to the retailers. This changeover took longer than expected because the Offenbach plant was not sufficiently prepared to assume the increased deliveries. Furthermore, the cost of purchasing the rights of the dealers exceeded expectations.

3. Tengelmann, Germany's largest chain of food stores, canceled its contract with Pepsi in July 1991.

4. Pepsico failed to follow up its initial 1990 success in eastern Germany and lost business there in 1991.

Coca-Cola had the same management team at the top as chairman and president from 1981 to 1993. They were Robert C. Goizueta, born in Havana, and Donald R. Keough, a native of Maurice, Iowa. Goizueta received his degree in chemistry from Yale in 1953 and went to work for Coke the same year. Keough got his B.S. degree from Creighton in 1949, went to work for Butternut Foods in Omaha, and joined Coca-Cola in 1967.

Goizueta and Keough led Coke through twelve very successful years. They regained market leadership over Pepsi in the cola wars here in the United States. Their management almost doubled sales between 1982 and 1991, from $6.2 to $11.56 billion. They pushed up the profit margin from 8.2 percent to 14 percent, and profits as a percentage of equity climbed from 18.4 percent to 36.6 percent in the same nine-year period. Earnings per share have gone from $0.44 to $1.22, and dividends as a percentage of profit have held at 40 percent and better.[4]

On a per capita basis, Germany is the sixth-best consumer nation for Coca-Cola. The following shows per capita consumption in 1990 by country in eight-ounce servings.[5]

United States	292
Mexico	263
Australia	224
Norway	200
Canada	180
Germany	149
Spain	148
Japan	112
Colombia	111
Argentina	105
United Kingdom	99
Brazil	99
Philippines	92
Italy	86

South Korea	63
Taiwan	48
France	48
Thailand	42
Morocco	32
Turkey	20
Indonesia	4

It is expected that per capita consumption in Germany will double and be equal to that of the United States by the year 2000.[6]

Coke sold about two-thirds of its output overseas in 1992. These sales increased an average of 31 percent per year from 1985 to 1992, while the increase in domestic figures averaged 7 percent.[7]

Germany is the largest buyer of Coca-Cola in the twelve-nation European Union, which contributed $767 million in 1991 to the global operating profits. This total exceeded operating profits generated in the United States, where sales were about twice the amount of the EU.[8]

Coke reported that in 1985 about 50 percent of its operating profits came from overseas. By 1990, this percentage had increased to 80 percent, making it one of America's most international companies. In 1990, Pepsico had 16 percent of its operating profits from foreign activities.[9]

Coca-Cola sales in Germany in recent years have been as follows:

1988	DM 3.2 billion
1989	DM 3.4 billion
1990	DM 3.6 billion
1991	DM 6.0 billion
1992	DM 6.8 billion
1993	DM 6.7 billion

Pepsi has reported:

1990	DM 950 million
1991	DM 850 million

Coca-Cola claims that it outsells Pepsico 4 to 1 outside the United States. Pepsico says the ratio is only 3 to 1.[10] Foreign sales of Pepsi grew 12 percent in 1991 over 1990. Only Germany failed to participate in this growth; sales there fell from DM 950 to DM 850 million, a drop of 10 percent.

Both of America's top cola drinks originated in the South—Coke in Atlanta in 1886 and Pepsi in New Bern, North Carolina, in 1892. Pepsi, like many other drinks, was brewed to enter the affluent market enjoyed by Coke, and long ago it became the only powerful competitor. Dr. Pepper/7-Up, in third place on the U.S. market, took 11 percent in 1992, compared with 41 percent for Coke and 32 percent for Pepsi. The total soft drink domestic market was $47 billion.

The fascinating cola wars between Coca-Cola and Pepsico still rage vigorously a century after their discoveries. In 1950, Coke domestically outsold Pepsi 5 to 1; but by 1984, Pepsi had 22.8 percent and Coke 21.6 percent. Then Coke put on a strong drive and regained leadership.

Coca-Cola and Pepsico both have acquired companies outside their main field. Thus, while Coke leads in soft drinks, its total sales are well below Pepsico. In 1993, Pepsi reported $25 billion in sales, compared with $13.9 billion for Coca-Cola. Coke's spectacular profit performance has overshadowed the impressive returns of Pepsico. In 1993, Coca-Cola reported $2.1 billion net income (15.7 percent of sales), while Pepsico had $1.5 billion (6.3 percent of sales). For the past five years, Coke's profit margin has consistently been at least twice that of Pepsico.

Comparing the two corporations as to profits as a percentage of equity, Coke made 47 percent in 1993 and Pepsi 25 percent. The differential has been fairly constant in recent years. Profits as a percentage of assets in 1993 were 18 percent for Coke and 7 percent for Pepsi.[11]

Analyst Emanuel Goodman at Paine Webber has estimated that Coke makes four times more profit on each gallon of concentrate sold in Asia than in the United States. In Europe, he calculates the ratio is 3 to 1.[12]

Fortune compiles a study every year of the 500 largest industrial corporations in the world on the basis of sales. The study for 1993 reported that in the beverage industry (alcoholic and nonalcoholic combined), only eighteen corporations were big enough to be listed. Pepsico and Coca-Cola placed first and second, with Anheuser-Busch third. Anheuser-Busch had $11.5 billion in sales and $0.5 billion in profits (a profit margin of 5 percent).[13] This was very favorable but less attractive than that of Coca-Cola.

It is also worth noting that no German company was big enough to appear in the charmed group. There are still more than 1,200 breweries in Germany, but none of them had sufficient sales to reach the world's top 500. Brau und Brunnen AG—with $1 billion—was first in 1993, well behind the beverage companies just listed; and profits were only 1 percent of sales. Brau und Brunnen is the resulting conglomerate of some thirty independent breweries, with such popular beers as Dortmund Union, Schultheiss, and Schlösser.

NOTES

1. *Wall Street Journal*, New York, February 3, 1994.

2. *Commerce Germany*, Frankfurt, American Chamber of Commerce in Germany, 4 (1992): 16.

3. *Frankfurter Allgemeine Zeitung*, April 10, 1992.

4. *Value Line*, New York, February 19, 1993, pp. 1536, 1538.

5. *New York Times*, November 25, 1991.
6. Ibid.
7. *Wall Street Journal*, New York, July 23, 1993.
8. *Business Week*, New York, April 13, 1992, p. 96.
9. *New York Times*, November 25, 1991.
10. *Financial Times*, London, January 16, 1992.
11. *Fortune*, New York, July 25, 1994, p. 164.
12. *New York Times*, November 25, 1991.
13. *Fortune*, New York, July 25, 1994, p. 165.

21

IBM, Hewlett-Packard, and Digital Equipment

The three largest U.S. computer manufacturers—IBM, Hewlett-Packard, and Digital—compete vigorously for business not only in America but also in Germany and elsewhere in the world. All three of these firms enjoyed impressive sales and profits until 1990. IBM revenues then began to fall apart as it suffered a drastic decline from $69 billion in 1990 to $62.7 billion in 1993, or 9.1 percent. Digital continued to grow in revenues after 1990 (when it reported $12.9 billion), to reach $14.3 billion in 1993, a gain of 10.8 percent.

Hewlett-Packard (HP) took this three-year period in fine style, climbing from revenues of $13.2 billion in 1990 to $20.3 billion in 1993, a jump of 53.7 percent. HP also continued to increase its profits every year ($739 million in 1990 to $1.1 billion in 1993). By contrast, IBM ran into brutal losses of $2.8 billion in 1991, $4.9 billion in 1992, and $8.1 billion in 1993. Digital followed the same pattern, losing $617 million in 1991, $2.7 billion in 1992, and $251 million in 1993.

Moreover, IBM had to reduce its work force from 344,000 in 1991 to 256,000 in 1993. Digital declined from 121,000 to 94,200 in the same period. Only Hewlett-Packard was able to avoid layoffs, increasing its total employees from 89,000 to 96,000.[1]

While IBM continues to lead the world in computer sales, HP has been closing the gap. It reported 11 percent as much as IBM in 1983, but by 1993, the ratio had grown to 32 percent ($20 billion for Hewlett-Packard and $62 billion for IBM).

Although IBM, Hewlett-Packard, and Digital ranked first, fourth, and sixth, respectively, in sales in the global computer industry in 1993, HP was far out in front in profits.

Siemens Nixdorf is a subsidiary of Siemens, the second-largest German industrial in sales after Daimler-Benz. Siemens itself had been the top computer manufacturer in Germany for many years. In 1990, it acquired Nixdorf Computer—its chief competitor—and created Siemens Nixdorf.

Nixdorf was founded in 1952 by Heinz Nixdorf, then 27 years old. He started out with limited borrowed capital in a basement in Essen. He became one of the more spectacular workers of miracles in Germany's postwar "economic miracle." In 1968, Nixdorf brought out its 820 general-purpose minicomputer, designed for most smaller companies that did not need the larger machines offered by IBM and Siemens. Sales climbed from DM 28 million in 1964 to DM 263 million in 1970. By 1978, Heinz Nixdorf's firm sold DM 1 billion in twenty-two countries through 10,000 employees. In 1984, sales were DM 3.7 billion, still climbing at 20 percent per year. The work force numbered 20,000.

In 1986, at the age of 51, Heinz died of a heart attack while dancing at a company party. His successor was unable to maintain the momentum. Profits of DM 264 million in 1987, the firm's peak, fell 90 percent to DM 26 million in 1988. The next year was a nightmare. First-half losses of DM 297 million snowballed and were almost twice as bad in the second half. For 1989 as a whole, Nixdorf lost DM 1 billion on sales of DM 5.2 billion.[2] In the same year, Siemens Data Systems had sales of DM 5.4 billion and net income of DM 0.2 billion.

Deutsche Bank had acquired 25 percent of Nixdorf stock in 1979. The Bank and the Nixdorf family (still owning 75 percent) were anxious to keep the company in German hands. Siemens was a happy solution for the Bank and the Nixdorfs, but Nixdorf Computer has not been an easily digested acquisition for Siemens.

In 1991, its first full year, Siemens Nixdorf had sales of DM 12.1 billion and lost DM 0.7 billion. In 1992, it increased its sales to DM 13 billion and reduced its loss to DM 0.3 billion. In 1993, sales were DM 11 billion and the loss was DM 0.4 billion.

The German computer market is by far the richest in Europe. In 1992, Germany absorbed 23 percent; France, 17 percent; the United Kingdom, 16 percent; Italy, 11 percent; and Spain, 5 percent of total European sales.[3]

The three U.S. computer companies mentioned above and Siemens Nixdorf were the dominant firms in dividing up the German market in 1993 in billions of DM in sales, as follows:[4]

IBM Deutschland GmbH	12,591
Siemens Nixdorf AG	11,900
Hewlett-Packard GmbH	6,600
Digital Equipment GmbH	1,800

Only Hewlett-Packard made a profit in 1993 to the tune of DM 69 million. IBM lost DM 582 million, Siemens Nixdorf DM 419 million, and Digital DM 145 million.

Hewlett-Packard in 1993 had a 23-percent increase in sales to DM 6.6 billion and a 2-percent growth in net income to DM 69 million. Hardware peripherals, measuring equipment, medical electronics, and services led the way. The company opened a logistics and manufacturing center in Böblingen in 1992. A new circuit board production facility for DM 100 million was finished in 1993. Investment plans called for DM 180 million in 1992 and the same in 1993. Eberhard Knoblauch moved up from chairman of the management board to chair the supervisory board. Jörg Harms, formerly head of Hewlett-Packard's European medical electronics division, became the new chairman of the management board.

The success story of William Hewlett and David Packard is one waiting for a good movie maker. In 1938, these two recent graduates in electrical engineering at Stanford University were encouraged by a professor to start their own business in a rented cottage behind Packard's home in Palo Alto, California. With $538 in capital they began to work part time on a resistance–capacity oscillator for testing sound equipment, which Hewlett had developed for his master's thesis. They assembled several models and baked the paint on the instrument board in Packard's kitchen oven. Their first big order was from Walt Disney Studios, which bought five oscillators to develop and test a new sound system for *Fantasia*.

On January 1, 1939, Hewlett and Packard signed a partnership agreement, tossing a coin to decide whose name came first. Hewlett took responsibility for technical development and Packard managed the business side. In 1947, Hewlett-Packard incorporated; and by 1950, they recorded sales of $2 million, with seventy products and 143 employees.

Primarily a manufacturer of instruments for analysis and measurement, Hewlett-Packard first developed a computer in 1966 for its own production control. At that time, it had no plans to enter the computer market.

Two years later, in 1968, the firm introduced the HP-2116A, the first desktop calculator capable of performing scientific functions. Then came the HP-3000, which put them in competition with IBM and Digital Equipment. Its first personal computer, the HP85, appeared in 1980. Hewlett and Packard brought in John Young as president in 1977 and made him CEO the next year. The founders became directors; and in 1987, their sons, Walter B. Hewlett and David Woodley Packard, were elected to the board.[5] David Packard is now chairman. Today, Hewlett-Packard has 92,000 workers.

Lewis Platt replaced John Young as president and CEO in 1992. Aged 51 at that time and with twenty-six years of company experience, Platt took over a well-tuned machine in no need of serious repairs. Platt said in June 1993 that Hewlett-Packard's main reason for its success is its domination in the desktop printer sector.

Hewlett-Packard opened its subsidiary in Böblingen, Germany, in 1959, long before it started to make computers in 1968. The German operations have been especially profitable. Also very impressive in view of huge layoffs by competitors, total Hewlett-Packard employment in Germany remained stable at 6,400 in 1993. Meanwhile, IBM had cut its work force 9 percent and Digital 22 percent.[6]

Reunification had a major impact on the German computer makers. Hewlett-Packard, IBM, and Digital all decided not to establish production facilities in what was East Germany. Instead, they would supply the easterners from existing plants in the West or from foreign countries.

Before reunification in 1989, IBM had DM 12.3 billion in sales, and Hewlett-Packard DM 3.76 billion. IBM remained about the same at DM 12.5 billion in 1993, while its rival moved up strongly to DM 6.6 billion. As previously mentioned, IBM's German subsidiary lost DM 582 million in 1993, while Hewlett-Packard's made DM 62 million.[7]

Digital Equipment Corporation, located in the Boston suburb of Maynard, Massachusetts, got its start in 1951, almost a replay of the Hewlett-Packard scenario. Two MIT graduates, Ken Olsen and Harlan Anderson, advised and encouraged by Professor George Doriot, borrowed $70,000 from a venture capital firm. They produced and sold $94,000 worth of printed circuit modules and made a small profit in their first year.

Digital produced its first computer in 1960. It was called the PDP-1 (Programmed Data Processor), which had a cathode-ray tube—a screen that allowed the user to see what was being entered and received from the central processing unit. The PDP-1 was no larger than a refrigerator and sold for $120,000. The only other computers available at that time were million-dollar mainframes being sold by IBM, Univac, and Burroughs.

In 1963, Digital designed the first minicomputer. It was offered for sale as the PDP-5 at a price of $27,000. By 1970, the PDP-11 was announced at a price of $10,000.[8]

Profits continued to grow until 1988 when they peaked at $1.3 billion, but then a decline set in: $1 billion in 1989, $524 million in 1990, $391 million in 1991, and then a bitter loss of $2.7 billion in 1992.

The board turned vigorously against Ken Olsen, the Digital founder (still president and CEO after thirty-five years). He was accused of refusing to make the tough cost-cutting decisions the company needed, particularly layoffs. Olsen finally resigned in July 1992 and was replaced by fifty-two-year-old Robert Palmer.

Palmer went to work on job cuts, 20,000 in his first year, thus reducing the work force to 97,000. He instituted an incentive pay system for salesmen for the first time in the company's history. Olsen had refused to pay commissions because, he said, they led to customer dissatisfaction.

Not only did Digital Equipment lose DM 145 million in Germany in 1992, but it was forced to announce in August 1993 the closing of a plant making magnetic disk drives and employing 600 people. The facility in Kaufbeuren had been operated by Digital since 1981; but it now had excess manufacturing capacity for magnetic disk drives, which are used for storing information in computers. Work at this German operation was to be phased out through the middle of 1994, and production continued at a Digital plant in Colorado Springs.[9] Digital had already, within the previous year, closed a number of production units in the United States and one in Ireland. In addition to the 600 to be laid off at Kaufbeuren, Digital announced that 700 more German workers would be cut by the end of 1994, bringing German employment in that country down from 6,200 to 4,900.[10] The company said it would negotiate individual labor contracts with each plant after the restructuring was completed. The workers insisted on a nationwide agreement before the reorganization. I .G. Metal (which, in 1986, had only 2 percent of Digital workers organized) had been able, in this labor climate, to increase union members to 30 percent by June 1993. The union called a strike against Digital (the first in the German computer industry), and within a week Digital agreed to negotiate a contract with I. G. Metal.[11]

In April 1993, IBM hosted one of history's liveliest annual meetings in Tampa. Some 2,300 stockholders, mostly retirees and mostly irritated, filed into the hall. Bill Steiner, with 1,000 shares, was fairly typical; his holdings were worth $175,000 in 1987 and $100,000 in 1992, but only $48,000 on the day of the meeting. Understandably angry, he spoke for many of those present: "IBM no longer provides for your old age, but it certainly hastens it."[12]

Louis V. Gerstner, Jr., the new chairman of IBM with barely a month in office, was able to answer the multiple complaints by merely stating his obvious innocence for past mistakes. The only time he was forced to defend himself was when questioned about his own pay package: $3.5 million in annual salary and bonus, a one-time payment of about $5 million, and $500,000 in stock options. One stockholder retorted, "I want to congratulate you on a no-lose situation. I think $5 million, whether the stock goes up or down, is not to be sneezed at."[13]

On the basis of market value of total outstanding stock, IBM in 1972 was by far the largest corporation in the world, worth $46.8 billion, while AT&T ranked second, with $29.2 billion. Twenty years later, IBM had fallen to twenty-sixth place with $29 billion. Exxon was now in first position with $75.8 billion market value.

In all fairness, it should be noted that IBM was not the only corporate giant to fall out of the top twenty in this two-decade period. General Motors, Xerox, Eastman Kodak, Sears Roebuck, and Ford were also toppled. In fact, only six of the top twenty in 1972 were still there in 1992: General Electric, Exxon, AT&T, Procter & Gamble, Royal Dutch/Shell, and Coca-Cola. General Electric enjoys the distinction of being the only company to have been on the list in 1900 and to have survived ninety-two years.

This once fabulous corporation known as International Business Machines did not receive that name until 1924. It actually began in the last century as the Tabulating Machine Company, which was organized by a talented engineer, Herman Hollerith. He invented a machine that would sort and count cards based on the pattern of holes punched in each card. He supplied the U.S. Census Bureau with these machines for the census in 1890 and 1900, and they were adopted by other organizations in need of rapid computation.

Thomas Watson, already famous for his work in building up National Cash Register, was hired in 1914 as general manager. He guided the destinies of this corporation for thirty-eight years until 1952 when he retired to be succeeded by his son, Thomas Watson, Jr. (1952–1972).

The Watson father-and-son team, both highly gifted, reigned for more than a half century over this glamorous organization. By 1939, IBM had become an incredibly profitable firm, earning $9.1 billion (23 percent of sales).

During World War II, IBM helped the armed forces build what is usually considered the first computer, the Mark I. This machine had a memory capable of retaining a set of rules, which could be applied to any subsequent input. It had 765,000 parts and 500 pounds of wire.

After the war, IBM came out with the 705, which swept the market. IBM tabulating equipment had already acquired the dominant role of being used in 85 percent of U.S. offices, which simply switched over to IBM computers. In foreign sales, IBM achieved much the same domination, except in Britain and Japan, where strong competitors forced it to settle for about one-third of the market.[14]

Over the years, sales continued to climb and so did profits. Net income peaked in 1984 at $6.5 billion, or 13 percent on sales of $50 billion. Although sales kept climbing to a record of $69 billion in 1990, profits dropped slightly in 1985, the first time in twenty years. Even so, IBM's profit margin in that year was a healthy 9.1 percent.

In 1992, revenues were down to $65 billion; but IBM was still the world's fourth largest industrial corporation after GM, Exxon, and Ford. IBM actually earned $1.4 billion in 1992 (2.2 percent in sales); but it elected to take restructuring charges of $6.3 billion, which resulted in a net loss of $4.9 billion. Despite the fall in profits, IBM continued to pay $4.84 per share dividend in 1990, 1991, and 1992.

While IBM has fallen from its pedestal, it still leads all other computer companies in sales by a large margin. With $62 billion in 1993, it was far ahead of second-place Toshiba, with $42 billion.

In the mainframe computer market, IBM in 1992 took 52.2 percent, down markedly from its 72.1-percent share in 1984. Fujitsu was a poor second, with 9.4 percent.[15]

It is estimated that sales of mainframe computers along with related storage disks and printers by IBM in 1990 came to $18.9 billion (27 percent of total revenues). This segment fell to $9.7 billion in 1993 (15 percent). Mainframe machines cost as much as $20 million; but they are often replaceable by microprocessor-based computers, costing one-tenth as much. In corporations and governments around the world, some 35,000 IBM mainframes are still in use, an investment of about $1 trillion.[16]

Very few companies are unplugging their mainframes. Competition from microprocessor-based alternatives and mainframes of Amdahl and Hitachi (which are compatible with IBM) is pushing prices down drastically. Prices that started at $65,000 per MIPS (million of instructions per second) in January 1993 had fallen to $35,000 to $40,000 by October of that year.[17]

On the personal computer market, however, IBM lost half its share between 1987 and 1992. It had only 12.4 percent of the market in 1992—barely leading Apple, which grabbed 11.9 percent.[18]

Within the United States, the personal computer market came to 11,761,000 units in 1992. Apple took 13 percent of the market (1,528,000), while IBM was second with 11.7 percent (1,374,000).

Third-place Compaq has grown very quickly since 1992. This Cinderella company produces laptop and desktop computers that are IBM compatible, selling its products through mail order and 21,000 outlets worldwide. In the first half of 1994, Compaq shipped 2.12 million personal computers, compared with 1.74 million for IBM.[19] It had 12 percent of the American and 12.5 percent of the European market. Sales of this firm grew from $329 million in 1984 to $7.1 billion in 1993. Profits in the same period jumped from $12 million to $498 million.

In 1993, the revenues of IBM came principally from the following sources:[20]

Sales of computers	57 percent
Sales of software	16 percent
Maintenance	11 percent
Services	9 percent
Rentals and financing	7 percent

An additional small source of revenue (probably less than 1 percent) came into existence in October 1992 when IBM announced that it was starting the IBM Consulting Group. This worldwide organization of some 1,500 staff offers both general business consulting and technical consulting in specialties ranging from computer networking to manufacturing logistics. IBM Consulting already had 150 clients, 80 percent of which came from referrals by the sales force. It is estimated by IBM competitors that the division could generate $250 million in revenues per year.[21]

IBM Consulting Group is competing in a crowded field of business consultants, including McKinsey, Boston Consulting, Booz-Allen, and Bain, as well as dozens of specialized consultants. The consulting arms of the Big Six accounting firms are also fighting for business in this area.

In 1993, it was estimated that IBM derived 47 percent of its revenues from foreign operations. One of the most profitable IBM foreign subsidiaries has been IBM Deutschland GmbH, which started in Berlin in 1910. This German subsidiary reports to IBM Europe (an American corporation chartered in North Carolina), with its head office in Paris. IBM Europe, owned by IBM, is responsible for Germany and other European operations, as well as Africa and the Middle East.

IBM Deutschland reached a peak in profits in 1985, with DM 825 million, a 6-percent return on sales of DM 13.3 billion. Profits were also outstanding in 1989, amounting to DM 755 million, or 6 percent on sales of DM 12.3 billion; but it lost DM 443 million in 1992 and DM 582 million in 1993. At its highest, IBM employed 31,500 workers in Germany in 1991. This had been cut to 26,900 by January 1, 1994.

IBM Deutschland GmbH was massively reorganized on January 1, 1993. It was dissolved and replaced by a brand new holding company, IBM Deutschland GmbH (Holding), with its domicile in Berlin. There were now five new principal operating companies as follows:

1. *IBM Information Systems GmbH*, located in Stuttgart, employs 15,000 workers and is the profit center of the group. It is responsible for marketing, service, and finance, as well as law and instruction of customers.
2. *IBM Production GmbH* (7,000 workers) does not have such a cheerful future. It controls production facilities in Mainz, Berlin, and Sindelfingen; but its costs are 15 percent to 20 percent higher than in the United States and Japan. It could be sold off or closed in the near future.
3. *IBM Systems and Networks GmbH* (1,800 workers) serves the internal computer needs of the company.
4. *IBM Education GmbH* (500 workers) handles training of company workers.
5. *IBM Development GmbH* (2,300 employees) is responsible for research and development.

Hans-Olaf Henkel, chairman of the managing board of IBM Deutschland (1987–1993), served notice that as of January 1, 1994, only the workers of IBM production will be subject to labor contracts with the giant union I. G. Metal. He hopes that this will enable him to secure longer hours and lower wages for employees in the other IBM companies. The union argues that the master contract will apply to all IBM workers until it expires December 31, 1998.[22]

In October 1993, he was promoted to president of IBM Europe, effective January 1, 1994. Henkel has made a name for himself as an outspoken public critic of German working habits and as an ax-wielder within the company. In 1980, when he headed IBM's semiconductor plant in Sindelfingen, Henkel became one of the first managers in Germany to defy normal labor practices and stay open on Sundays. Edmund Hug, deputy to Henkel, succeeded him as chairman of the management board at IBM Deutschland.[23]

In 1992, IBM Deutschland had DM 9.5 billion revenues in Germany (down 7.8 percent from 1991) and DM 4.3 billion generated overseas (down 4.8

percent). According to Henkel, IBM—like many other firms—had a false sense of confidence when the Berlin Wall was breached in November 1989. It received large orders from big western German customers, and investment in the East was high. In June 1992, new orders began to slow down. Big customers not only reduced purchases but even started to buy from competitors.[24]

Unlike its competitors, IBM was active in East Germany during the Marxist era (1945–1990). It had a license agreement with Robotron Combine, under which the East German licensee built computers. In April 1990, the two firms signed a letter of intent for a joint venture covering sales of IBM equipment and software in the East bloc. IBM has no production projects for the East but has built a distribution chain and service centers. It also established an extensive educational program, including projects in cooperation with ten universities in the East.

In retrospect, there are many reasons for the global decline of IBM, but the following seem to be the most important:

1. The stifling bureaucracy of the company has been a major factor in the downfall. One critic said that getting action out of IBM was like swimming through "giant pools of peanut butter."[25] Total employment came to 84,000 in 1963 and the introduction of the sensational System 360 computer with six different models in 1964 was an enormously complex and costly process. By 1966, sales had climbed 97 percent, but the work force had jumped 130 percent to 198,000. Peak employment reached 407,000 in 1986. By the end of 1993, it was 267,000 and further cuts were still planned.[26]

2. Until recently, it was a matter of sacred writ that IBM offered lifetime employment with no layoffs in recessions. Only with the greatest reluctance did IBM finally give up this article of religious faith.

3. IBM failed to exploit the reduced instruction set-computing (RISC) technology. Although it invented the RISC microprocessor in 1974 and knew that it offered simplified and faster computing, IBM hesitated too long before moving into minicomputers then growing in popularity. Understandably, IBM saw and feared RISC as a rival to its globally dominant mainframe technology, but competing firms rushed in with no reluctance. Some critics think this may have been the most damaging of all mistakes made by IBM.

4. Perhaps even worse was IBM's failure to move vigorously in personal computers in the early 1980s.

5. Arrogance unquestionably played a role in the downfall of IBM, an arrogance based on the company's unprecedented string of greater and greater financial gains. Like GM, Sears Roebuck, and Xerox, top executives underestimated competitors until it was too late.

6. Antitrust suits caused post-Watson chief executives to be more (and probably excessively) cautious. Tom Watson, Jr., suffered a heart attack in 1970, which led him to retire in 1972. Two antitrust cases against IBM—one by Control Data and the other by the Department of Justice—contributed to his decision.

Vincent Learson (1972–1973) succeeded Watson and settled the Control Data action. Then came Frank Cary (1973–1981), a careful executive by nature, whom antitrust litigation made even more conservative. This strategy worked, and in 1981, the U.S. government gave up its suit without having forced the desired breakup of IBM.

Some analysts even argue that IBM would be better off today if the Department of Justice had won the case. They point to the AT&T breakup, which has generally proved beneficial to the slimmed-down AT&T and the now-independent regional operating companies.

7. Poor service alienated customers, causing them to switch to competitors. A much-publicized example was the Wal-Mart account. Because of sloppy service in 1991, IBM lost maintenance contracts for 400 of the 1,900 Wal-Mart stores nationwide, involving a loss of $2.3 million in revenue.[27]

8. Fierce and effective competition by younger companies both in the United States and abroad has hurt IBM's revenues and profits. Repeatedly it has been forced to cut prices. In Germany, IBM reduced its quotations by 33 percent between 1985 and 1990.[28]

9. Some critics place primary responsibility for IBM's decline on the less-qualified top executives who followed the Watson era (1914–1972). Certainly, they must bear some blame for the erosion taking place under their leadership, but objectively it should be noted that IBM during the Watson era faced far less competition and approached the status of a monopoly. The antitrust suit filed by the Department of Justice against IBM may have failed, but it had solid evidence of monopolistic practices.

John Akers was chairman of the board of IBM for eight years before he threw in the towel in 1993. He must accept a major part of the blame for IBM's problems, which Louis V. Gerstner, Jr., inherited on April 1 of that year. The task for Gerstner was enormously complex. He had to convince some 250,000 employees in 140 countries to change the way they think and act. It was one of the toughest jobs in America.

Gerstner, born in 1942 in Mineola, Long Island, New York, became an engineering graduate at Dartmouth and received an MBA from Harvard. His first job was as a consultant with McKenzie. He then went on to distinguish himself as top executive at American Express and RJR Nabisco Holdings Corporation before moving to IBM.

Six weeks after taking office, Gerstner said that he did not believe in breaking up and selling off parts of IBM as had been planned by his predecessor, John Akers. Gerstner remarked that "the whole of IBM is greater than the sum of the parts."[29] Time alone will tell if this is a mistake: trying to keep IBM a full-service company, offering everything from software to personal computers to mainframes along with microchip and consultancy.[30]

Gerstner himself admits he is not a technical expert, and that may prove his downfall. It would seem that the top boss of the dominant firm in the turbulent, fast-changing computer industry should combine both technical and management expertise. He faces highly dynamic competitors, which have undermined IBM repeatedly with technical innovations in the past. Certainly, Gerstner's job would be easier if he had a better understanding of these scientific breakthroughs.[31]

Gerstner has also revived an idea, often expressed previously in the computer industry, including IBM. He wants to present an objective sales staff that will recommend equipment of competitors to customers when it outperforms IBM. This old chestnut ought to be buried once and for all; it is very disrespectful to consumer intelligence.

Gerstner's first full year at the helm of IBM was 1993; it was not too impressive. Sales fell 2.8 percent to $62 billion; and losses came to $8.16 billion, compared with $4.9 billion in 1992.

Finally, in the first quarter of 1994, sales turned upward and IBM made a profit. Sales of $13.3 billion exceeded by 2.3 percent those of the first quarter of 1993 ($13 billion). Profits were $392 million, compared with a deficit of $399 million in 1993. In the second quarter, sales were $15.3 billion, 2.7 percent higher than in 1993. Net income came to $689 million, compared with a loss of $8 billion in the same quarter of 1993.

These figures are encouraging; but one cannot tell if IBM can generate significantly higher revenue, which is necessary to sustain long-term growth. By comparison, Hewlett-Packard reported sales of $11.9 billion in the first six months of its fiscal year ending October 30, 1994. This was a growth of 24 percent over the first half of 1993. Profits were $776 million ($608 million in 1993), a jump of 27 percent.

Meanwhile, Digital closed its 1994 fiscal year on July 2, 1994, with sales of $13.4 billion ($14.3 billion in 1993). It reported a loss of $519 million ($251 million in 1993).

NOTES

1. *Fortune*, New York, July 25, 1994, p. 166; July 26, 1993, p. 214; July 27, 1992, p. 198.

2. Thomas Derdak (ed.), *International Directory of Company Histories*, Vol. 3 (Chicago: St. James Press, 1991), p. 154.

3. *Financial Times*, London, May 26, 1993.

4. *Frankfurter Allgemeine Zeitung*, July 5, 1994.

5. Derdak, *International Directory*, p. 142.

6. *Financial Times*, London, June 22, 1993.

7. *Frankfurter Allgemeine Zeitung*, July 5, 1994.

8. Derdak, *International Directory*, p. 132.

9. *New York Times*, August 20, 1993.

10. *New York Times*, September 21, 1993.

11. *New York Times*, June 22, 1993.

12. *Wall Street Journal*, New York, April 27, 1993.

13. Ibid.
14. Derdak, *International Directory*, p. 148.
15. *Der Spiegel*, Hamburg, 14 (1993): 132.
16. *New York Times*, October 26, 1993.
17. Ibid.
18. *Der Spiegel*, Hamburg, 14 (1993): 132.
19. *New York Times*, July 30, 1994.
20. *Value Line*, New York, July 29, 1994, p. 1093.
21. *New York Times*, October 20, 1992.
22. *Frankfurter Allgemeine Zeitung*, September 9, 1993.
23. *Wall Street Journal*, New York, September 9, 1993.
24. *Financial Times*, London, April 22, 1993.
25. *Fortune*, New York, May 3, 1993, p. 41.
26. *Frankfurter Allgemeine Zeitung*, April 28, 1993.
27. *New York Times*, July 5, 1992.
28. *Wall Street Journal*, New York, April 6, 1990.
29. *Financial Times*, London, May 17, 1993.
30. *The Economist*, London, October 23, 1993, p. 75.
31. *Business Week*, New York, October 4, 1993, p. 87.

22

Anheuser-Busch and Boston Beer Company

THE TWO BUDWEISERS

St. Louis–based Anheuser-Busch rightfully boasts about brewing 43 million barrels of Budweiser annually (one-half its beer output). It is understandably reluctant to state that it cannot legally sell this brand in Germany. On the other hand, Germans consume with great pleasure some 75,000 barrels of Budweiser (one-quarter of total production) brewed by the tiny Budweiser Brewery in Budweis, Czech Republic.

Under Germany's Unfair Competition Act, a product bearing a geographical name cannot be sold on the German market unless it is produced in the place named. Thus, Budweiser (which in German means a person or thing coming from Budweis) brewed in Budweis can be marketed in Germany, but the St. Louis Budweiser is banned. This same law prevented German makers of sparkling wine from calling it Champagne, a name reserved for products of that famous French province. Hence, the German vintners call their bubbly Sekt.

The fascinating story of the two Budweisers began more than seven centuries ago in 1265 in a Bohemian village called Budweis. The Kingdom of Bohemia was then one of hundreds of member states in the Holy Roman Empire, and the king granted a charter to the people of Budweis to operate a brewery. It was a good brew, so good that in 1431 the Holy Roman Emperor Ferdinand ordered it served at his court.[1]

In 1795, a group of ethnic Germans in Budweis organized a corporation under the laws of Austria, which then ruled over Bohemia. In 1895, Budweiser Brauerei AG was founded and the name registered.

The St. Louis Budweiser came into existence in 1876 when Adolphous Busch, a German immigrant with brewing experience in his native country, announced the development of a new beer by Anheuser-Busch. Busch claimed in a letter written in 1894 to have thought up the name himself, choosing Budweiser because it was easy for Americans to pronounce and sounded German. The name was registered in 1878.[2]

In 1911, the Bohemian brewery objected to this registration in the United States; but the dispute was settled by an agreement, under which Anheuser-Busch paid a substantial sum to the Bohemians. The agreement is still confidential, but it divided up the markets in which the two competitors could use the Budweiser label.

At the end of World War I, Bohemia was taken away from Austria-Hungary and made part of the newly created state of Czechoslovakia. *Budwar*, the Czech word for "Bud brew," was added in smaller print to the Budweiser label.

Again in 1939, trouble arose when some of the Bohemian Budweiser was imported into the United States. Negotiations led to a second agreement under which Anheuser-Busch paid $50,000 to the smaller brewery. This agreement also remains confidential, but the Czech firm understood both settlements to grant the American brewery rights to use "Budweiser" outside Europe while it retained the trademark in Europe.

After World War II, Czechoslovakia fell under Communism and the Budweiser Brewery was nationalized. The Marxist rulers maintained the beer's quality, and sales provided a valuable source of chronically short convertible currencies. Bohemia's Budweiser continued to be one of the leading beer imports in Germany, not far behind the even more famous Pilsner Urquel, brewed in Pilsen, Czechoslovakia. With the overthrow of Communism in 1990, Budweiser became the property of the new democratic state. The town of Budweis, with about 100,000 residents, is a depressed area heavily dependent on Austrian charitable organizations. Many of its citizens commute to Germany or Austria, where they work illegally but bring home wages many times higher than those paid in the Czech Republic.[3]

The St. Louis management approached the Czech government to purchase the name Budweiser. In 1992, it offered to buy 30 percent of the company.[4] Although some forty other breweries, mostly German and British, are in competition, Anheuser-Busch executives are optimistic about victory. There are three reasons for this optimism. First, Anheuser-Busch with its trademark difficulties has more to gain and thus can afford to pay more than its German and British rivals for a share of the Budweis brewery. Second, Anheuser-Busch has financial resources far greater than its competitors. As one wit remarked, the St. Louis giant could afford to buy the whole country. Third, the

Budweis brewery has much to gain from the capital infused by Anheuser-Busch and settlement of its trademark dispute, which would open up new markets. On January 1, 1993, Czechoslovakia divided itself peacefully into Slovakia and the Czech Republic. Budweis is located in the latter.

THE TRADEMARK ISSUE

The two secret agreements of 1911 and 1939 are still in force as to the division of world markets between the two users of the Budweiser trademark. In general, these contracts seem to limit the Bohemian brewery to continental Europe with the exceptions of Portugal, Denmark, and Finland (where it is also excluded). There are sixteen countries where court actions are pending. In 1989, the two breweries signed a moratorium on such litigation so that they could seek a solution out of court.[5]

The St. Louis brewery changed its label to plain "Bud" to get around the trademark problem in several European countries. By 1993, it was using this strategy in Italy, Belgium, Switzerland, France, Holland, and Russia.[6]

In 1994, "Bud" appeared in Germany in Berlin's famous department store, Ka De We (short for Kaufhaus des Westens, meaning Department Store of the West). In 1993, Anheuser-Busch's Michelob was on the shelves of this largest department store in Germany; but, of course, it presented no legal difficulty. Samuel Adams was also for sale in 1993. By July 1994, Coors, Miller, and Genesee were also in this beer department of Ka De We.

None of these U.S. brews was selling very well. In the first place, Germans do not like American beer. Second, the brands carried amazingly high prices in comparison with leading German labels and well-established imports. Miller and Coors had price tags equal to $2.48 a bottle, while the other U.S. beers sold for $1.86. On the same shelves, Warsteiner—one of Germany's top quality brews—sold for $0.93, as did Pilsner Urquel and Budweiser, the highly popular Czech imports. Berliner Kindl, widely drunk by the German in the street, was priced at $0.54.

Actually, the St. Louis executives found out in 1984 what a dim view Germans take toward their beer. Anheuser-Busch tested its Michelob beer in West Berlin because of legal barriers against using the Budweiser label.[7] Jerry Ritter, executive vice president, stated that the test marketing was quickly terminated because the beer was too expensive to brew.[8] Brewing executives and consumers in Berlin say that the American brew was too light and bland for German taste. Anheuser-Busch officials were smart enough to have known all these facts in advance, and the test merely confirmed them.[9]

Until 1987, there was another legal obstacle to selling America's Budweiser in Germany. The German Beer Purity Decree (*Reinheitsgebot*) dating back to 1487 banned all beer unless made solely from water, malt, hops, and barley with no additives allowed and no acceleration of nature's own slow brewing process. In 1987, the European Court of Justice struck down the decree as violative of the Treaty of Rome of 1957 in barring free commerce between Germany and the other members of the European Union. To meet the court's decision, Germany has revised the law. It now provides that any recipe can be used to make beer as long as the deviations from the old decree are clearly marked on the label.

German breweries decided to voluntarily follow the now-invalid Beer Purity Decree because this was the beer preferred by their consumers. Most foreign brewers (other than the Americans) have adopted the same policy. However, Samuel Adams (brewed by Boston Beer) follows the German formula on all its beer.

All available evidence suggests that the executives at Anheuser-Busch have no great desire to sell their Budweiser on the brutal German market against 1,280 other highly competitive breweries. Germany's biggest brewer has a market share of 7 percent and makes 1 percent profit on sales, while Anheuser-Busch had 44 percent of the U.S. market in 1993 and made 5 percent. Why risk global prestige and diluted profits by taking on the German sharks with their enormous home-court advantage? The German press would have a field day over a failure by America's biggest selling beer for which it has long shown little respect. "Otto Six-Pack" has been drinking his local beer for centuries; he is fiercely loyal. He cannot be manipulated by advertising like his American counterpart, "Joe Six-Pack," into drinking a beer that departs from his strict criteria.

If the St. Louis management team acquires the "Budweiser" name now owned by the Czech government, it will probably shorten its own "Budweiser" to "Bud." In this way, there will be no confusion on the world markets, particularly in thoses countries such as Germany, Italy, France, and Spain, where Anheuser-Busch is now selling its beer under the "Bud" label. It can promote the Czech "Budweiser" in the United States as a top premium beer to beer drinkers looking for such quality in a brew. American consumers of the St. Louis Budweiser are already accustomed to buying the brew under the "Bud" name. In those other countries now closed to the Czech Budweiser, it should prove to be an attractive new product, a strong profit center for the American brewing giant.

BOSTON BEER COMPANY

Boston Beer Company, a brash newcomer on the American beer market in 1984, seems to have done everything right, both in the United States and Germany. By way of contrast, Anheuser-Busch, with 120 years of experience, has generally made astute moves in America but shown less talent on the German market. At present, these two breweries are the only serious U.S. competitors in that fabulous beer-drinking country.

Sales for both these American brewers are so small in Germany that neither the Boston Beer Company nor Anheuser-Busch is boasting about them.

However, industry sources say that Boston Beer enjoys a small lead over Michelob, produced by the St. Louis giant.

AB has long ranked first both domestically (44-percent market share) and globally (with annual output of some 80 million barrels). Boston Beer, ranked fourteenth among U.S. brewers with production of only 450,000 barrels in 1993, has made a much more favorable impression on the sophisticated beer drinkers of Germany.

Boston Beer showed genius at the outset by adopting the name of Samuel Adams, not only one of America's most colorful rebels during the Revolution but also a Boston brewer. He went to work in his father's "mash business" after the elder Samuel Adams lost £1,000, loaned to his son's business failure. The older man saw to it that young Sam was a sufficiently junior partner that he never threatened the beer enterprise. Who cares? Sam went on to become a true hero and later governor of Massachusetts. It was a superb choice of a name for the new beer, far more stirring than the meaningless labels of competing brews.

James Koch (pronounced "Cook"), the founder of the brewery, says that Samuel Adams was chosen because he symbolizes the Boston Beer revolt against imported European beers, such as Heineken, Beck, St. Pauli Girl, and others. Koch uses the slogan: "When America asked for Europe's tired and poor, we did not mean their beer." Koch claims his beer is purer than these leading imports because the latter are doctored by their makers with extraneous materials to preserve them for long trips and to make them more acceptable to American beer drinkers.

Boston Beer is a limited partnership with Koch as the sole unlimited partner. He invested $100,000 at the start, while friends and relatives came in as limited partners with $400,000. The first full year of production (1986) resulted in sales of $4.9 million and profits in six figures. Production has increased from 23,000 barrels in 1986 to 450,000 in 1993. Although sales and profits after 1986 are not reported, sales have increased about 50 percent annually for the past two years. The firm has been profitable every year. Prices are higher than those of other American beers, about equal to those of the leading imports.

Koch must be the world's best-educated brewer, having earned a B.A., an M.B.A., and a J.D. from Harvard. He also spent nine years as a business consultant with the prestigious Boston Consulting Group before leaving it to start Boston Beer.

Koch likes to joke about his ancestors, who left Bavaria in 1830 for America: "We have a great tradition of running bankrupt breweries." His great-great-grandfather, Louis Koch, started a brewery in St. Louis in 1870, which was merged into several other small breweries in 1889. Nevertheless, the recipe used in that brewery later became the formula for Samuel Adams Boston Lager. Koch's father is a former *braumeister* and an investor in Boston Beer.

Another wise decision of Boston Beer was to contract out its brewing for three years and save on costs at the start of the enterprise. It did not begin production itself until 1988, and then at a renovated old brewhouse purchased in a run-down area of Boston in Jamaica Plain with bargain real estate prices.

Koch wisely decided to make all his beer, for both domestic and foreign sales, according to the venerable German Beer Purity Decree of 1517.

While the Beer Purity Decree no longer has any force, all 1,280 German breweries still follow its formula because that is the way Germans want their beer to taste. Boston Beer has adopted the same strategy, while AB ignores the old decree and sells beer to Germans like that sold in America.

Boston Beer began exporting Samuel Adams to Germany in 1985, its first year of production. Boldly, it presented the brew in two Munich pubs. One of the owners was quoted in the local press as saying, "This is truly the first American beer which I can in good conscience offer to spoiled German beer drinkers."

Koch's next strategic move came in 1988 when Boston Beer became the first and still the only American brewer to make its beer in Germany. It licensed Gabrinus Brauerei, a small brewery located in southwestern Germany, to make and distribute its brew. This brought enormous advantages because Samuel Adams was no longer an American import but a respected German-brewed beer. In 1993, the license to brew Samuel Adams was shifted to Anker Brauerei in the same town, but Gabrinus continues to handle distribution.

GERMAN BEER MARKET

Beer is not a German invention, but many believe that the Germans have developed the beverage to its highest perfection. Scholars think that the Mesopotamians may have begun to make beer by 8000 B.C., when they domesticated barley. A long-standing debate in archeology revolves around the question of which came first after man domesticated barley: bread or beer.[10]

History records that the German tribes produced beer in the first century B.C. because Julius Caesar gave it a glowing testimonial as a "high and mighty liquor." Tacitus in the first century A.D. was less complimentary: "Their beverage they prepared from barley or wheat, a brew which slightly resembles an inferior quality of wine."

Regardless of what these two famous Romans thought, the present-day Germans know a good thing when they taste it. Year after year they lead the world in per capita consumption. The 1,280 breweries produce 6,000 different brands.[11]

In 1993, the Germans drank 139 liters of beer per capita. The Czechs gulped down 130 liters for second place, and each Dane 126 liters for third. The United States was in tenth position with about 90 liters per capita.

However, a disturbing story came out of an Augsburg factory in the summer of 1994. Siemens Nixdorf, the computer firm, has launched a cost-cutting program that has gone overboard. The facility had cut the work force from

1,300 to 1,000 since the start of the year, added a third shift, and tied pay scales to meeting quality and volume goals—all quite understandable. It has also taken beer out of the employee cafeteria.[12]

Bavarians make fun of these beer statistics, pointing out that the State of Bavaria leads the other fifteen German states with 200 liters per capita year after year. They also seem to have more fun than other Germans.

Bavaria also boasts the largest number of breweries. It still has far more than all the other German states combined. As of 1987, Bavaria had 1,122 breweries out of 1,280 for the country as a whole, but they were mostly small. With 68 percent of all breweries, the Bavarians only produced 27 percent of the beer. North Rhine–Westphalia led all states, with 29 percent of the output.

On the issue of draft versus bottled beer, the Germans consume 29 percent out of the tap. The percentage is only 12 percent in the United States. The Irish lead the world with 80 percent, which may or may not explain some complexities of Irish behavior.

Total beer production in Germany in 1993 was 115 million hectoliters, 4.5 percent lower than in 1992.[13] A hectoliter is 10 liters, or 2.64 gallons (equivalent to five six-packs). Western German brewers in 1993 accounted for 101 million hectoliters, while easterners produced 14 million. By contrast, there are only about fifty older established beer makers in the United States, not counting recently built microbrewers. Germans are astounded to find that we have so few breweries and are not satisfied with our excuse of prohibition (1920–1933). The vast majority of German brewers sell only in their own localities, supported by intense neighborhood loyalties.

TOP GERMAN BEERS

The leading beer brand in Germany on the basis of production is Warsteiner—5.9 million hectoliters in 1993 (up 2.5 percent over 1992). This single brand had only a 4-percent share, a good measure of the competitiveness of the German market. Sales were DM 1 billion in 1993 (up 3.6 percent over 1992); and profits, though unreported, were good.

Warsteiner concentrated on eastern Germany in 1992 and saw its sales there reach 500,000 hectoliters, a jump of 70 percent over 1991. The brewery expressed itself as "particularly happy" over its exports to Italy, Spain, Greece, and the United States. Total exports were not released, but they were reported to be up 17.5 percent in 1992.[14] It is hard to find in the United States but worth the effort. In the not-so-humble opinion of the American coauthor, Warsteiner is the finest in Germany.

Some Germans will argue that Bitburger ("Bit") should be listed as number one because it is the largest seller of tap beer. Much can be said to support this logic, and Bit sold 3.4 million hectoliters in kegs in 1993. Bitburgerbrauerei Thomas Simon, as the name indicates, is an individual proprietorship.

Total beer production in 1993 was 3.6 million hectoliters (up 1.5 percent); sales were DM 562 million (up 4.7 percent). Bit brags a little about the 4,300 upper-class hotels and other places serving Bit in Germany and outside its boundaries.[15]

EXPORTS AND IMPORTS

Germany exported 7 million hectoliters in 1993, or 5.9 percent of its production. Over half of foreign sales (57 percent) went to the eleven members of the European Community, and the United States took 16 percent.[16] Braueri Beck & Co. of Bremen is by far the largest exporter, making 30 percent of all foreign sales. It is even more dominant in exports to the United States, supplying 85 percent of the German beer to that market.

Beck produced 4.8 million hectoliters in its fiscal year ending June 30, 1993 (up 1.2 percent over 1992). Exports by Beck came to 2 million hectoliters, about 44 percent of production. Approximately half of Beck's exports, 1 million hectoliters, went to the United States.[17]

The management of Beck has diversified in recent years. It produced 1.4 million hectoliters of soft drinks in fiscal year 1993. Beck entered a licensee arrangement in 1992 to bottle Coca-Cola in eastern Germany.

Löwenbräu of Munich deserves mention here because for many years it was the leading German export to the United States. It was also the leading American import until toppled by Heineken of Holland. Löwenbräu AG dates back to the fourteenth century, and it refused to cut its prices when Heineken began to lure away its U.S. customers. In 1972, Löwenbräu entered a license agreement with Miller Brewing Co. of Milwaukee to make the German product in the Miller breweries in the United States. This failed to restore Löwenbräu's position for two reasons. First, it carried a higher price than American brews. Second, many U.S. beer drinkers will not buy German beer made in America. By 1988, Heineken was first among imported brews in sales in the United States, and Corona from Mexico was second. Beck was third, followed by Molson and Moosehead, both from Canada.

Imported beers have never done very well in Germany. In 1993, they amounted to only 2.3 million hectoliters, equal to 2.5 percent of domestic production. By comparison, U.S. imports were 4.3 percent.

Danish brewers led all other nations in exports to Germany in 1991, as the following list illustrates:

Danish (Tuborg and Carlsbad)	500,000 hectoliters
Dutch (Grolsch and Amstel)	350,000 hectoliters
Czech (Pilsner Urquel and Budweiser)	170,000 hectoliters
Belgian (Stella Artois)	150,000 hectoliters

The Danish statistics are misleading because three-fifths of this is returned to Denmark by thrifty Danish shoppers, who want to buy their own beer more reasonably under lower German taxes. The Danish value-added tax alone is 25 percent, compared with 15 percent in Germany.

Pilsner Urquel, brewed in Pilsen, Czech Republic, has long been the favorite foreign brand of German beer drinkers. The name is German and means "original Pilsner." It was founded in 1842 when this area was part of the Austrian-Hungarian Empire. Pilsner became famous for its golden clarity and somewhat bitter taste. Other beers at the time were often murky, and Pilsner's popularity spread through Europe. Pilsner type beer is now brewed all over the world.[18]

Pilsner Urquel and Budweiser were the only Czech beers the Marxist government allowed to be exported before 1989. The other seventy breweries produce much the same type of brew, which probably would have been popular in Germany. Radegast Brewery AS, built under the Communist regime in the late 1960s, has the largest brewing capacity in the country. It went private in 1992 and is now exporting 10 percent of its production to Germany, Japan, the United States, Spain, and other countries. As a modern plant, it enjoys a substantial cost advantage over Pilsner and Budweiser. Radegast shares are in great demand on the Prague stock exchange.[19]

EASTERN GERMAN BREWERS

Before reunification, there were 180 breweries in East Germany. Many of them have gone out of business, and a majority of the 108 still operating have been purchased by western German breweries.

Real beer drinkers will not mourn the passage of most of these brewers. Many of them produced a beer so bad it would not even sell in the United States. Some came up with the alibi that they were forced by the Marxist authorities to employ rice supplied in countertrade with China instead of barley. Their beer tasted more like overflow from the local sewers.

When the Berlin Wall fell in 1989, the eastern Germans rushed to buy western beer, foods, household appliances, and other goods, no matter whether they were superior to products made in the East. Eastern breweries at first lost almost all their customers; then eastern Germans began to realize that this rush into western goods at higher prices was costing them jobs and money. Meanwhile, the quality of eastern beer and other products began to improve.[20] Today, the eastern brewers have won back about 70 percent of their customers.

There were two breweries in East Germany that deserve the highest praise because they produced outstanding beer during the Marxist era: Radeberger and Wernersgrüner. In fact, they were too good because they were mostly sold in western countries to obtain badly needed hard currencies. Delivery trucks for both breweries were often seen in West Berlin. The ordinary East German seldom tasted these beers, unless he took them as a tip for rendering some service in short supply like plumbing or auto repairs.

It is a pleasure to report that both Radeberger and Wernersgrüner are alive and doing well today. Radeberger was sold to a western German conglomerate, the Oetker Group in Berlin, which makes Berliner Kindl. Wernersgrüner received takeover offers but has managed to remain independent. Treuhand holds 49 percent of the stock. The original family owners, the Männels, have 51 percent and are trying to get 100 percent.[21]

The best news about German beer has been its declining cost. In 1938, the average German had to work twenty-four minutes to earn enough to buy a bottle of beer. By 1958, a bottle cost him sixteen minutes; and in 1985, a mere three minutes. That should contribute powerfully to peace in our time.[22]

While on the subject of alcoholic beverages, western Germans—in addition to their annual 143 liters of beer per capita—also put away 27 liters of wine and sekt (German sparkling wine), while the easterners consume 17 liters. As for hard liquor (cognac, whiskey, vodka, schnapps, etc.), the East outdrinks the West 12 to 6 liters per capita or 2 to 1. As for pure alcohol, the Germans as a whole take on 12.1 liters per year per capita—the world's highest consumption. The easterner absorbs about 1 liter more than his western cousin. The French hold second place.[23] In view of these facts, it should not be necessary (but both authors feel a duty) to urge the reader: "Do not ever try to outdrink a German under any circumstances."

NOTES

1. *Wall Street Journal*, New York, April 3, 1992.
2. *Frankfurter Allgemeine Zeitung*, April 18, 1988.
3. *Der Spiegel*, Hamburg, 32 (1993): 119.
4. *Financial Times*, London, March 5, 1992.
5. *Frankfurter Allgemeine Zeitung*, August 7, 1993.
6. *Wall Street Journal*, New York, September 20, 1993.
7. *Frankfurter Allgemeine Zeitung*, March 28, 1988.
8. *Los Angeles Times*, May 31, 1988.
9. *Frankfurter Allgemeine Zeitung*, October 10, 1984.
10. *New York Times*, December 30, 1992.
11. *Frankfurter Allgemeine Zeitung*, February 7, 1994.
12. *New York Times*, July 17, 1994.
13. *Frankfurter Allgemeine Zeitung*, April 19, 1994.
14. *Frankfurter Allgemeine Zeitung*, January 7, 1994.
15. *Frankfurter Allgemeine Zeitung*, January 19, 1994.
16. *Frankfurter Allgemeine Zeitung*, June 15, 1994.
17. *Frankfurter Allgemeine Zeitung*, December 13, 1993.
18. *International Herald-Tribune*, Paris, May 17, 1990.
19. *Wall Street Journal*, New York, May 6, 1994.
20. *Wall Street Journal*, New York, October 9, 1992.
21. *Frankfurter Allgemeine Zeitung*, June 10, 1994.
22. *Frankfurter Allgemeine Zeitung*, September 13, 1986.
23. *Frankfurter Allgemeine Zeitung*, April 21, 1994.

Selected Bibliography (English)

NEWSPAPERS

Financial Times. London.
International Herald-Tribune. Paris.
Los Angeles Times. Los Angeles.
New York Times. New York.
Wall Street Journal. New York.
Wall Street Journal Europe. Brussels.

PERIODICALS

Business America. Washington, D.C.: U.S. Department of Commerce.
Business Week. New York.
Commerce Germany. Frankfurt: American Chamber of Commerce in Germany.
Economic Bulletin. Berlin: Deutsches Institut für Wirtschaft (German Institute for Economics).
The Economist. London.
Forbes. New York.
Fortune. New York.
German-American Business Journal Midwest. Chicago: German-American Chamber of Commerce.
German Brief. Frankfurt: Frankfurter Allgemeine Zeitung.
International Financial Statistics. Washington, D.C.: International Monetary Fund.
Monthly Report. Frankfurt: Deutsche Bundesbank.
Survey of Current Business. Washington, D.C.: U.S. Department of Commerce.
Value Line. New York.

BOOKS

Adenauer, Konrad. *Memoirs*. Chicago: Henry Regnery, 1966.

Ardagh, John. *Germany and the Germans*. New York: Harper & Row, 1987.

Bailey, George. *Germans*. New York: Macmillan, 1991.

Barzini, Luigi. *The Europeans*. New York: Penguin, 1984.

Berghahn, Volker R. *The Americanization of West German Industry 1945–1973*. New York: Berg, 1986.

Berghahn, Volker R. *Imperial Germany 1871–1914*. Providence: Berghahn Books, 1994.

Bölling, Klaus. *Republic in Suspense*. New York: Praeger, 1964.

Botting, Douglas. *From the Ruins of the Third Reich*. New York: Crown, 1985.

Carroll, Paul. *Big Blue: The Unmaking of IBM*. London: Crown, 1994.

Childs, David. *The GDR: Moscow's German Ally*. London: Allen & Unwin, 1983.

Childs, David. *Germany since 1918*. New York: St. Martin's, 1980.

Cohn, E. J. *Manual of German Law*. Dobbs Ferry, N.Y.: Oceana Publications, 1971.

Craig, Gordon A. *The Germans*. New York: Times Mirror, 1982.

Craig, Gordon A. *Germany: 1866–1945*. New York: Oxford University Press, 1978.

Dahrendorf, Ralf. *Society and Democracy in Germany*. New York: Doubleday, 1969.

Derdak, Thomas (ed.). *International Directory of Company Histories*. Chicago: St. James Press, 1988–1991.

Dill, Marshall, Jr. *Germany: A Modern History*. Ann Arbor: University of Michigan Press, 1961.

Donhoff, Marion Grafin. *Foe into Friend*. New York: St. Martin's, 1982.

Dornberg, John. *The New Germans: Thirty Years After*. New York: Macmillan, 1975.

Erhard, Ludwig. *Germany's Comeback in the World Market*. London: Allen & Unwin, 1954.

Erhard, Ludwig. *Prosperity through Competition*. London: Thames & Hudson, 1962.

Fest, Joachim C. *Face of the Third Reich*. New York: Vintage, 1972.

Fest, Joachim C. *Hitler*. New York: Vintage, 1973.

Foster, Nigel. *German Law and Legal System*. London: Blackstone, 1993.

Frankfurter Allgemeine Zeitung. *Germany's Top 300*. Frankfurt: Maxim Worcester, 1993.

Garten, Jeffrey. *A Cold Peace: America, Japan, Germany and the Struggle for Supremacy*. New York: Random House, 1993.

German-American Chamber of Commerce. *U.S. Firms in Germany*. New York: The Chamber, 1993.

German Foreign Trade Information Office (GFTIO). *Doing Business in Germany's New Federal States*. Cologne: GFTIO, 1991.

Goodhart, David. *The Reshaping of the German Social Market*. London: Institute of Public Policy Research, 1994.

Grosser, Alfred. *Federal Republic of Germany: A Concise History*. New York: Praeger, 1964.

Grosser, Alfred. *Germany in Our Time*. New York: Praeger, 1964.

Hart, David (ed.). *Membership Directory and Yearbook 1994*. Frankfurt: American Chamber of Commerce in Germany, 1994.

Horn, Norbert, Kötz, Heinz, and Leser, Hans. *German Private and Commercial Law*. Oxford: Clarendon Press, 1982.

International Bureau of Fiscal Documentation. *The Taxation of Companies in Europe.* Vol. 2, *Germany.* London: The Bureau, 1993.

Kritsch, Henry. *The German Democratic Republic.* Boulder, Colo.: Westview Press, 1983.

Laquer, Walter. *Germany Today: A Personal Report.* Boston: Little, Brown, 1985.

Leonhard, Wolfgang. *Child of the Revolution.* Chicago: Henry Regnery, 1958.

Lynch, Richard. *European Marketing.* Burr Ridge, Ill.: Irwin, 1993.

Marsh, David. *The Bundesbank: The Bank That Rules Europe.* London: Heinemann, 1992.

Marsh, David. *The Germans: The Pivotal Nation.* New York: St. Martin's, 1990.

Marsh, David. *The Germans: Rich, Bothered and Divided.* London: Century, 1989.

Meador, Daniel John. *Impressions of Law in East Germany.* Charlottesville: University of Virginia Press, 1986.

Merkl, Peter H. *German Unification in the European Context.* University Park: Penn State Press, 1993.

Merkl, Peter H. *The Origin of the West German Republic.* New York: Oxford University Press, 1963.

Mueller, Stiefel, and Brücher. *Doing Business in Germany: A Legal Manual.* Frankfurt: Fritz Knapp, 1971.

Nyrop, Richard F. *Federal Republic of Germany.* Washington, D.C.: U.S. Army, 1982.

O'Donnell, James P. *The Bunker.* Boston: Houghton Mifflin, 1978.

Orlow, Dietrich. *A History of Modern Germany, 1870 to Present.* Englewood Cliffs, N.J.: Prentice-Hall, 1987.

Pünder, Volhard, Weber, and Axeter. *Germany.* Chicago: Commerce Clearing House, 1990.

Read, Anthony, and Fisher, David. *Berlin Rising, Biography of a City.* New York: W. W. Norton, 1994.

Rheinstein, Max. *Collected Works.* Tübingen: J. C. B. Mohr (Paul Siebeck), 1979.

Rüster, Bernd (ed.). *Business Transactions in Germany.* 4 vols. New York: Matthew Bender, 1991.

Ryan, Cornelius. *The Last Battle.* New York: Simon & Schuster, 1966.

Schalk, Adolph. *The Germans.* Englewood Cliffs, N.J:. Prentice-Hall, 1971.

Schmidt, Helmut. *Defense or Retaliation.* London: Oliver & Boyd, 1962.

Sinn, Gerlinde, and Sinn, Hans-Werner. *Jumpstart.* Cambridge, Mass.: MIT Press, 1992.

Smith, Gordon, et al. (eds.). *Developments in German Politics.* Durham, N.C.: Duke University Press, 1992.

Spaeth, Lothar, and Henzer, Herbert A. *Can the Germans Still Be Saved?* 1993.

Speer, Albert. *Inside the Third Reich.* New York: Macmillan, 1990.

Strobel, Kilius, and Vorbrugg. *Business Law Guide to Germany.* Chicago: Commerce Clearing House, 1988.

Thurow, Lester. *Head to Head.* New York: William Morrow, 1992.

Turner, Henry Ashby, Jr. *Germany from Partition to Reunification.* New Haven: Yale University Press, 1992.

Turner, Henry Ashby, Jr. *The Two Germanies since 1945.* New Haven: Yale University Press, 1987.

Twain, Mark. *The Complete Travel Books of Mark Twain.* Vol. 2, *A Tramp Abroad,* edited by Charles Neider. New York: Doubleday, 1967.

U.S. Army. *Federal Republic of Germany: A Country Study*. Washington, D.C.: U.S. Army, 1983.

Wallich, Henry. *Mainsprings of German Revival*. New Haven: Yale University Press, 1955.

Selected Bibliography (German)

NEWSPAPERS

Frankfurter Allgemeine Zeitung. Frankfurt.
Handelsblatt. Dusseldorf.
Suddeutsche Zeitung. Munich.
Tagespiegel. Berlin.

PERIODICALS

Der Spiegel. Hamburg.
Die Zeit. Hamburg.
DIW-Wochenbericht. Berlin: German Institute of Economic Research.
Focus. Munich.
Ifo Schnelldienst. Munich.
Ifo Studien. Munich.
RWI-Mitteilungen. Essen.
Statistisches Jahrbuch. Wiesbaden.
Wirtschaft und Statistik. Wiesbaden.
Wirtschaftsdienst. Hamburg.
Wirtschafts-Konjunktur. Munich.

BOOKS

Bölling, Klaus. *Die Letzten 30 Tage des Kanzlers Helmut Schmidt: Ein Tagebuch*. Hamburg: Spiegel Buch, 1982.
Büchting, Hans-Ulrich. *Beck'sches Rechtsanwalts Handbuch*. Munich: C. H. Beck, 1989.

Deutsche Bank. *Die neuen Bundesländer*. Frankfurt: Deutsche Bank, 1990.

Egger, T. Jan, and Gornall, John (eds.). *Handbuch-USA-Geschäft*. Wiesbaden: Betriebswirtschaftlicher Verlag Dr. Th. Gabler, 1989.

Horn, Norbert. *Das Zivil-und Wirtschaftsrecht im neuen Bundesgebiet*. Cologne: RWS-Verlag, 1993.

Kampe, Dieter. *Nachruf auf die Treuhand: Wer uns kennen-lernt, gewinnt uns lieb*. Berlin: Rotbuch, 1993.

Maiburg, Hermann. *Gesellschaftsrecht*. Munich: Oldenbourg, 1986.

Reinfried, Hubert, Langels, Rudolf, and Bartsch, Günther (eds.). *Handbuch Deutsches Recht*. Berlin: Walhalla, 1992.

Schiller, Karl. *Der schwierige Weg in die offene Gesellschaft*. Berlin: Siedler, 1994.

Schmidt, Helmut. *Die Deutschen und ihre Nachbarn*. Stuttgart: Siedler, 1990.

Schmidt, Helmut. *Handeln für Deutschland*. Berlin: Rowohlt, 1993.

Stephan, Rainer (ed.). *Beck'scher Ratgeber Recht*. Munich: C. H. Beck, 1983.

Index

ABOUT THE AUTHORS

JAMES A. HART is an international lawyer specializing in German business. He practiced in Chicago for thirty years before joining the Berlin law
firm of Ackermann & Schultze-Zeu in 1988. He holds a doctorate in economics from Fordham University, a J.D. from Georgetown University, and has
taught international finance at Fordham, DePaul, and San Diego Universities.
A past president of the Academy of International Business and a member of
the American Chamber of Commerce in Germany, his clients have included
Motorola, Schlitz Brewing, Procter & Gamble, CBS, Continental Bank,
American National Bank, Bank of Indiana, Bank of Boston, and Arthur
Andersen. His articles have appeared in various international journals and
other media. He has broad television and public speaking experience in both
Germany and the United States.

DIETER SCHULTZE-ZEU has earned a J.D. after study at Berlin, Frankfurt, and Kiel universities. He served as a District Judge in Mainz and then
for ten years as a corporation lawyer for Vickers-Zimmerman in London and
Frankfurt. In 1972, he became a founder and a senior partner of Ackermann
& Schultze-Zeu in Berlin. As a lawyer and notary, he has represented numerous American clients. He authored "Foreign Trade Laws of the German
Democratic Republic," published by Chase World Information Corporation
in 1977, was editor of *Berlin Law Letter*, and has published many articles in
German law reviews. He is also a member of the American Chamber of Com-
merce in Germany.